WHAT PEOPLE ARE SA

THE RINGTONE AN

Fuses the traditions of great travel writing with a deep and sophisticated knowledge of the fast-changing politics and cultures of West Africa. The result is a truly engaging and informative book that provides a rare tour of one of the world's poorest and least understood regions.
Doug Saunders, Globe and Mail, Canada

The Ringtone and the Drum is high-energy food for wanderlust. Teeming with interesting facts, it turns Weston's perspicacious eye on some of the least visited countries on earth. The result is an accessible, unique and enchanting account. But beware: it will tempt even the least daring to pack their bags for West Africa!
David Bloom, Professor of Economics and Demography, Harvard University

A wise and compelling book, which offers a real picture of what daily life is like in West Africa. Weston is a brave and resourceful traveller, who has entered the heart of some of the most fascinating and least visited parts of the world.
Toby Green, author of *Meeting the Invisible Man: Secrets and Magic in West Africa*

This is a courageous book, which sheds much-needed light on a corner of Africa that rarely gets media attention. Weston's first hand reporting and analysis will help anyone seeking to understand how poor countries work and poor people live.
Seth Kaplan, author of *Fixing Fragile States*

The Ringtone and the Drum

Travels in the World's Poorest Countries

The Ringtone
and the Drum

Travels in the World's Poorest Countries

Mark Weston

Winchester, UK
Washington, USA

First published by Zero Books, 2012
Zero Books is an imprint of John Hunt Publishing Ltd., Laurel House, Station Approach,
Alresford, Hants, SO24 9JH, UK
office1@jhpbooks.net
www.johnhuntpublishing.com
www.zero-books.net

For distributor details and how to order please visit the 'Ordering' section on our website.

Text copyright: Mark Weston 2012

ISBN: 978 1 78099 586 1

A CIP catalogue record for this book is available from the British Library.

Design: Stuart Davies

Printed and bound by CPI Group (UK) Ltd, Croydon, CR0 4YY

We operate a distinctive and ethical publishing philosophy in all
areas of our business, from our global network of authors to
production and worldwide distribution.

CONTENTS

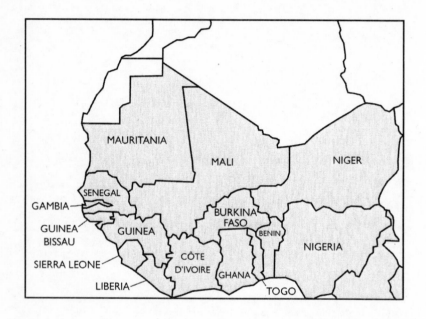

For my parents, and for Ebru

'The great affair is to move, to feel the needs and hitches of life a little more nearly, to get down off this featherbed of civilisation and to feel the globe granite underfoot and strewn with cutting flints.'

  Robert Louis Stevenson

'If God dishes your rice in a basket, you should not wish to eat soup.'

  Mende proverb, Sierra Leone

Prologue: Senegal

No sooner do you step out into the darkness from the Air France 737 than West Africa smothers you in her treacherous embrace. With one hand she plies you with the sweet, earthy smells of the tropics and anaesthetises you under a wave of damp heat; with the other she dismantles your defences, chipping away at the control you thought you had over your life, stripping you of your layers of protection, and leaving you naked, vulnerable, powerless to stave off her arsenal of threats.

At first, the losses of control are minor. In the airport, the unofficial porter who makes off with your bags can probably be trusted to take them to a waiting taxi, but as you are swallowed up by the dimly-lit throng outside the terminal and lose sight of both porter and luggage, you are hit by a moment of doubt as it occurs to you that the bags' contents would be worth much more to their bearer than the meagre tip you will give him. In the taxi your control is limited by the decrepit state of the ancient vehicle, the absence of seat belts or headlights, and the carefree driving of the alarmingly young driver. In your hotel you chance the food, praying it has not been touched by unclean hands, washed in contaminated water, or left for too long in the pounding sun. And in the town the following morning, when you allow a "guide" to show you to the transport park, you hope your payment for his services will be acceptable; proffering a few hundred francs, however, you are rebuffed and then threatened, more serious trouble averted only when you raise your voice, cry 'thief,' and discover with relief that your aggressor is unwilling to run the risk of vigilante justice at the hands of an angry mob.

As you move around the country the dangers mount up, your grip on your life loosens. The long journey south in the battered seven-seater Peugeot estate car that is the region's only form of public transport, along a rutted dirt road littered with overturned trucks: one stray cow or unnoticed boulder, perhaps obscured by dust thrown up by a passing jeep, and that could be you. Nearing the border a different threat looms. A low-lying rebellion has simmered here for years, occasionally boiling over into horrific violence. Not long before our passage, a Red Cross worker had been kidnapped and then executed by rebel soldiers; not long after, a nine-year-old girl would be shot dead in a bungled attack on a village. Commercial transport makes a three-hundred-mile detour to avoid the area. This is expensive and slow, but the money and time saved by taking the direct route are judged not to be worth the risk.

Fewer than fifty miles away, across a different frontier, more trouble lurks. A World Food Programme representative is here in Senegal's south-eastern corner, staking out the territory in case civil war breaks out in neighbouring Guinea and a flood of refugees pours in. A military junta seized power there a year ago and is equipping itself for a fight. Weapons are being stockpiled, South African mercenaries recruited to train the new president's supporters in the arts of war. Earlier in the year the junta had put down a protest in a stadium by killing dozens of unarmed civilians. Weeks after we passed by, the president himself would be shot in the head at point blank range by an aide. He would survive, miraculously, only to be spirited overseas for treatment, his brief hold on power consigned to history.

On reaching the border you breathe a sigh of relief. You cling to the delusion that it is you that is responsible for your fate, that it is your own resourcefulness that has got you through the first tests. In reality, of course, it is Africa that has allowed you to survive. It is she that controls your destiny, and if she so decides, although you are loath to admit it to yourself so early in your journey, this capricious continent can take it all away from you on a whim.

In the end, to retain your sanity, you must surrender. Your panic must soften into resignation. You must loosen the reins and, faced with no other choice, accept a higher degree of risk.

This, after all, is how West Africans cope. The daily dangers they face in their lives are more threatening than any that confront the wealthy Western traveller. Fatalism, the resigned acceptance of whatever the gods throw at them, is their only rational response.

We break our journey at the small frontier outpost of Kolda. One of the hottest towns in Africa, it is a mosquito-infested froth of sweat, noise, industry and filth. Everywhere you turn there is a bicycle repair shop, a mechanic, a tyre seller or a wholesale store, all servicing the thin stream of cross-border traffic. The air judders with the roar of generators, the clink of metal on metal, and the rumble of idling engines. A central square clogged with mopeds and trucks hosts a single fuel pump. Along one side of the square winds a sluggish river, oozing litter and grime. Bloated pigs trawl its banks for scraps. Only in the evenings does the stench of traffic fumes recede, elbowed gently aside by the dank smell of raw sewage.

But although unlovely, Kolda is a friendly place, its inhabitants surprised and pleased to see foreign visitors. In the late afternoon, as the heat is beginning to relent and the first squadron of brilliant white egrets flies by in V-formation to roost, an old Muslim rice-seller in a sky-blue robe and white skullcap beckons us over to sit with him in front of the dark cavern of his shop. Tall and thin, with a hooked nose and slightly sunken cheeks, his crooked teeth are blackened and the skin on his flip-flopped feet chapped. His dark eyes are warm and welcoming, and he seems pleased to be able to fulfil his dual duty, as an African and a Muslim, of showing hospitality to strangers. He motions us to sit beside him on his wooden bench, and from a passing vendor orders three plastic cups of *café touba*, a strong, peppery black coffee that is reputed to have medicinal properties and to improve the eyesight. When I offer to pay, he laughs me off paternally. To our right, sitting on low stools, two young men wash their feet with water from a kettle in preparation for the

3

afternoon prayer. Another man, already washed, kneels on a green straw mat on the dusty ground next to them. Facing Mecca, he prostrates himself in submission to Allah, oblivious to the motorbikes churning past a few feet east of his bald scalp.

The rice-seller's French is limited, my Diola nonexistent, but we manage to establish that before he grew too old he had been a truck driver, and had travelled to Guinea-Bissau, Guinea, Mauritania, Mali and Niger. He can tell me the distance to the Guinea-Bissau border, the most effective means of reaching it (another seven-seater), and the state of the roads on the other side (a comfortable journey sounds unlikely). He still owns a truck but his son now drives it, leaving him to concentrate on his new business of selling rice imported from Vietnam and Thailand. (Senegal's farmers once produced enough rice to meet the nation's needs, but the combined effects of French colonial encouragement to grow cash crops for export rather than staples for domestic consumption, post-colonial underinvestment in roads and irrigation, and the disruptive effect on agriculture of the rebel uprising mean that South East Asian rice is now both cheaper and more abundant than the West African variety.)

Later that evening we are reminded that our growing sense that life is slipping from our control is as nothing to how West Africans must feel. We have dinner in the spartan, strip-lit restaurant of our hotel. The room is vast – someone clearly once had grand plans for it - with long wooden tables laid out as if a large group is expected, perhaps a school party or wedding guests. We, however, are the only diners. In the corner of the room a television is switched on, but the screen is so fuzzy it is impossible to watch. A clock is stopped on the wall behind the bar. Outside the window behind us, a blizzard of bats screeches past in the darkness.

We are served by Ibrahima, a stocky, light-skinned young waiter with a shy, polite manner. He brings us fried chicken and chips – the only item on the menu. As we battle with the stringy bird he hovers by our table, smiling shyly but expectantly at us, evidently hoping for a chat. His eyes are narrow and watery. His broad, pale face bespeaks both openness and vulnerability; it is the sort of face to which bad things happen. He speaks good French, and when we reciprocate his smile he grasps the opportunity to unburden himself of his troubles.

His parents were groundnut farmers. Funds were tight, but they scraped enough of a living to send their son to school until suddenly, when Ibrahima was in his mid-teens, they both died in quick succession of undiagnosed illnesses. They left no money, so he had to give up his education. 'Kolda is poor and there was no work here,' he says, 'so I left for the coast. There were no jobs there either – people employ their family or their neighbours, not strangers. That's how things work here: there aren't enough jobs to go around.' He speaks quietly, barely opening his mouth, no trace of resentment in his voice.

In the coastal town he tried his hand at buying and selling fish in the market, which gave him just enough to live on. Then, after a few months, he had a lucky break. A local businessman, impressed by his linguistic abilities (he speaks six of Senegal's forty languages as well as French and a little English), gave him a job in a seaside hotel frequented by wealthy Senegalese and a trickle of French tourists. Aware of how fortunate he had been – 'if you don't have connections here you need fate to help you,' he says – Ibrahima worked hard. He learned the trade and took groups of tourists to Guinea-Bissau and Guinea. 'I had got back on my feet,' he says. 'It was going well. I married a girl from Thiès, a city near Dakar, and we had a son.'

Success in this part of the world, however, is as difficult to hold onto as it is to achieve; at any moment, often through no fault of your own, the rug can be pulled from under your feet. The seaside hotel, bereft of guests, closed. Ibrahima's boss was reluctant to let him go and promised to try to find him another job. He waited around for a while, but with a wife and child to keep soon ran out of money. He was out of work again, back among the struggling masses, a precious opportunity gone.

He rocks slowly on his heels as he comes to the most difficult part of his tale. His broad hands tense, the skin tautening over his knuckles as they grip the back of the chair next to me. His sad eyes narrow to a squint. 'Kolda is my home so I thought I might be able to find work here,' he says. 'I told my wife I was coming back and asked her to join me. But I had lost my job and had no money, so she didn't respect me any more. Her mother and father didn't want her to be with someone who was out of work, so they tried to dissuade her from coming with me.' His wife heeded her parents' advice and went back to Thiès to live with them, taking the child with her. Now divorced and still lacking the means to earn his in-laws' respect, Ibrahima is allowed to see his young son only twice a year.

He has worked in the hotel restaurant for a few years now, putting in a long shift from six-thirty in the morning until ten at night. He lives alone. After work he goes home and sits for a while, reflecting; he tries to forget about the hotel, the empty restaurant, the second-rate job he has no enthusiasm for. Then, in the middle of the night, he goes out on his bicycle. 'Je suis athlète,' he says with a flicker of pride, explaining his fit, muscular frame. Sport provides an escape, a way of forgetting the past, something to look forward to. Every night he cycles fifteen miles in the dark through the forest. He has no helmet and his bicycle no light (and there are no streetlights), but there is little traffic at that time, donkeys and sheep presenting more of a hazard. When it is really dark he uses the torch on his mobile phone to light his way. I ask if he could find another wife now that he is back in work. 'First of all I want to get myself organised and settled,' he replies, his wounds still unhealed. 'I'm quite sensitive. I don't want to go through that again.'

The next morning, after a short but bumpy ride in another decrepit Peugeot, we reach the border. We are the first to cross that day. The Senegalese border post is a dusty yard with a well in the middle. When we arrive, the customs official, a tall, authoritative man in a white, knee-length tunic, is standing chatting to a woman who is drawing the morning's water in a bucket. Once they have finished their discussion, the man leads us into the dark, bare, brick-built office that abuts the yard. He takes out a tatty A5 notebook and with a biro and a ruler carefully draws up three columns on a fresh page. He writes in our names, passport numbers and nationalities, and after stamping our passports and wishing us 'bon voyage' directs us down a track across two hundred yards of scrubby no man's land to Guinea-Bissau.

The day is overcast, dulling the lush green of the dense surrounding forest. It is the beginning of the dry season and the rains' fecund legacy is still evident in the range and depth of greens on display. The border is unmarked; there is no fence or watchtower, no line of waiting guards; the forests of Senegal merge seamlessly with those of her southern neighbour. All is quiet and still, the only sound the occasional cackle or caw from high up in the trees. Rounding a bend in the track, we come upon the Guinea-Bissau customs post. Under a straw shelter held up by wooden poles, two khaki-clad border guards are draped sleepily over brown plastic chairs. I am apprehensive – border police across West Africa are notorious for extracting bribes - but their laid back smiles put me at ease. I open my rucksack for their inspection, but instead of rummaging through it one of the guards, a cheery young man with bulging eyes and round cheeks, asks me in Portuguese if I have any bombs. 'No,' I reply, surprised. 'Any guns or drugs?' 'No.' Relieved, I offer the men a cigarette as a thank you for our painless passage. They decline and wave us on with a grin. Inevitably there is another Peugeot waiting beyond them. We climb into the back, happy, uplifting West African pop music blasting from a huge speaker in the boot, and hurtle through the jungle down the cratered road to Bafatá.

Guinea-Bissau

1

West Africa is nobody's idea of a dream holiday destination. This troubled region, which was once mooted as a dumping ground for transported British convicts, contains most of the world's poorest countries and many of its least stable. Tourist attractions are sparse, amenities for travellers meagre (the convicts were eventually sent to Australia instead, West Africa deemed too disease-ridden and too uncomfortably hot even for the dregs of British society). Back home in southern England, where few people I knew had heard of Guinea-Bissau or Burkina Faso and where Sierra Leone was known only as the scene of a bitter civil war, my plans to spend half a year travelling around the three countries met with a mixture of incredulity and alarm.

In England I had carved out a comfortable life, with a mortgage, a marriage and an interesting career. I had been fortunate to stumble upon the latter when I responded to a newspaper advertisement for what was described simply as a "Good Job" but which turned out to involve working with eminent American professors to research and write about ways of tackling the problems of poor countries. Having no particular calling or ambition but thinking, with the naive arrogance of youth, that it would be wasteful not to put any abilities I had to a useful purpose, I buckled down, and within a few years had become sufficiently established to set up on my own. Chance had given me a leg-up, but I now felt I had some control over my destiny. I had attained contentment, and was happy with my lot.

Contentment, however, can breed boredom, and I worried that if I continued along this smooth path the slow creep of middle-age would accelerate. In my mid-thirties I retained an adolescent urge to have a life that was unconventional, unpre-dictable, romantic. I had a hazy notion that I could fend off

9

stagnation by seeing and doing new things, as if, like a character in a computer game which acquires extra lives each time it completes a task, consuming new experiences would somehow buttress me against time's onslaught.

In the past I had sated this need through travel (I had inherited a certain restlessness from my father, a peripatetic dealer in antique scientific instruments who on returning from his innumerable buying trips abroad would delight in showing me the globes, astrolabes and sextants that had guided voyagers of centuries past). But long trips to India, Turkey and South Africa had become steadily less fulfilling, with a diminishing return in extra lives. As I grew older and harder to impress, and as globalisation made these countries more like what I knew at home, I felt that travelling in them had become too easy. Whether it was the last, desperate throes of youth or the first symptoms of a mid-life crisis I am unsure (they are perhaps the same thing), but I now found myself confronted with a new yearning: to jettison comfort and control and advance to the next stage of the game, the next level of intensity.

I cast about for a means of soothing this itch, and soon had another lucky break. A chance trip to the West African nation of Ghana to write about a malaria programme was to introduce me to a part of the world which, as well as giving me the convulsive experience I was seeking, would force me to question much of what I thought I had learned in my work. Africa's western reaches are widely considered its most inhospitable and least attractive. A friend of mine, an old Africa hand, warned me that 'nobody goes there unless they have to,' and the little I was able to glean from my preparatory reading (there were few recent books in English and most of those in French dated from the colonial era) suggested his gloominess was justified. The region offered few luxuries to the visitor - paved roads were scarce, electricity and water supplies anaemic, and there were minimal facilities in the way of hotels and restaurants. Grinding discomfort, on the other hand, was easy to come by. Coastal West Africa is hot, humid and a fruitful hunting ground for lethal diseases. The interior is bone-dry, witheringly poor, and prone to devastating famines. Both coast and hinterland, moreover, are chronically unpredictable. History is still in the making, nothing is settled or certain. Governments rise and fall, wars erupt and subside, people live and die. At all times there is a sense that from one minute to the next a sudden tremor, a small twist of the kaleidoscope, could transform the social and political landscape beyond recognition, reshaping entire countries, entire lives.

Ghana in many ways lived up to this image - hot, poor and ramshackle, it boasts few monuments, palaces or museums, and travel around it can be exhausting. But during my month-long stay I saw that there was more to the country than dilapidation. As the sun and the heat and the damp ate away ravenously at everything humans had made, Ghanaians appeared to be fighting off decay in a stubborn display of vitality. There was music everywhere, upbeat, joyful music that lifted you above the surrounding squalor. There was bustle, movement, commerce, noise. To the visitor there was warmth and kindness. In a remote northern village a blind old woman performed a little shuffling dance to welcome me to her crumbling, mud-built compound. At a pavement bar in the capital, where I sat watching acrobats performing outlandish feats in the oil-lit street, a group of skinny boys on an adjacent table treated me to a plate of kebabs. And in yet another hour-long traffic jam on the way home from work, as lilting hip-life tunes floated on the sticky, petrol-fumed air, smiling hawkers ribbed me good-naturedly as I refused their offers of chewing gum, mattresses and seemingly everything else in between. These unfamiliar and beguiling encounters, the poise and spirit of the people, convinced me that West Africa was worth getting to know, and the idea of an extended visit began to take root in my mind.

Ghana challenged my preconceptions. In my work I had

written about Africa's many problems – disease, poverty, bad governments, and so on – and on television I had seen the terrible images of starvation and war and genocide. But Ghana presented a different picture, suggesting that the continent was more complex, and therefore more interesting, than I and many other outsiders assumed. For years I thought I had been working to better the lot of people in poor countries, but I realised I lacked a strong enough sense of how life there was really lived. It occurred to me that a journey around Africa's western fringes could have a more constructive purpose than satisfying my self-indulgent craving for adventure. What did West Africans talk about? What do they do every day? How are they adjusting to the onrush of modernity that is transforming the rest of the developing world? I felt I needed a deeper understanding of this neglected corner of the planet, and thought that perhaps, by writing about it, I might help bring its inhabitants' lives a little closer to ours.

As I began to plan a trip, I discovered that Ghana's near-neighbours Sierra Leone, Burkina Faso and Guinea-Bissau were the poorest countries in the world. Of the seven billion people on earth, the citizens of these small, seldom-visited backwaters were the very worst off, the least fortunate. This was Africa at its most exacting. In these ill-starred lands, things that we in the West take for granted – being born without killing yourself or your mother, reaching your first birthday, surviving colds, diarrhoea and other minor illnesses, reading and writing, toilets, switching on a light or turning a tap, eating a regular meal – all these things are privileges few are accorded. Slavery, colonial plunder, dictatorship and war had left the three countries reeling. More recent afflictions, from Islamic terrorism and international organised crime to climate change and the population boom, threatened to thwart their hopes of rising out of poverty.

Volatility, however, brings highs as well as lows, and even here, amid the most gruelling living conditions to be found anywhere, there was good news among the bad. Guinea-Bissau and Sierra Leone had recovered from crippling civil wars and defied the doomsayers by enjoying a decade of peace. Burkinabes had begun to mobilise against a despotic, violent regime, demanding greater democracy and freedom. As in Ghana, it seemed, the reality was more complex than the news headlines suggested, and I felt sure that exploring the three countries would give me a clearer picture of West African life, and a better idea of how the world's poorest people make it through the day.

Having decided where to go, there remained one final task: to convince my wife, Ebru, that this was a journey worth making. Although she had accompanied me on previous visits to India and South Africa, and although herself brought up in far from affluent surroundings in south-eastern Turkey, Ebru was nervous about my choice of countries for this trip. She had heard my friend's unenthusiastic assessment of West Africa, and a brief look at the UK Foreign Office's website confirmed her fears (the mandarins described in vivid detail the instability and insecurity in and around the countries on our itinerary, informing us that in Guinea-Bissau alone, as well as the usual problems of crime, unsafe roads and unpreventable killer diseases, we would do well to guard against the less familiar threats of banditry, armed uprisings, land mines and Colombian drug traffickers).

My raptures over Ghana and a short holiday together in Gambia were of only limited effectiveness in assuaging Ebru's concerns, but the combination of a curiosity kindled by the diet of African novels I passed on to her and a perception that I was too incautious to undertake the journey alone eventually persuaded her to join me. Her acquiescence came with three conditions: that we buy a plane ticket with an adjustable return date, that since she has a mortal dread of the snakes with which West Africa teems we stay in no mud huts in forests, and that we avoid rather than gravitate towards potentially life-threatening situations. Delighted to have her company for what would be a long and difficult trip, I gratefully agreed to her demands (although as it turned out, only the first two of them would be met). We booked our flights before she could change her mind.

Bafatá provides a gentle introduction. Guinea-Bissau's second city, home to just twenty-two thousand inhabitants, is little more than a large village. Built on a black rock above a bend in the languorous Gêba River, it is slowly emptying out. The old colonial quarter hugs the riverbank, snoozing in a permanent siesta. Crumbling two-storey Portuguese villas shade its deserted cobbled streets, their white paint peeling off and balustraded balconies sagging in the heat. Most are abandoned, their roofs caved in, door and window apertures gaping like the mouths of sleeping grandmothers, but a few have been occupied, by child-heavy Guinean families who have replaced terracotta roof tiles with corrugated-iron sheets and whose women hang clothes washed in the river over the balconies to dry.

At the water's edge, life proceeds slowly. Boys in torn T-shirts fish with bamboo rods, a man rinses a bicycle, young women soap their naked bodies. In an adjacent, weed-strewn field, as kites circle overhead in the pearly afternoon light, a child and his mother hack at the dry soil with tiny hoes. The far bank of the river, perhaps seventy yards away, is thick with forest. In the shade of its trees an orange-breasted Egyptian plover pecks in the mud. The plover has mystical qualities – according to Herodotus its ancestors were allowed to pluck scraps of meat from between the teeth of crocodiles; that it could maintain such a close relationship with such a dangerous animal was regarded as proof of the bird's special powers.

A few yards from the riverside, between an abandoned covered market with arched Moorish entranceways and a children's playground where rusting chains which once bore swings now hang loose, a small, unobtrusive statue offers a clue to the state of neglect that cloaks the town. For a brief period in the 1970s Guinea-Bissau shuffled out of obscurity and onto the world stage, as the country's bitter fight for independence from Portugal became a cause célèbre for students and leftist movements in Europe and America. The struggle was led by Bafatá's most famous son, Amílcar Cabral. It is his bust that stands near the market, seemingly the only new construction in the old town in the last forty years. (Thousands of miles away in a different world, another monument, Amílcar Cabral Court, a scruffy 1970s apartment block which today houses refugees from East Africa, still stands near Paddington Station in London).

The Portuguese were the first Europeans to establish a colony in West Africa. In the late fifteenth century they settled the hitherto uninhabited Cape Verde archipelago, three hundred miles off the coast, and began using it as a base for trade. For the next four hundred years their only use for what is now Guinea-Bissau was as a source of slaves, first for cultivating the islands and later for export across the Atlantic. It was only after the Berlin Conference of 1884, at which European powers carved up the continent into private colonial fiefdoms, that the Portuguese pressed for greater control. Their wars of "pacification" lasted until the 1930s, when the "savages" were finally brought to heel. The campaigns were long and brutal. One Portuguese officer had to be withdrawn to Lisbon when his barbarity proved too much for even his superiors to stomach; his methods, which would be deployed again a century later in Sierra Leone's civil war, included burning villages, massacring civilians, gouging out eyes and shooting pregnant women in the womb.

Having been the first to arrive, the Portuguese were the most reluctant to leave. The 1930 Colonial Act had emphasised the importance to the Portuguese nation of 'civilising the indigenous population' of its overseas territories, but in practice the colonisers did nothing to elevate their subjects. Ryszard Kapuscinski, the great Polish writer on Africa, remarked that in

Luanda, Angola, 'in the course of four hundred years, the Portuguese did not dig a single well for potable water, or illuminate the streets with lanterns.' The Patriarch of Lisbon announced in 1960 that the colonies needed schools, but only within limits, 'to teach the natives to write, to read and to count, but not to make them doctors.' In Guinea-Bissau, even this was considered a step too far: at independence in 1974, only one in fifty Guineans could read and write.

But despite Portugal's apparent indifference to her colony, as the winds of change blew across the continent after the Second World War and Britain and France let go of their West African territories, Guineans who expected the same treatment were to be disappointed. Antonio Salazar, the Portuguese dictator, was unwilling to accept his country's diminished status in Europe, and believed that holding onto the colonies would demonstrate her continued international clout. While the French and British moved Africans into positions of power, therefore, in preparation for a peaceful handover, nationalists in Portugal's territories were ignored, and all their demands for dialogue dismissed.

Guineans who yearned for freedom would have to seek other means to achieve it, but although weak relative to France and Britain, Portugal was a mighty force compared with Guinea-Bissau. The overwhelming majority of Guineans could afford to eat only what they grew themselves; most lived on the brink of starvation. Disease was rife, with average life expectancy just thirty-eight years. The population seemed too enfeebled even to think of rebellion, and the idea that a ragtag group of impoverished peasants might overcome his well-equipped military was of little concern to the strongman Salazar.

2

Born in 1924, Amílcar Cabral left Bafatá for the Cape Verde islands as a young child. His family's poverty was nearly fatal, for when he was in his teens Cape Verde was hit by a series of droughts and famines. Cabral would later estimate that between 1940 and 1948 famine killed a quarter of the islands' population. 'I saw people die of starvation,' he said. 'This is the fundamental reason for my revolt.'

He was in no doubt that the colonisers were to blame. At the age of twenty-one he won a scholarship to study agronomy in Lisbon, and it was here that his political consciousness awakened. Many Cape Verdeans felt closer to Portugal than to Africa, but contact with other educated young Africans shifted Cabral's perspective. Inspired by black American civil rights leaders and by "Négritude", a concept developed by French West African intellectuals who rejected colonialism and argued that black culture was the equal of white, he began to meet regularly with like-minded Lisbon-based Guineans, Mozambicans and Angolans. Their aim was "re-Africanisation". At the meetings they discussed African literature, geography and culture, and made covert plans for a reconquest. Cabral, a charismatic, popular participant whose goatee beard, woollen cap and half-rim glasses gave him the classic look of a twentieth century intellectual revolutionary, was becoming convinced that his future lay not in Europe but in freeing his continent from the imperialist yoke.

His conviction was strengthened on his return to Guinea-Bissau in 1952. He took a job with the colonial service as an agricultural engineer, and was asked by the Governor of Guinea to conduct a survey of the territory. He travelled the entire country, studying land use, crop production and trading conditions. For the first time he got to know his homeland. He saw the ubiquity and depth of rural poverty, and noted how Portuguese demands for peanut and cashew exports to balance the colonial budget were hastening soil erosion. Guinean farmers responded to these demands by burning fields to speed the soil's recovery and cutting down forests to create more space. Such methods – effective in the short-term but devastating when used over long periods – exhausted the soil, bleeding it of precious nutrients; the colonisers' insistence on intensive cultivation of cash crops was jeopardising Guinea-Bissau's future for Portugal's temporary gain.

In 1956 Cabral founded the Partido Africano da Independência da Guiné e Cabo Verde. Like its South African contemporary, the African National Congress, the PAIGC began by agitating peacefully but clandestinely for change. Its members infiltrated trade unions and organised industrial action. An early strike demanding higher pay for dock workers was successful, but after police quashed a further protest by shooting dead fifty dockers at the Pidjiguiti waterfront in the capital, Bissau, Cabral realised peaceful dissent was futile. Like Angola and Mozambique, Portugal's other African colonies, Guinea-Bissau would have to fight for its freedom.

Leading up the rock away from old Bafatá is a once-tarred road. It is flanked on one side by dark forest and on the other by wasteland and a few crumbling buildings on whose porches sit pairs of Guinean men smoking and chatting. Sleepy donkeys pull carts up and down the hill. Occasional trucks bringing water or removing sewage traverse in a wide zigzag to avoid the numerous potholes, many of which are so deep that the red earth shows through. A thin breeze whispers up from the river.

At the top of the hill sits the African quarter. When the Portuguese moved out of the colonial town on the riverbank, no Guineans moved in. Instead of occupying the large, comfortable European villas with their bougainvillea-filled gardens and airy balconies, the Africans remained where they were, huddled in their simple, ramshackle township on the great black rock. The quarter's main street winds between crepuscular shops built of wood and corrugated iron. Women sit in the dust by the road, touting little piles of fruit and bags of peanuts laid out on cloths on the ground before them. There are few cars, so shoppers and idlers walk down the middle of the street, many of them in groups of two or three, smiling and talking, or haggling with hawkers. Compared with the old part of town it is bustling, but after eighty yards the activity peters out and gives way again to quiet.

Wandering through one day in the fading late afternoon sun, we buy oranges from a young girl. She has peeled off the skin, leaving a rough white orb. She lops the top off with a knife and, in the West African way, we squeeze the sweet juice into our mouths, spitting the surfacing pips onto the ground. The girl has the spindly, undeveloped limbs of a child; she appears no older than eight or nine. She wears a blue and white school dress, her hair tied in short plaits pushed back from her brow. Delighted to be selling to "brancos", she tells us she comes here after school every day to sell oranges. Each orange costs twenty-five francs (about six cents). She has about twenty in her bucket. If she has a field day and, having fended off stiff competition from other vendors, sells an entire bucketful, she will earn just over a dollar – and that does not take into account the cost to her of buying or growing the oranges or the less direct, longer-term costs of tiredness and time spent away from her homework. Her mother sells bananas nearby for about seven cents each. On a good but not stellar day, they might make a profit of a dollar or so between them, just enough to buy a kilo of rice.

Further along the street we come upon a roadside coffee shack. We push aside the old grey sheet that shelters the interior from the heat and dust and take seats on a wooden bench. We order Nescafés. On the opposite side of the single table sits an old man. He is thin and frail, the skin of his face drawn and slightly dry, but his small eyes are bright and alert, giving him a cunning, somewhat feline air. He wears a white shirt, its undone top buttons exposing his bony chest, over baggy blue trousers and flip-flops, and sits bent-backed with his legs crossed and hands clasped lightly around his knee. He greets us with a smile, and asks to look at our guidebook. He peers at it, holding it upside down – few of his generation can read – and explains in Portuguese that he speaks no English.

He introduces himself as Eduardo Gomes. He is a carpenter by trade, and although old does not yet consider himself retired. 'If I could afford the materials I'd work,' he says, 'but I have no money to buy wood.' His first wife died a few years back and he has recently married a younger woman. He had six children, but two died; his latest son, with his new wife, is a toddler. It is a struggle to feed his young family and he relies on his older children for financial support, but despite his troubles he is cheerful and sprightly, and chuckles often as we talk.

He tells me about the war of independence. When it began, he was a young man living in the capital. He had no hesitation in joining the nationalist cause. Like many older Guineans, Eduardo has bitter memories of Portuguese rule. 'They did nothing to raise us up,' he complains. 'They treated Africans very badly. When I was seven my father had several big rice fields near Bissau, and eight dugout canoes to take rice to the Bijagós islands off the coast and bring palm wine back to the city. A Portuguese man called Manuel Pinto came one day and took all my father's fields. He took his canoes too, and his rice, goats, pigs and chickens. My father had no choice but to give them all up. Pinto was strong and because he was Portuguese he could do what he wanted.' He sips at his coffee. The young coffee seller sits beside him, washing glasses in a tub of soapy but grey water. 'My father lost his strength after that,' Eduardo continues. 'It changed him. We became poor overnight, and he had to take me out of school. From that time I hated the Portuguese.' Although the years must have diluted the anger, a trace of hatred still flashes in his sharp little eyes.

He joined the PAIGC soon after its formation. When the fifty dockers were massacred he was working near the Pidjiguiti waterfront. He saw the police running towards the port and heard the shooting. 'It was then that everyone realised we had to get rid of the Portuguese. Everyone saw what they did at Pidjiguiti. There is a Guinean saying: When your house is burning, it's no use beating the tom-toms. We had a meeting of Africans and said we would fight them – maybe they would kill us but we would fight.'

3

The nationalists faced an enemy with vastly superior firepower and manpower. Portugal had shown at Pidjiguiti that it could keep a lid on protest in the capital, that it was strong enough and well enough organised to snuff out unrest in the cities. Amílcar Cabral and his colleagues realised this, and switched their attention instead to the countryside. Cabral suspected that the colonial machine would not be so formidable outside the main population centres, and that if forced to stray too far from its urban fastness it might be vulnerable. Taking his lead from guerrilla campaigns in Latin America, therefore, he turned his back on the cities, and plotted a peasant revolt.

But how to mobilise the masses? How to bridge that huge gulf between the educated, cosmopolitan city-dwellers who would lead the rebellion and the conservative, illiterate villagers whose participation was essential for its success? The peasants had known nothing but colonialism; their instinct, inculcated over the centuries, was to defer to rather than resist authority. Revolution would require putting down their tools and interrupting the life-giving cycle of planting, nurturing and harvesting. It would mean surrendering the little security they had for the possibility – and it was no more than that – of a better future. Most villagers had little interest in who would govern them from a far-off capital; they were more preoccupied with basic survival, with finding enough food to make it through the week.

Cabral's time touring the country had sensitised him to these difficulties. He was an engaged and understanding listener ('he was interested in the personal life of any individual,' one of his successors would say of him after his death), and in his meetings with chiefs and farmers he had felt and learned to soften country-dwellers' mistrust of sophisticated urbanites. He spoke the peasants' language and trained his supporters to do likewise; although a socialist himself, he refrained from using Marxist jargon in his speeches. His recruitment methods were based on friendly persuasion, not force. From his base in Conakry in neighbouring Guinea, to which he had fled to escape the Portuguese secret police, he sent out envoys into Guinea-Bissau's villages to hold discussions with chiefs and their subjects. His followers worked their way patiently around the country, cajoling and negotiating, listening and reassuring.

They backed up their words with actions. 'Always remember,' the pragmatic Cabral told his party, 'that the people are not fighting for ideas…they fight and accept the sacrifices demanded by the struggle in order to gain material advantages, to live better and in peace, to benefit from progress, and for the better future of their children. National liberation, the struggle against colonialism, the construction of peace, progress and independence are hollow words unless they can be translated into a real improvement of living conditions.' The party set up schools and hospitals in the villages; it established health brigades – mobile training teams which taught villagers the rudiments of hygiene, disease prevention and basic treatment; and it provided training to farmers, introducing new techniques and encouraging them to diversify away from peanuts so that they would be better protected in times of scarcity.

The nationalists recruited thousands of villagers to their guerrilla campaign, bringing together people from dozens of ethnic groups and speaking numerous different tongues. All were unified by the desire to evict the colonial oppressors. Like their contemporaries in South Africa's ANC, they began the armed struggle with acts of sabotage. Later, as their numbers grew and they gained in confidence, they attacked enemy barracks, police stations and military convoys. The Portuguese, overstretched as Cabral had predicted, lost one district after another. The south and parts of the north were quickly liberated, but the cities remained under the colonists' control.

The Portuguese response drove more peasants to the nationalists' side. Unable to match the guerrillas on the ground, they turned to an aerial campaign, bombing rice fields and dikes and, following the fashion of the time, napalming liberated villages. They set up networks of informers, executed prisoners, and tortured and killed villagers suspected of harbouring nationalists. They deliberately targeted the rebels' schools and hospitals, which were forced to move several times a year. Driven out of their villages, many peasants were at first too afraid to flee into the forests, where dangerous spirits were thought to lurk, but after Cabral convinced them that the spirits too wanted rid of the colonisers, they took cover under the trees and launched attacks from their shade.

In contrast to the Portuguese, the rebels conducted a clean war. Captured soldiers reported being well treated, and Cabral's arguments and his troops' comportment impressed even senior Portuguese army officials. 'The longer a subversive war lasts,' mused one high-ranking officer, enunciating the growing sense of unease among his troops, 'the more one assimilates the ideas of the enemy, the oppressed.' As their losses accumulated, so did military dissatisfaction with the fascist government in Lisbon, now headed by the bookish Marcelo Caetano. With young Portuguese fleeing their country in droves to avoid being conscripted to what had come to be seen as a useless and unwinnable war, the first rumblings that a coup d'état might be imminent were heard at home.

By 1972 the insurgents had gained control of most of the country. Cabral compared Guinea-Bissau's situation to that of an independent state, 'part of the national territory of which – notably urban centres – is occupied by a foreign power.' He described national liberation as a 'return to history;' only when his country was free of foreign domination, he believed, would it resume its natural trajectory.

He would not live to see that day. On the evening of 20 January 1973, with the war almost won, he was shot dead by a colleague outside the PAIGC headquarters in Conakry. It remains unclear whether his killer, who was later executed, was recruited by disgruntled elements within the party or, more likely, by the Portuguese secret police, who had been trying to eliminate Cabral for years. But the assassination did not stop the war effort: the nationalists' declaration of independence eight months later was recognised by the majority of United Nations member states. The following year, after the Caetano regime was overthrown in a coup, Portugal, bowing to the inevitable, recognised Guinea-Bissau as a free and independent country.

Eduardo spent much of the war in Conakry, screening new recruits to ensure they were not agents for the Portuguese secret service. On his return to Bissau he was arrested and thrown into jail, released only when the gates were flung open at independence. 'We won because we were right,' he says now, supping the last dregs of his coffee. 'It is not always the hare that wins the race. Sometimes the one who starts slowly wins.' In his words are traces of Cabral's legacy – a unified nation proud of defeating a better equipped enemy and of conducting a clean, just war. Its totems are still in evidence today: memorials to fallen soldiers still stand in Bissau, independence and Pidjiguiti are commemorated as national holidays, and T-shirts emblazoned with Cabral's grainy image are a common sight on young Guinean torsos.

As we stand up to leave the coffee shack, Eduardo invites us to dinner at his house. Aware of his financial straits, and not wishing to deprive him and his family of precious food, we decline. He smiles and shakes our hands, wishing us a good stay in his country. We leave him chatting to the coffee seller and head back down the darkening hill to the old town.

4

When dusk falls in Bafatá, something extraordinary happens: Guinea-Bissau's second city, like all its other cities, towns and villages, is plunged into darkness. The shops in the African quarter are blotted out. The Portuguese villas recede into the gloom. Streetlamps hang unlit, the little wood fires kindled on the ground below them a quaint but ineffective substitute. Only the lighters of the fires are visible – everyone else is swallowed up, their dark faces and limbs melding into the night.

Since the state power company ran out of money and closed down in 2003, Guinea-Bissau has had no electricity. For nearly a decade, no fan has turned, no streetlight shone. Ice, refrigeration, the very concept of coolness are mere memories. Businesses cannot light their stores, power their machines or try out new technologies. Families, cast back in time, rely on candles and oil lamps to illuminate their homes. Even the wealthiest are affected: to charge their mobile phones government ministers must take them to internet cafés, which unlike their ministries have functioning generators. Seen from space at night, the country is a black hole.

We pick our way carefully down the potholed hill and slowly our eyes adjust. Ebru points out the dazzling equatorial starscape up above, the pinpricks of light almost merging in intense, brilliant clusters. At Cabral's statue we turn left along a cobbled lane parallel to the river and come to Bafatá's only restaurant. It is easy to find in the darkness because it has the old town's lone generator and is suffused with a faint electric glow, like a single light in the bottom of a large swimming pool. On the cracked and uneven pavement outside it, four young children sit around a table, taking advantage of the lamp above the door to do their homework. Further along the street their mother sits in front of a house, cooking over a low fire. The children's chatter and the chirruping of crickets rest lightly on the pregnant silence of the

African night.

The owners of the restaurant are the last Portuguese in Bafatá. Dona Celia, a small, motherly figure now in her late fifties, her grey hair tied tightly back from her tanned, sun-worn face, came here in the final years of the colony to marry José, who had stayed on after completing his military service. Most of their compatriots left for the motherland in the early 1970s, as defeat in war and independence loomed. A handful clung on, but without their privileged status and with the economy in post-oil crisis freefall life was hard. One by one they gave up the struggle and boarded the plane home. A brief but destructive civil war in 1998, which saw foreigners evacuated by boat to Senegal and Guinea-Bissau's already tiny economy contracting by a quarter, flushed out the stragglers.

'It is too late for us to go home now,' says Dona Celia as we sit outside on heavy wooden Iberian chairs, the looming darkness kept at bay by the fly-flecked light above us. 'Portugal is a better place because it has electricity and facilities, but I've been here too long. I'm used to it now. It would be hard to go back.' Three of her four children have moved to Europe, and the youngest, Bruno, a strapping, dark-eyed teenager whose energy and verve sleepy Bafatá could never contain, will follow as soon as he finishes school. 'You can't make money here,' he explains, standing beside his doting mother's chair. 'There are no jobs. I have problems with epilepsy so I need money for treatment. There is no free healthcare in Guinea-Bissau and the nearest hospital is seventy miles away. If I want to get on in life, I have to go to Portugal.'

The smell of woodsmoke drifts up from the fire along the street. Dona Celia brings us huge plates of omelette and spaghetti, the only item on today's menu. (We have ordered in advance. The restaurant has few customers and to keep down fuel costs the generator is powered up only at night. This renders refrigeration impossible and means food must be bought in and served on the same day; since buying too much would be wasteful, diners must give warning of what they will need.) After we finish eating, the father of the homeworking children, Anton, a studious-looking young teacher in round, metal-rimmed glasses, wanders up the street and takes a seat next to us. He greets Dona Celia and tells us how fond he and his family are of her and José. He even named one of his daughters after her, he says, the general Guinean distrust of the Portuguese as a nation running up against the warmth of the individual human relationship.

As a teacher, Anton is theoretically in a privileged position, for unlike nearly all his countrymen he has a salaried job. In Guinea-Bissau, however, employment does not guarantee financial security. 'It is hard to make ends meet,' he tells us, brushing away a large mosquito that has been droning around his head. 'The government doesn't pay us on time. Sometimes they go months without paying, and then they only give us one or two months' wages. I worry that I won't be able to put all my children through school. Even clothing and feeding them is difficult when I don't receive my salary.'

I ask him what has happened to Bafatá. He knows instantly what I mean. It is not just the Portuguese quarter that is decaying, he says: the African town is also thinning out. The city used to have electricity, and its roads were paved and intact. A cotton factory employed four thousand local people, and many more cultivated rice on the surrounding flatlands. But the post-independence socialist government, carried away by dreams of rapid Soviet-style industrialisation, neglected the hinterland in favour of the capital. There was no investment in irrigation or in upgrading agricultural techniques. Rural roads were left to crumble, making it impossible to take produce to market (despite a doubling of the population, the country has the same road mileage today as in 1974). Grand promises to stimulate the economy failed. In 1982 the government declared a "Year of

Production and Productivity"; 1983 was the "The Year of Action, not Words". Neither lived up to its name – in 1987 the same government, unabashed, announced another "Year of Production".

The cotton factory in Bafatá has closed down, Anton tells us. Rice, once sufficiently plentiful to export, is now imported from Thailand and Vietnam. Thousands have left for Bissau, abandoning the second city to the vultures and the encroaching bush. Early the next morning we make the same journey. As we are humping our bags up the pockmarked hill towards the transport park, a man in a pick-up truck pulls up beside us and gives us a lift.

5

In Bissau we stay at a hostel run by evangelical Christian missionaries. Very few tourists or foreign businesspeople come to Guinea-Bissau, so there is no competition to attract their custom. Hotels are therefore expensive. The mission hostel is cheap, but as the only non-missionary guests we have the additional cost of guilt. There are probing questions at first, suspicious glances, particularly from the Americans, but my book seems to meet with approval (a young woman from Ohio promises to pray for it to 'open people's eyes to what life is like here'), and we are for a time left in peace while they go about their good deeds.

For many young Guineans from the interior, Bissau is the promised land, a great metropolis where their dreams will be realised, where they will escape the eternal agricultural treadmill and step into a modern, Westernised world of possibilities and change. At independence three-quarters of today's city was uninhabited bush, but in the past thirty years its population has quadrupled. A great flood of humanity has converged on the capital, gushing in from all corners of the country. Like a deserting spouse who has grown out of a long marriage, rural Guinea-Bissau has gathered up its belongings, said goodbye to its past and decamped for the city. All the emptying villages and provincial towns of the hinterland, all the abandoned rice fields, the forlorn forest hamlets with their decomposing mud houses – all come down to this.

What has triggered this exodus? What has ruptured the ancient cycle of planting and harvesting, the slow rhythms of village life, the unquestioned acceptance of the cards life deals? Guinea-Bissau once had a proud agricultural tradition. In pre-colonial times, while most of Africa was struggling to feed itself, Guineans, expert in wet-rice farming and using manure from cattle and goats as fertiliser, produced surpluses of rice, yams and millet. They traded these staples with early Portuguese explorers, and exported malaguetta peppers and kola nuts across the Sahara to North Africa. An eighteenth century English visitor to the country was dazzled by its great orchards of 'orange, lime, lemon, fig, guava, banana, cocoa nut, and plantain trees, and also pine apples, water melons, cucumbers and cassava plants.'

Slavery and then colonialism disrupted this Eden. With the advent of the Atlantic slave trade, harvesting souls became more lucrative than harvesting crops; after its demise the European colonisers transferred the subjugation of Africans from the international to the domestic arena, forcing their vassals to grow crops for export. Farming had once been a venerable occupation, regarded by most Guineans as the only truly honourable form of work. Now it was reduced to drudgery, a mindless, joyless slog for a hated foreign master.

Independence could not halt the slide. Amílcar Cabral's return to history never materialised. The farmers who were supposed to lead this revival and shepherd their nation to prosperity were stopped in their tracks by a new blight, for the colonists' departure coincided with a population explosion. Health improvements in the West had filtered through to Africa – vaccination against measles, smallpox, whooping cough and tuberculosis prevented millions of early deaths; improved hygiene and new treatments for diarrhoea and other maladies saved the lives of millions more. Instead of dying within a few months of birth, African babies began to make it to childhood, and then to adolescence. Women who had previously had eight or ten pregnancies in the hope that one or two infants would survive suddenly found themselves with five or six healthy children to bring up. There was a continent-wide baby boom - Guinea-Bissau's population, which before independence had remained static for decades, more than doubled in forty years.

Although for their parents a bigger household means more hands to help in the fields and at home, for the children it is a disaster. Food must be shared between more mouths, so each child grows up less strong and healthy. Parental time and money must be parcelled out, meaning less attention is paid to the health and education of individual children. And when the baby boomers reach adulthood and ask the village elders for a plot of land to farm, there is nothing left to give them. While communities had remained stable and small there was enough land to go around; sons took over their fathers' fields, plots were passed down from one generation to another. But as the population mushrooms and the ranks of young adults swell, land must be sliced more thinly, between five or six claimants rather than one or two. Where farmers had once had sufficient acreage to produce and sell surplus crops, now there is barely enough space to grow enough to eat, and with plots ever more cramped it becomes uneconomical to use machines or animals to cultivate them. The boomers must bend over the ground themselves, and hack at the dry soil with hoes. They know that these methods cannot compete with the more efficient, mechanised techniques of farmers in less crowded countries, but there is no alternative – they have run out of room.

The problems for farmers do not end there. To keep up with the rest of the world, and to be able to offer their crops at prices that will attract domestic and overseas consumers, Guinean farmers do not just need the same amount of land; they need more land. The Portuguese demanded that their subjects grow cash crops – peanuts and, later, cashews – which would be sold in Europe to balance the colonial budget. But cash crops are at the mercy of global forces, particularly if, like Guineans, you lack the know-how and technology to offer anything more sophisticated than the raw product. Manufactured goods are constantly refined and developed – even a humble peanut can be cooked, flavoured, combined and packaged in numerous different ways. But the quality of raw produce improves little if at all over time; a cashew nut plucked from a tree in the 1970s is no different from one picked today. While the price of manufactured goods increases, therefore, that of raw commodities declines. Since independence the value of the unprocessed crops in which African farmers specialise has collapsed: between 1987 and 2007, the price of a ton of cashews halved.

To earn the same income as he did in the 1980s, then, a modern-day Guinean cashew farmer must plant double the number of trees. To do this he must either use more land - but there is no more land - or work his existing acreage more intensively. He tries the second approach, but quickly runs up against the exhaustion of the soil foreseen by Cabral. It becomes impossible for the farmer (who now, remember, also has more children to feed) to maintain his standard of living.

As farming becomes ever more difficult and unattractive, the country dweller casts around for alternatives. In the past, when everybody lived in villages and all life revolved around agriculture, he had nowhere to go; now, however, drawn by the promise of jobs in industry, government or the aid sector, a few intrepid pioneers have taken the plunge and left the bush for the capital. From time to time they come back to their villages to visit. They bring with them the trappings of success: a moped, a mobile phone, perhaps a music player. They wear different - modern - clothes: jeans, baseball caps, training shoes, short skirts. And they tell villagers of the bounties of the city, of the abundant jobs, the shops overflowing with exotic foreign goods, the market stalls teeming with fish and meat.

Our country-dweller is entranced. At last there is a solution to his problems. His choice is simple: he can stay in the village and struggle or move to the city and thrive. Tired of breaking his back in the pitiless fields for tiny, and dwindling, rewards, he follows the pioneers to the capital.

6

The old European quarter of Bissau saw few of the new arrivals. A low-rise town of wide avenues and pastel-coloured colonial villas and mansions, it nestles sleepily below a canopy of palms and shady mango trees, its western edge divided from the still, sun-pounded ocean by a thin green line of tangled mangroves. It must once have been elegant, with European traders thronging the port area and colonial officials and their frayed wives sipping at sundowners and peering from their balconies at the street life below, but after the Portuguese fled it lay vacant: with the exception of a few embassies and government ministries, and despite a massive influx of African villagers to the city, old Bissau never filled up. Instead of occupying the grand and spacious brick-built villas, the peasants, the inheritors of the colonial legacy, built their own city, a city of mud, thatch and tin, adjacent to but separate from the abode of their former masters. Where the colonisers had clung to the shoreline, which provided proximity to home, access to trade goods and occasional relief from the exhausting heat, the new arrivals spread inland, back towards where they had come from. The focal point of life in the capital shifted, and the Portuguese quarter was reduced to an irrelevant relic, a mere curiosity for the dribble of visitors who pass through on their way somewhere else.

Today the old town is silent and almost deserted. In Bissau as in Bafatá, the Portuguese buildings are collapsing, many of them no longer safe to live in even if anyone felt so inclined. Nature, never long kept at bay in the tropics, has crept back in and filled the gap. Thick bushes occupy living rooms, cracks in plastered facades expose red-brick scars, the slender trunks of climbing trees wind like pythons through windows. The central market too has been vacated and begun the process of decay; a few stall-holders have moved onto the pavement outside, where they charge high prices to stray tourists and newly arrived aid workers. A couple of cafés on Che Guevara Square see a steady traffic of politicians, World Bank staffers and South American drug traffickers, but otherwise life is elsewhere.

Those newly arrived from the country brought it with them on their backs. Today's capital is a patchwork of villages. Neighbourhoods are dominated by a single tribe, a single family, or by migrants from a single village. The dividing lines between them are impermeable: within the lines, everybody knows one another, and knows one another's business; beyond them, although still in the same city, you are an alien, a stranger - the people you encounter live by different rules and with different customs. Your loyalty, unchanged since time immemorial, is not to these outsiders but to those inside the lines, to your fellow villagers. That they, like you, have left the countryside behind is not important; you belong to your family and to your ancestral community, not yet to your city.

As in the countryside, life is lived outdoors, in the unpaved streets that are indistinguishable from the lanes that wind through forest hamlets. The mission is in one of the poorest *bairros*, a quarter dominated by the Pepel, a tribe of fishermen and farmers from the malarial swamps north of Bissau. It lies at the end of a dusty track that zigzags between rusting metal fences, shacks selling liquor or basic provisions, patches of untidy scrub, and a few simple one-room houses with tin roofs. Pigs rummage in the drifts of refuse that have washed up against the buildings. Children throw stones listlessly at stray dogs. The squalor is interrupted only by the few mango and neem trees that have not yet been felled for firewood or construction, and by the tiny, bright-red firefinches that flit among their leaves.

There are people everywhere, re-enacting village scenes in the city. Teenage girls sit in front of their houses, plaiting each other's hair. Children draw water from a well and wash in the open. Young men play chequers or table football, or lie sleeping on porches. Housewives in headscarves and patterned skirts bend at the waist like pairs of compasses to sweep the dust with palm-frond brooms or scrub clothes against wooden washboards; they hang the clean clothes to dry on lines suspended from trees. At the far end of the street, near the mission, a small boy lies face down on an old tyre, observing the road intently like a cat stalking a bird. A huddled old lady, white hair cropped short above her wrinkled brow, sits near him on the ground, selling peanuts and lumps of charcoal. A few yards further on, a middle-aged man, newly washed, sits on a chair pontificating, naked but for a blue towel wrapped around his waist; three women, perhaps his wives, crouch beside him over a little stove, cooking pungent-smelling fish. There is chatter, laughter and an occasional raised voice scolding an errant child. Pied crows squawk, piglets snort. But the sounds are not of a city. The roar of traffic is absent, the road too uneven and the dust too deep for most cars. There is no electricity, so no television or stereo blares. And there are no sirens, since the police have no vehicles. The only sign of industry is a tenebrous baker's oven, sheltered from the dust by rusting corrugated-iron walls; the baker runs out of loaves in the early morning, and spends the rest of the day sprawled on his mud floor snoozing in the gloom.

The village ways die hard. Like their rural cousins, the people of the *bairro* are wary of strangers. Our arrival in their midst is greeted with hostile stares and muffled discussion, as if we were brash Londoners striding into a remote country pub. Modern Guineans are unused to white visitors, but their ancestors' experiences have not been forgotten. As we walk down the dirt road, attempting vainly to be inconspicuous, a few children shout 'branco' (white man) or 'oporto' (Portuguese) at us from the safety of doorways. But their parents do not return our smiles and greetings, instead staring at us blankly or uttering disapproving or mirthful comments to their friends. We have a bleak sensation of being very far from home.

Slowly, however, and perhaps won over by our dogged refusal

to ignore them back, the people of the neighbourhood begin to lower their defences. In many poor countries merely having white skin assures immediate attention and popularity, but in Guinea-Bissau you must earn affection. At first one or two of the more confident men return our greetings. The youngest children sally forth from their doorways to hold our hands or follow us home. We buy peanuts from the old lady, who thereafter salutes us with a cheery smile. After a fortnight, people begin to wish us good day; those who speak Portuguese ask how things are going and whether we are missionaries (in a community that is predominantly animist, they seem pleased that we are not). Some days later a serious, rugged-looking man, who has never previously acknowledged us from his street corner seat on a plastic jerrycan, suddenly beckons us over. He pulls up two more jerrycans and offers us a glass of sweet green tea that he has brewed in a little red kettle on a metal stove. Other young men come up and join us. Relieved at gaining some degree of acceptance, we chat happily with them for a while, about the mission, our trip and the situation in Guinea, and when we rise to leave, our new friend refuses to accept payment for the tea.

7

Since there is no power and the heat quickly rots anything perishable, Bissau's residents must lay in a new supply of food each day. Every morning, therefore, we walk down the paved but potholed road that leads from our *bairro* to Bissau's main market at Bandim. The market is a labyrinth, its narrow dark lanes winding between rickety wooden stalls whose tin roofs jut out threateningly at throat height. A press of brightly-dressed shoppers haggles noisily over tomatoes, onions, smoked fish and meat. The vendors know their customers – you can buy individual eggs, teabags, cigarettes, sugar lumps and chilli peppers; bread sellers will cut a baguette in half if that is all you can afford; potatoes are divided into groups of three, tomatoes into pyramids of four; matches are sold in bundles of ten, along with a piece of the striking surface torn from the box. In the days leading up to Christmas and New Year, which all Guineans celebrate regardless of their religious persuasion, the market is crowded and chaotic, but after the turn of the year, when all the money has been spent, it is empty and silent.

Only the alcohol sellers do a year-round trade. On a half-mile stretch of the paved road there are thirteen bars or liquor stores. They sell cheap Portuguese red wine, bottled lager, palm wine and *cana*, a strong rum made with cashew apples. Bissau has a drink problem. Its inhabitants' love of alcohol is well-known throughout West Africa. Back in Senegal, a fellow passenger on one of our bush taxi rides had warned us that Guineans 'like to drink and party but they don't like to work.' Later in our trip, on hearing we had spent time here, Sierra Leoneans would talk in awed tones of Guineans' capacity for alcohol consumption. The liquor stores near our *bairro* are busy at all hours of the day and night. Christians and animists quaff openly, Muslims more discreetly.

For there is little to do but drink. When the hordes of wide-eyed villagers arrive in the capital, there is nothing here - no neon lights, no buzzing shopping malls, very few private cars or motorbikes. All they see is poverty, filth and a jumble of crowded neighbourhoods that bear an alarming resemblance to what they have left behind. Nor is there any work. The aid jobs have been colonised by foreigners, government is in the hands of a small clique of elders, and the few public sector positions in a city with scant public services are handed out to the friends and relatives of the powerful, not to humble, uneducated peasants. The new arrivals are too late – there are too many people and not enough jobs; the threadbare urban economy, like the villages they have forsaken, has no room for them.

The only option available to them is commerce. But how can they lower themselves to hawking in the markets? These are people used to real work: hard physical labour in the fields, hunting, fishing, work for which you need strength, determination, patience, where you are judged by the size of the yams you produce, the sacks of rice you harvest. A man's work. Commerce is for women and for Fulas, those flighty Muslims from the east who are too lazy, too eager for a fast buck, to bend their backs in the fields. Bandim market is dominated by women, Fula men and foreigners. Coffee sellers from Guinea-Conakry, medicine men from Niger and pale-skinned Mauritanian shopkeepers compete for business with Senegalese, Gambians and Malians. Even if they could put aside their hauteur, Guineans would not easily find a niche – the foreigners and Fulani are well ensconced; they have taken the prized pitches, honed the sharpest sales techniques, cornered the best customers. Here again the villagers are crowded out, here again they have arrived too late.

So instead they idle. They drink, play chequers, or brew green tea. Many survive on one meal a day – they call it "um tiro", one shot. The well-connected crowd into small houses with relatives or friends, six or seven sharing a room; those without contacts must sneak into the market at night to sleep under the tables. I ask a local headmaster, Carlito, if he thinks the migrants would be better off staying in the villages. He replies without hesitation: 'If I could afford a tractor, I'd go back to the village myself.'

But the new arrivals have their pride. While they were back home toiling in the fields, those who came from the city to visit were the ones who had prospered, who had made it (the others, who did not come back, were presumed to be too busy to take time out from their soaring new careers). With them these pioneers brought not just mobile phones and sports shoes, but an aura of glory, of achievement, of success. Can those who followed them now go back as failures? Can they give up their dreams of betterment and return – forever – to a life of drudgery? Of course, they cannot. It is too late for that, as well. Their aspirations have left the fields behind. The village is the past, not the future. In their minds they have moved on, and turning back is impossible to countenance.

Next to the mission in a small, whitewashed one-room building, a young Christian convert named Tino has a shop. He built it with his own hands, having saved enough money as a hawker to buy bricks, cement and a plot of land. From behind the metal grid that fronts it he sells basic provisions – washing powder, sachets of water, tinned sardines, pencils, exercise books and other sundries. The shelves are only thinly stocked, however, and since he opened up a few months ago business has been quiet. He spends most of the day sitting on the raised platform out front, reading the Bible or playing chequers with his friend, Joka. I sometimes join them in the sultry late afternoons after buying teabags and eggs from the shop for the next day's breakfast. Tino without fail gives me his plastic chair and pulls up a less comfortable wooden stool for himself. Small children run around squealing in the street below us as we talk.

Neither of them is happy. Joka, tall and languid, sprawls

across his plastic chair like an octopus. He is often asleep when I pass, his head lolling pendulously over the back of the chair, a living image of Orwell's 'boredom which is inseparable from poverty; the times when you have nothing to do and, being underfed, can interest yourself in nothing.' He came to Bissau as a child from a village in the north. Although he completed several years of schooling and speaks three languages, he cannot find a job. He complains about the lack of opportunities for young people in the city. 'The government does nothing for us,' he spits, his general air of sloth betraying an angry streak that I have encountered before among young men in more combustible parts of West Africa. 'All they do is stuff their pockets. The only people who can find jobs here are the family and friends of politicians. They live in big houses and drive big cars. Nobody else has a chance.' Tino, smaller and more compact than his friend and with a less cynical demeanour, nevertheless concurs. 'People in the countryside think conditions are good here in Bissau,' he says, 'but they are wrong. There is nothing here.'

Their resentment is trained on the older generation. The heroes of the war of independence have reneged on their promises. Instead of development they brought impover-ishment; since the colonists departed, incomes have plummeted. Although a handful of the country's leaders have prospered, the wealth has not been shared. The elders allowed – encouraged! – the spread of corruption, and excluded the next generation from prosperity and power.

Until recently the young have kept quiet, mindful that Africa expects deference towards its elders. But look around Bissau and you see signs of change. In the shade of an abandoned Portuguese building in the old town is a stall selling cheap replica football shirts. They are in blue and white stripes or green and white hoops – the colours of Porto FC, or Sporting Lisbon. Some are in the deep red of the Portuguese national team. Teenage boys wear T-shirts emblazoned with photos of Deco or

Ronaldo, the modern heroes of Portuguese football. Most young Guineans do not want Ghana or the Ivory Coast to win the upcoming World Cup; they are supporting their old colonial masters. To the dismay of the elders, their children and grand-children do not despise but look up to Portugal. Tino and Joka are among numerous young people who talk of "taking the boat to Europe," where you can get ahead through merit and hard work rather than deceit and nepotism. The journey, they know, is dangerous and often fatal, claiming thousands of West African lives each year, but their patience is running out.

The political scientist Samuel Huntington once wrote that it is not invasion by foreign armies that is the main threat to stability in traditional societies, but invasion by foreign ideas. Across West Africa, foreign ideas are fuelling a clash of the generations. In the city, Guineans are exposed to Western products and Western culture. They see foreign aid workers driving around in European cars and tapping away at laptops. They see them chatting on mobile phones, dining in Western restaurants, wearing Western clothes. And they meet fellow Guineans who have done well in Europe and returned to flaunt their success. Realising that a better life is possible, and that millions in the West enjoy electricity, running water, a steady income and an array of other luxuries, their frustration with those running their country is growing.

The latest slight against the older generation is perhaps the most painful. A popular rap song is playing on radios all over the city. It harangues the elders, the veterans of the independence struggle, and tells them that life was better under the Portuguese. Imagine the shock, the betrayal! All that they fought for, all those brave friends who gave their lives for freedom. Was it all a waste of time? Was all that blood spilt for nothing? Have their heroics been forgotten so quickly?

The youths are unrepentant. They want more than Guinea-Bissau can offer them. Until recently, all but a few have been reluctant to undertake the journey to Europe – Guineans are not great risk-takers and family ties at home are strong. But as the population grows and resources decline and they find their government neither willing nor able to give them a chance, the ocean crossing beckons like a Siren. Several of Tino and Joka's friends have already boarded makeshift motorised canoes for the perilous trip up the Atlantic coast. If Joka does not find a job soon, he says, he will have to follow. Many of those who depart West Africa are arrested en route and sent back, unwanted; many more drown, their vessels unfit for the ocean. But a few make it, and grow prosperous enough to send money back home, and a handful of success stories is all it takes to persuade their desperate peers, whose journey to the city has brought nothing but disillusion, to make the next, much greater leap.

8

The mission compound sits behind high walls studded on top with broken glass. Built of brick and freshly whitewashed, it boasts a basketball court, an outdoor cafeteria in a pleasant, grassy garden, and two large, two-storey classroom blocks. In such a tumbledown neighbourhood the mission's size and solidity appear incongruous, but this juxtaposition has a purpose. The compound conveys a simple message to those living around it. If you mend your heathen ways, it tells them, you too can be orderly, affluent, whitewashed, and sheltered from the tumult outside the walls.

The hostel lies at the rear of the complex, behind the basketball court. Our first-floor room overlooks the compound on one side and on the other a wide expanse of lush green rice fields, bordered in the far distance by a dark line of palm trees. It is where the city ends and the country begins. The room is spartan but comfortable. It has a bathroom with a cold water shower, and a ceiling light and fan. The latter are only occasionally of use, however, for the electricity, which relies on a private generator, is strictly rationed (the mission was once hooked up to the old city grid, but the connecting copper wires were stolen and the collapse of the national power company rendered replacing them pointless). To save on expensive fuel, the generator is only fired up quite late in the evening, often well after dusk. It is switched off again at ten o'clock sharp.

The absence of electricity has surprising effects on one's state of mind. As darkness falls, the guest finds himself longing for the moment of illumination. This is not just a practical matter – being unable to read, cook, remain cool or see those you are talking to are all bothersome but, after a period of acclimatisation, bearable. No, it is more than that. Living in the dark is miserable. Conversation is muffled, eating becomes an ordeal rather than a pleasure, you feel and probably are less safe (criminals and dangerous animals and insects all thrive in the dark), and there is nothing to do to while away the hours before bed. You are plunged back to a simpler but less secure time. You find yourself, like the renegade Egyptian pharaoh Akhenaten, worshipping the light. As the generator's ugly drone - sweet music! - finally cranks up and dormant bulbs flicker into life, great joy and relief wash over you. You feel ashamed, of course, at your pettiness - most Guinean homes are never electrified - but everyone you meet is embarrassed by the country's powerlessness. Local people complain as lustily as spoilt foreigners; for them, it is the ultimate symbol of the government's failure.

The hostel's five rooms see a steady traffic of guests. There are two long-term residents: Dan, a lugubrious, middle-aged Californian whose gaunt frame and sunken cheeks bespeak years of subsisting on a meagre African diet, and Missael, a jolly young Guatemalan music teacher. They are joined from time to time by temporary lodgers - earnest students from the Americas, here to teach for a term in the mission school, or doughty evangelists from the interior who have business in the capital or are in need of a break and some comfort. Freddy, a jocular Brazilian with a grey beard and bottle-thick glasses, visits frequently from the south of the country. He and his wife Raquel, a nurse, have set up shop in the Islamic stronghold of Quebo, a hot, dreary town whose resident Muslim holy men, or marabouts, draw pilgrims from all over West Africa in search of healing or wisdom. Freddy is building a small mission there, and he comes to Bissau to buy building materials and classroom equipment, which are not available in the south. The venture is not going smoothly, he tells us. Many of Quebo's Muslims are angry that a Christian mission is going up in their town, and are keen to sabotage the project. They have repeatedly torn down the perimeter fence and blocked the access road. Anyone tempted to take up the mission-aries' offer of schooling is hounded into backing down. Night after night, moreover, the remarkably unflustered Freddy adds cheerfully, enraged locals surround the house where he and Raquel are sleeping and stone it.

Another Brazilian guest, a chubby, unshaven, serious young scholar named Tony, lives in the eastern forests. He is a linguist, and is translating the Bible into Sarakole, a language of the predominantly-Muslim Soninke people. Translation is always painstaking work, but this is a particularly laborious under-taking. To do it, Tony has had to learn four languages: Sarakole, English, Kriolu (Guinea-Bissau's lingua franca) and koine Greek, the language of the first New Testament manuscripts. When he translates, he tells me, he starts by reading the Greek Bible. He then checks his interpretation against the English and Portuguese texts (he has three different versions of the Portuguese) to make sure he has not missed any subtleties in the original. Next, in order that his translation will be at home in a Guinean context he consults the Kriolu Bible. This, however, does not help with the most difficult cultural conundrums. Mark 8:34, for instance, where Jesus tells his disciples and various bystanders that anyone wishing to follow him must 'deny himself, and take up his cross,' makes sense to Kriolu speakers, who have had long exposure to Christianity and understand the symbolism (the earliest Portuguese explorers of West Africa planted wooden crosses to mark their progress down the coast). But to speakers of Sarakole, far from the sea and barely touched by the Portuguese presence, the cross is meaningless. 'I puzzled over this for days trying to find a suitable translation,' says the patient Tony. 'The cross wouldn't do, so I needed to find another symbol. I asked around and discussed it with people in my village in the east, and finally I lit on the *casanke*, a sheet the Soninke use as a shroud. Every Soninke owns one of these sheets in preparation for death, so they will all understand its meaning.' He beams with satis-faction.

The Jesus of the Sarakole Bible therefore tells his followers to take up their *casanke*. Few are likely to hear. Most Soninke are based in Mali and Senegal. Since they speak a different dialect to their brethren in Guinea-Bissau, Tony's translation will be unintelligible to them. There are just seven thousand Sarakole speakers in Guinea-Bissau. Nearly all are Muslim, but even if they convert en masse to Christianity and show a sudden interest in the Bible, literacy rates are so low in that part of the country that only a handful will be able to read it. Tony, who has calculated that the whole project will take him ten years, expects a readership of around a dozen. This does not deter him, for he knows he is doing God's work and that the path to salvation is never smooth. One day, he believes, the Soninke, who have hitherto shown little enthusiasm for the missionaries' message, will be won round. 'Who knows when the Lord will speak to them?' he asks. When at last He does, Tony's Bible will be there waiting.

To some extent, the missionaries' motives for being in West Africa are similar to my own: to be of some use in life, to assuage our wracked consciences, to burrow ascetically among the wretched of the earth. But whereas my beliefs are rooted in the shallow rubble of hope rather than the deep clay of conviction, the evangelists are in no doubt that they will be bountifully rewarded for their labours. 'I know I'm doing good here,' says Dan, the doleful Californian, sounding simultaneously both smug and melancholy. 'I know I'm going to heaven.'

Doing good has as its focus the spreading of the Gospel. The South American missionaries seem equally interested in Africans' spiritual and physical well being, but for the North Americans improving the lives of local people is not a target but a tool, a means to an end. Children are taught English so that they can attain high rank in their careers or communities and use their influence to spread the Word; young men are given business coaching so that they can support themselves as pastors; computer training and basketball are offered as incen-

tives to lure fresh recruits; Dan, who has no medical qualifica-
tions, runs a clinic where he distributes medicines in the name of
Jesus. Although subtler than the methods of the eighteenth-
century Muslim jihadis who gave the forest peoples of the
interior the choice of converting to Islam or being attacked, the
intent is the same. Bringing Jesus into Africans' lives, the missionaries believe with chilling certainty, will be more beneficial to
them – in this world and the next – than the secular goals of
health, education and the elimination of poverty in which the
international aid community places its faith.

Before he found Jesus, Dan, who is lanky and greying but still
fit-looking in his fifties, was 'a pretty normal Californian kid.' He
excelled at baseball and golf, smoked marijuana, chased girls and
cheated at cards. As a Roman Catholic, however, whose Irish
ancestors migrated to the United States in the late nineteenth
century, he had been inculcated at a very early age with a bleak
fear of hell. When he was in his late teens he decided to find out
how to avoid eternal damnation. He began to study the Bible, and
after months of reading and ruminating came to the conclusion
that only by submitting his life to Christ would he be saved. At
the age of just nineteen, he was born again; for the three and a
half decades since, his entire existence has revolved around his
religion.

We sit one hot afternoon on a comfortable bamboo sofa in the
garden, drinking tea. Large grey lizards dart across the high
walls around us. A praying mantis waits patiently on the armrest
of the sofa. In the far corner of the garden three Guinean boys lay
bricks; they are building a workshop that will train Christian
mechanics, labouring under the watchful eye of a young man
from Michigan (the mission's American founder did not yet trust
Africans to run projects themselves: 'We still need to hold hands
with them,' he had told me with a paternal smile).

Dan tells me about his father, Ed. A tough Irish policeman of
the old school, Ed smoked heavily, womanised and gambled, and

did not shrink from dealing out beatings to suspected criminals. His Roman Catholicism was nominal; he entered church only for weddings and funerals and prided himself on living a perfectly godless life. Only once was he spotted praying, when the family car broke down one evening in a crime-ridden district of Detroit – 'we're gonna die, Dad's praying!' shrieked Dan's terrified sister when she saw her father murmuring to the heavens.

When Dan told him about his conversion, the father felt he had lost a son. 'You're a goddamn Jesus freak!' he yelled, horrified. 'You're a goddamn fucking Jesus freak!' Seven times he repeated the same thing. Dan's attempts to calm him were futile. 'Give Him up or get out of my house! Renounce Him!' his father bellowed. Dan, shellshocked, left and went to stay with a friend.

Son and father made up after a few months. They resumed their weekly golf games, but Dan never succeeded in converting Ed to his new creed. Even when the years of smoking two packs of cigarettes a day finally caught up with him and he was struck down by Legionnaires' disease, Ed remained steadfast. When he was on his deathbed, Dan made one last attempt. 'I told him it's never too late Dad,' he says with a resigned but sad smile. 'He knew what I was talking about, and even though he could hardly breathe for all the tubes that were wrapped around his face, he still managed to tell me to get the fuck out of there.'

Dan didn't laugh. For him, his father's refusal was spiritual suicide, a one-way ticket to hell. But living up to Dan's standards is exacting. Simply believing in God and accepting the existence of Jesus are not enough. Even living a virtuous life will not help you reach Dan's heaven. Unless you give yourself to Jesus and relegate everything else in your life – love, friendship, work, pleasure – to mere appendages, you are doomed. The mission-aries' demand that you shed your old, sin-tainted skin and become, born again, a completely different person; nothing less will save you.

For the first few days after our arrival Ebru and I had been left free to continue along our benighted path, but the missionaries cannot resist for long. Dan tells me that by refusing to devote myself to Christ I have 'chosen darkness over light.' During an evening game of cards he informs me that Satan has me in his grip. This is an unsettling revelation, and a highly effective diversionary tactic: I duly lose the next hand.

The assaults quickly become relentless, not just from Dan but from the other North Americans and their zealous Guinean converts. I fight back, but my plaintive arguments that belief in God and living a good life will surely help one to escape damnation are brushed off peremptorily, like a mosquito from your arm. Dan claims that doing good will make no difference to your prospects of salvation. You can spend most of your life in sin, but as long as before you die you give your life to Jesus, you will enter the kingdom of heaven. Live a saintly life without converting, on the other hand, and you will flounder forever in hell. Stunned by this nihilistic philosophy, you find yourself playing devil's advocate (providing the knowing missionaries with further proof of your allegiances). But they have answers for everything, as if they have memorised a manual of responses to infidel questions. Ask them why an all-good God allows Guinean infants to die of pneumonia or malaria and they tell you that sinful mankind has failed to prevent the deaths, and that anyway the children are now in a better place. Ask if the children can go to heaven without having given their lives to Jesus and they tell you that the Bible contains exceptions for those who die too young to have found Him (the age threshold for this is unclear). Few of the answers are watertight, but the missionaries have no doubts – everything can be explained, everything is part of the divine schema. Even when you lose your temper and balk at their inconsistencies (Ebru is so exasperated by their obduracy that she tells Dan he is in danger of turning her away from belief), they remain unruffled; Jesus told them in the Bible that people would think his followers mad, so your behaviour too is already in the blueprint.

It was not until after his death that Dan discovered his father had been a devil-worshipper. 'I went round to my sister's house in California one day and saw all these books in the living room about Satan and the occult. I was shocked. I said, Debbie why have you got all these books? You can't follow Jesus and have all this evil around you!' Debbie told him they were Ed's books. She had found them in a closet after he died, and had kept them for sentimental reasons.

After some persuasion, Dan convinced her to throw them on the fire that was warming the living room against the chill winter afternoon. One by one the books were burned. As the pages crackled and shrivelled, Dan noticed that his sister's cat was acting strangely. 'Debbie had a cat and a parrot, and they'd always got on very well. But as the books were going up in flames I saw the cat staring intently at the parrot. Her jaws were quivering in a way I'd never seen before. And then, suddenly, she jumped up at the bird and grabbed its neck between her teeth, trying to throttle it. My sister managed to pull them apart, but then the cat ran to the other side of the room and sank her teeth into my little niece's finger. She bit really deep and wouldn't let go.' Both parrot and niece survived, but the following day the cat went out of the house and started running back and forth across the busy road in front – a road she had always previously avoided – until she was hit by a truck. 'It was only later,' Dan says, 'when I read in the Bible that Jesus said spirits can inhabit living things, that I realised the evil spirits must have jumped from Dad's books into the cat.'

Similar stories are commonplace in West Africa, which is a much more fertile hunting ground for Christian evangelists than the desiccated wastes of the developed world (Dan mournfully describes Europe as 'spiritually dead'). Whereas Islam had to adapt to attract converts, by allowing them to meld the stories and preaching of the Koran with their existing beliefs in ancestors and other spirits, Christianity had to make less of an adjustment. For while Islam's stark austerity has little time for miracles, saintly mediators or ecstatic trances, its more baroque rival shares much with the old religions of Africa.

The animists of West Africa attribute great powers to the spirits which reside in water, trees, the soil and rocks (there is a divine creator, but he is a distant entity who has little to do with everyday human affairs). These spirits are amoral and, like Greek gods, must be regularly propitiated if they are to do you good rather than harm. They are reached with the help of your ancestors, who fulfil a mediating role that bears some resemblance to that of Christian saints. Miracles, too, are common to both Christianity and animism. I met several Guineans who believe people can turn into snakes, for example. One, a well-educated, sensible young follower of Christ, told me that he once saw his own uncle make this very transformation. The uncle metamorphosed into serpentine form and slithered into a nearby hut. His nephew, amazed, followed him inside, only to find his relative standing there chatting calmly to the hut's inhabitants, not a reptile to be seen.

When you believe that your president can make himself invisible, as many Guineans did of the late Nino Vieira, who reportedly vanished when soldiers broke into his palace to kill him, reappearing only when the intruders had beaten his wife to within moments of death, it is not a great conceptual leap to place your faith in a miracle-working son of a virgin who came back from the dead and claimed to be God's heir. The Portuguese made little effort to convert Guineans to Catholicism, using religion instead as a front to justify slavery and colonial domination ('When the missionaries came,' the Kenyan independence leader Jomo Kenyatta observed, 'we had the land and they had the Bible. They taught us to pray with our eyes closed. When we opened them, they had the land and we had the Bible'). But the Scottish explorer Mungo Park, who trekked through West Africa in 1795 in search of the Niger River, recognised the region's potential as a target for more sincere evangelists. A Muslim salt trader who had heard that Park was a Christian offered him a rice supper if he would write him some verses as protection against wicked men. 'The proposal was of too great a consequence to me to be refused,' wrote Park, who existed on the edge of starvation, often going days without food when the wretched villages he passed through had nothing left to give or sell. He took a piece of chalk and covered the trader's writing board with verses from the Bible. When he had finished, the trader 'washed the writing from the board into a calabash with a little water and, having said a few prayers over it, drank this powerful draft.' Then, 'lest a single word should escape, he licked the board until it was quite dry.' The episode persuaded Park that since Islam had only recently taken root in the region and was not yet entrenched in people's hearts, it would not be difficult to convert West Africans to a more enlightened creed such as Christianity.

Today, Islam has gained a firmer foothold. Along with animism it is the predominant religion in Guinea-Bissau and most of the rest of West Africa. The fundamentalist Christians are undeterred by this, for it too is part of the plan. It was prophesied, they tell me, that Christ would return before the generation which saw the re-establishment of Israel dies out. Taking 1948, when Israel was born again, as a starting point, this gives us another thirty years, at most. In the season before the return of Christ, the Bible says, there will be a period of world rule by the Antichrist, with whom Christians will fight a long battle. This battle will culminate in Armageddon.

For the missionaries, Muslims are the Antichrist, the rise of Islam a fulfilment of the prophecy. The final battle is already underway – the End of Days has begun – and they are the Christian soldiers charged with fighting it (this perhaps explains

Freddy's equanimity in the face of the stoning of his mission house in the south). I could find no reference in the Bible to Islam, and no evidence to back up their story, but the missionaries have no doubts, and no hesitation in telling the people of Guinea-Bissau, where relations between followers of different faiths have hitherto been peaceful, that Muslims are bent on eradicating Christ's followers from the earth.

9

Although Christians remain a small minority in Guinea-Bissau, in recent years the evangelists have begun to make inroads, and the proportion of converts is edging upwards. When all else fails – and in this part of the world all else very often does fail – the religion of the white man can be a tempting last resort.

Lalas, a burly, dark-skinned young Pepel man with an uncomfortably penetrating gaze, is helping to build a new mission in the town of Mansoa in the interior. He lives in a small house at the edge of the rice fields in Bissau, with his wife, his two baby children, his mother and three sisters. A few years ago he renounced his playboy ways and converted to Christianity ('I used to have many girlfriends at the same time,' he admits with embarrassment, 'I broke a lot of hearts'). He is now a zealot. Over a coffee in the mission canteen one morning he sets about winning us around to his new creed. He asks the usual questions about why we do not attend church and why we have let Satan overpower us, and then pulls out his trump card. Last week, he announces, he was preaching in a village near Mansoa when two teenage boys ran to him and told him that their friend had been killed playing football. The unfortunate boy had been kicked in the chest and died immediately. They asked Lalas to help, so he went to the pitch, stood over the prostrate young footballer, who had by now been dead for several minutes, and prayed. Miraculously the boy recovered. Lalas sees the miracle as proof of Jesus' power; that the boy might not have been dead but merely winded or unconscious does not occur to him. He looks at me defiantly, silently challenging me, asking how I can continue to doubt in the face of such overwhelming evidence. His icy stare is unnerving but his fanaticism renders argument futile, and as Ebru fixes me with a glare that tells me to back down I manage not to rise to the provocation.

A few days later Lalas takes us to his house by the rice fields.

He introduces us to his mother, Maria, who gets up from her seat on the veranda to welcome us. In her sixties and the bearer of seven children, she remains elegant, slender and upright in a boldly patterned blue, green and beige dress which matches the headscarf that covers her close-cropped grey hair. Her skin is smooth and clear, a few lines around her squinting, tired-looking eyes the only signs of aging and of the difficult life she must have led. The house was built for her by Lalas. Half of it, where she and her three daughters live, is made of mud; the other half, in which Lalas resides with his young family, is whitewashed brick. A corrugated-iron roof covers the whole, propped up on wooden poles. Around the small, bare garden, where two goats munch at weeds in the shade of a single papaya tree, a few sticks of bamboo mark out a border, beyond which stretch acres of brilliant green. A light chatter rises like woodsmoke off the fields, as women with babies straddling their backs bend to pluck sheaves of rice grass in the fading early evening sun. We sit on stools on the narrow veranda, and Maria tells us how she converted to Christianity.

'When I was a child I would have liked to go to school, but my father refused to send me,' she begins, her voice a slow, dignified murmur. 'The Portuguese ran the schools in those days, and he thought they would kidnap us and sell us into slavery.' Maria's tribe, the Pepel, provided the first slaves to be taken from the country by the Portuguese - a century after it ended, the trade was still terrorising minds and distorting lives. 'As a young teenager I lived in Bissau. I got a job as a cleaner for a Portuguese family, but when my father found out he took me away to my village in Biombo and told me to get married. He didn't trust the Portuguese, so he found me a husband and I had to marry him.'

Fortunately, Maria was pleased with her father's choice of groom. 'He was handsome and I liked him, but it didn't matter what I thought - I had no choice. I couldn't have refused my father's wish.' The wedding celebrations went on through the night. She was happy at being married, but disappointed to have lost her job with the Portuguese, who contrary to her father's fears had treated and paid her well. As we talk and the weakening sun sinks behind the palm trees, swallows divebomb the sides of the house, braking just in time to slip into their nests under the eaves. The rice fields slowly empty, as the women make their way home for the night. They greet us with a wave and a smile as they pass.

Maria's husband was a weaver, and she helped out by taking the clothes he had made to the market. Soon they had a son, Lalas, but by then her husband had contracted the illness that would kill him. 'We don't know what he died of,' says Lalas, who is now in his thirties and cannot remember his father. 'In those days you didn't know the cause – people just fell ill and died.'

Left alone with a baby boy, Maria had no plans to remarry. 'When I married I was a virgin, and I didn't want another man to know my body,' she explains. 'My mother was keen for me to marry again so that I could have more children, but for four years I resisted.' Among the Pepel the family line passes through women rather than men, and her mother needed granddaughters to ensure the survival of her lineage. Eventually her persuasion bore fruit, and Maria married her late husband's brother. She would already have been close to this man, for in a Guinean child's life uncles are often of more importance, and more involved, than fathers (a father may die, but a child has many uncles, and in such a hazardous environment it is prudent to spread the risk). The brother-in-law, who had played a part in Lalas's upbringing, would have seemed a natural choice of second husband.

The new couple moved back to Bissau, and Maria bore her husband five daughters and two sons (three of the daughters, pretty young teenagers, sit near us as we talk, combing and plaiting each other's hair). Her husband was good to her at first, but as time passed and she grew older his interest in her waned and he took a second, younger wife, to whom he devoted most of his attention. This is not unusual; a number of other Guinean mothers would tell me similar tales. Like the tradition of marrying your late husband's brother, polygamy evolved as a means of helping communities cope with a dangerous environment - safety in numbers was a critical defence mechanism, and close conjugal bonds had to be discouraged in favour of looser and larger groupings. The survival of the custom into modern-day Guinea-Bissau, however, has left a wreckage of embittered wives. Maria left her husband and took her children with her. When he refused to support them she took to buying fish at the port and selling them in Bandim market. Somehow, with help from her brothers, sisters and cousins, she scraped by.

Then her youngest son died of malaria, and it was this tragedy which prompted her conversion to Christianity. Most of Maria's tribespeople are animists. As rice farmers in the coastal wetlands the Pepel have an especially strong relationship to the spirits of water and soil, and the Muslim proselytisers who swept through the interior in the eighteenth century therefore gained few converts among them. When faced with disasters such as the death of a child, the Pepel rely on *irãn* – the spirits that dwell in sticks, trees, animal horns, the earth and the sea - to identify the origin of the problem and combat the sorcery that caused it (no misfortune is accidental or undeserved: either someone has cursed you, or you have sinned or neglected your religious duties). The *irãn* are reached with the help of a living middleman, a witch doctor, who communicates with them via the spirits of your ancestors. You must propitiate the ancestors with regular offerings and sacrifices if you want them to intercede in your favour.

Maria had performed her share of these rituals, but they prevented neither her son's death nor her husband's betrayal. Her ancestors were failing to honour their side of the bargain. 'I was tired of the things of the world,' she says. 'I was tired of performing sacrifices. I bought and sacrificed many cows and pigs to change my life, to make my family healthier and protect them against bad things, but nothing changed. I saw my family falling sick and dying.'

Her son had found Christ some years earlier, persuaded by a friend after many months of discussion. Unlike Dan, who believes the errant Ed is now burning in hell, Lalas cannot accept that his own father, an animist, is suffering the same fate. 'At that time people didn't hear the Word of Christ,' he explains, 'so he didn't have the chance to find Jesus.' The consequences of acknowledging that Portuguese and Latin American mission-aries were working the country throughout his father's lifetime, and that he may well have been exposed to Christ's message, are too painful for the son to bear. Although he aspires to complete submission to the hard-line fundamentalist creed, Lalas is as yet unable to take the final step; he retains vestiges of softness, of flexibility, of mercy, and cannot quite reconcile himself to such an intransigent God.

'Christianity has made my life better,' Lalas says. 'I have achieved my dream of building a house for my mother, I have work at the mission, and I have a young family.' He links these improvements unquestioningly to his religion; since they came to him only after he converted, he concludes, it must be his conversion that brought them about. It is easy, of course, for the Western observer to be cynical about such logic, but in this country, in this dirt-poor district of a dirt-poor city, these things – a job, a house built of brick, a healthy family – must indeed seem miraculous. Lalas must be almost unique among his peers. How else to explain what has happened to him, then, but as a signing-on bonus from his new God?

I ask Lalas about *irān* children. According to Pepel belief, a child born albino, epileptic, blind or with a deformity is likely to harbour harmful spirits. Such children bring misfortune to their families, potentially imperilling an entire lineage, and must therefore be sent back. Traditionally, babies suspected of being *irān* were "taken to the sea", from whence *irān* children come, and left on the beach by the water's edge. Those who cried out or screamed were clearly unhappy and did not wish to return to the ocean, so they were spared and taken back to the village. But some babies lay quietly, and allowed the lapping waves to carry them away. These children – *irān* children - were said to have gone back to their real home. Taking children to the sea is now illegal, but Lalas is one of many who suspect it still takes place in secret. 'I think it happens,' he says. 'I have heard about it, but these days it is hushed up. It is the work of the devil.'

While her son has been talking, Maria has busied herself cradling her baby granddaughter in her arms and whispering her praises to her daughter-in-law. Seeing Lalas at peace had an effect on her. 'I saw my son healthy and happy and realised that the Lord was working for him. I had had enough of all the ceremonies, so I became a Christian. God has set me free now.' This is the other part of the missionaries' offer, the part that goes deeper than the material improvements Lalas has enjoyed: join us, they promise, and you will be liberated from the stern gaze and stringent demands of the ancestors. I ask Maria how it felt to stop communicating with her forefathers after they had dominated her life for so long. 'It was very difficult,' she replies, 'but I don't miss them. I am happier now and my family is healthy. Finding salvation in the Lord has given me happiness.'

Not all Guineans are so easily won over. Fernando, a young zealot who teaches English at the mission, is the only Christian in his family. He wants to convert his mother, but she says she has too many sacrifices to perform first. Giving up animism does not just mean cutting the centuries-old link with the ancestors; to truly follow Christ you have to believe that the ancestral spirits do not exist, that they are nothing more than a primitive myth. Although there are similarities between the two belief systems, this killing off of the ancestors requires a greater psychological rupture than is demanded of the born-again American mission-aries, who were brought up with the mysteries of the Holy Trinity and the Resurrection before they devoted their lives to Christ. Fernando describes conversion as a process. Many Guineans do not complete the journey, he says. 'Some people gradually come closer to the Lord and forget the ancestors. Others go some of the way and then turn back to animism. Satan is very powerful.'

10

The next day, a Sunday, we go with Dan to the morning service at the local Evangelical church. We arrive about halfway through, two hours into the service. The church is a whitewashed rectangular block on a dusty square, hidden from the market road by a line of scruffy houses. The congregation, numbering around three hundred, sit on comfortable, cinema-style chairs as a well-fed Sierra Leonean pastor lectures them from a stage at the far end about Jesus' healing powers. The churchgoers are turned out in their Sunday best. The men wear shirts and trousers or jeans, the women colourful dresses, their hair freshly oiled and plaited. Children, also dressed up, wander around freely. We are shown to seats near the back, just as the bread and miniature plastic cups of wine of the communion reach our row. Beside us sit three serious-looking young boys, listening intently to the pastor. Behind us a tall man and his plump wife take turns holding a baby. Although the ceiling fans do not turn, the many windows and the cool tiled floor keep the heat from becoming oppressive. It is a comfortable and, by Guinean standards, opulent environment. Like the mission building with its high whitewashed walls, it tells the congregants that prayer will bring them material as well as spiritual wealth – an escape from a life of deprivation.

At first, the service proceeds in an orderly fashion. The trays of bread and wine are passed around quietly and the pastor, whose voice is amplified by a generator-powered microphone, holds most people's attention. Then the choir replaces him on the flower-bedecked stage, and things begin to go awry. Two electric guitarists lead the twenty young choristers through a series of upbeat hymns in the Gospel style. The first few are sung in harmony, but the synchronicity gradually breaks down. Some of the singers begin to race through their verses, leaving more sluggish colleagues lagging behind. Others stop singing altogether. Members of the congregation join in, although not everybody sings in time and a few experiment with completely different hymns. One or two content themselves with loud wails. Most people remain seated, but a few decide to stand up. It is as if a dormant computer virus has been activated, causing multiple and apparently random malfunctions in the system. Behind us, the tall man passes the baby to his wife and rises to his feet. He closes his eyes in prayer.

Slowly - and there is no more accurate way to describe it - all hell breaks loose. The Sierra Leonean pastor has reappeared on the stage. This time he is more animated, his face bulging and sweating as he shouts his way through a passage from the Bible. The choir sings louder to try to compete, which prompts the dissident singers dotted around the pews to ratchet up their own discordant hollering. The tall man standing behind us has begun to sway, his eyes clenched shut. He is shouting, 'Rema! Rema! Rema!' (the Word, the Word, the Word), and then 'Kema! Kema! Kema!' (I burn, I burn, I burn), each word louder than the last. He repeats the mantra again and again, increasing the volume each time. When he finally reaches a crescendo, he yells out at the top of his voice, 'KEMA! KEMA! KEMA! O nome de JESUSSS!' Children look up at him, alarmed. Even a few adults glance round, although the cacophony building in the rest of the hall means only those in the nearest rows can hear him. To our left we see a woman in a red dress staggering down the aisle, her head in her hands, sobbing. A few rows in front of us a man in a suit is standing with his back to the stage, his hands and face turned beatifically upwards, singing and smiling, his song bearing no relation to any of those chanted by the different factions of the choir.

Then the sound of a woman moaning breaks through the din like a shudder. On the stage a chorister in an orange and white print dress is looking to the heavens and whimpering, her face anguished, transported. Her moans grow louder and more piercing, until suddenly she collapses and falls backwards to the floor. She is quickly led away by two men, still wailing as she passes down the aisle. Another choir girl, infected by her colleague's delirium, soon follows suit. Among the pews, congregants shout or murmur different prayers. Several wave their hands above their heads. The air is heating up. The atmosphere is intense, frenzied, uncomfortable for Ebru and I as outsiders. I look around, but people I recognise barely acknowledge me. Two of Maria's daughters stare as if seeing me for the first time. Young children gaze up at their ecstatic, keening parents with a mixture of confusion and fear. The pastor is still on the stage exhorting into the microphone, but his voice is drowned out. His flock have taken flight into their own private worlds. 'God is here today,' explains one of the boys sitting next to us with a smile. 'Rema! Rema! Rema!' begins the man behind us again, his wife breast-feeding their baby next to him, no sign of emotion or surprise on her face. 'Kema! Kema! Kema!' Anarchy prevails, until finally the Sierra Leonean gives way to a young Guinean pastor and suddenly the place is calm, as if nothing has happened.

'None of these people are drunk,' the new pastor announces, twice, no doubt addressing the sceptics among us. We make our exit soon after, feeling shocked and drained, religion's role as an opiate never more evident. Dan, who seems nonplussed by this outpouring of emotion, his Anglo-Saxon conservatism clearly better suited to a more sober style of worship, tells us that the services are not always so rapturous. There is a hint of condescension in his tone, un-erased by several years of living among Africans (it is an attitude we have come across before in his compatriots' reluctance to allow Guineans to take charge of mission projects).

We walk through the market, reflecting on what we have seen. On a street where a few days earlier we had seen a crowd of revellers and drummers dancing around two sacrificial cows which were lying on the tarmac with blood gushing from their freshly slit throats, a new throng has gathered. In its midst a young woman in a white T-shirt and jeans lies curled up on the ground, the merciless sun beating down on her thin body. She has fainted in the heat. Dan, who although not medically qualified runs a clinic that distributes herbal potions and aspirin, crouches to feel her pulse. Her heart is beating fast and he says she probably has anaemia. Before long, the woman rises to her knees. Her large eyes look dazed and her high forehead is caked with dust. A crucifix hangs from her neck. She starts to pray, gazing beseechingly to the heavens, but appears to be on the verge of another collapse. I buy her a bottle of Coke from a nearby shop in the hope that the sugar and water will revive her (the crowd parts to let the white man through). At first she ignores me and continues to pray, but eventually she takes the bottle and gulps down its contents. Dan assures me that the Coke will be sufficient to 'get her where she wants to go,' like a top-up of petrol in a car. The woman stands up, and wanders off down the street without thanking me. She probably thought God had sent me. Maybe He had...

11

In need of a break from the nightly attacks on our secularity, we leave the mission and take the small passenger ferry to the island of Bubaque in the Bijagós archipelago. It is late December, and although the Bijagó people are predominantly animist, Christmas and New Year are public holidays and the ferry is full of people returning from the mainland for the festivities. It leaves Bissau's Pidjiguiti harbour two hours late, and the passengers take advantage of the delay to get drunk. Some have brought jerrycans full of palm wine; others buy bottles of beer from the on-board café. On deck a speaker belts out loud West African pop music. Passengers lean on the railings, drinking and chatting merrily. A few dance, clutching beer bottles and waving their arms in the air; the women jerk their backsides provocatively, in time with the music. The sea is flat and calm, the air hot and moist.

The forty-mile journey takes four hours. Two smaller boats, which have hitched a ride to save fuel, bob at the end of ropes in the ferry's wake. After two hours we pass the first of the archipelago's eighty or so islands: a muddy strand of beach, a long fringe of palm trees, thick dark forest behind. Only a handful of the islands are inhabited, with a few more settled temporarily during the rice-growing season. This one appears deserted, although from this distance we cannot be certain – many Bijagó villages are hidden deep in the jungle, away from the shore where they would be exposed to flooding and attack. (The Bijagó are notoriously hostile to outsiders. As far back as 445 BC the Phoenician captain Hanno, who sailed down the African coast from Cadiz, was shocked to find the islands inhabited by 'hairy, swift, monstrous wild women who could not be subdued even with bonds.' Two thousand years later the first Portuguese explorers met their deaths here. Early slavers, too, encountered fierce resistance and quickly switched their attention to the mainland. And in the colonial wars of pacification, the islanders were the last to be quelled.)

Half an hour later we pass another far-off islet. It is long and low, barely rising above the still sea; in the haze of the late afternoon it shimmers like a mirage. This island too appears empty of humanity, but with the aid of binoculars I make out a small village, thatched roofs resting atop tiny mud houses, nestling among the trees behind the mangroves. A villager, a tiny speck even through the lenses, emerges from the forest, perhaps after a day spent hunting bush rats. A woman is sitting on a stool beside a house, sifting rice. In the foreground a lone sacred ibis scours the beach, its curved black bill burrowing for grubs.

Dusk draws in, and as we pass through a narrow channel between two jungly islands we can feel the archipelago closing in on us, its tropical intensity enveloping the boat in heat, damp and stillness. As we round the far end of the starboard-side island the pungent smell of smoked fish reaches the deck. It is the first sign that we are nearing a human settlement. Ahead of us we see wisps of smoke rising through the palm trees of Bubaque. The ferry carves a wide arc to avoid a submerged sandbar and sweeps round to the right along a channel, with the island and the smoke and the palm trees now close by to our left. A man stands in the darkening sea with a broad fishing net. Behind him two women bend to pluck shellfish from rockpools. On deck the drunken dancers, their numbers now swelled to several dozen, whoop and cheer as we near our destination.

At last the dock comes into view, a high cement platform supported by thick iron pillars. A dense, jostling, hundred-strong crowd is waiting for the ferry, held back from the jetty by a thin rope. They are there to meet relatives returned from the mainland or to trade with the new arrivals or wheelbarrow their belongings to their homes. There are hustlers, ready to grab the few white visitors and lead them to hotels. A fellow passenger warns us that there are probably pickpockets too. It seems the whole island is there.

Once again you are forced to relinquish control. We scrum with the others for a place on the narrow gangplank, leaving behind the safety of the well lit deck and plunging into the littoral darkness. We barge through the expectant crowd, pretending we know where we are going. Ignoring the many offers of assistance we choose a rough dirt track to escape the throng, and hope it will lead to a hotel. After fifteen minutes humping our backpacks through a labyrinth of unlit lanes, we stumble with relief on a guesthouse.

The islands are full of mysteries. On our first morning, on the terrace of Bubaque's only bar, which overlooks the jetty, we meet Michel, a middle-aged Senegalese conservationist with a 1950s crew cut who has come here to teach local people how to fish without depleting stocks to extinction. As we walk in he greets us in French and asks us to sit with him at his small table. He looks tired, his eyes swollen, and is drinking strong black coffee. We exchange pleasantries and establish one another's business, but we cannot help noticing that his mind is not on the conversation. He keeps shaking his head, as if recovering from a shock, and gazing thoughtfully out over the calm sea. Ebru asks him if he is all right. 'You see many things here,' he replies darkly. 'What kind of things?' I ask. *'Inexplicables,'* he whispers.

He has spent the previous night on the island of Canhabaque, an hour's boat ride southeast of Bubaque. Even by Bijagós standards, Canhabaque is traditional, replete with forest spirits, shrines containing the dead souls of the ancestors, and giant cotton trees harbouring malevolent *irān* that must be constantly placated with offerings. The island's inhabitants guard jealously its many sacred sites; despite a long campaign of "pacification" they were never fully subdued by the Portuguese, and were exempted from the hut tax to which the rest of the country was subjected. A close-knit community of rice farmers and bushmeat hunters, whose economy is still based on barter, not cash, Canhabaque is closed off from the modern world, and remains wary of strangers.

Michel was unprepared for its enigmas. Walking down a village lane in the early evening he saw a dead snake on the ground, its body twisted like dried kelp. He was told it had been killed by the amulet, or *gris gris*, of a passing witch doctor. The witch doctor had been unaware of the snake's presence, but his *gris gris* was so powerful that the snake only had to approach and its fate was sealed.

At night Michel was given a hut to sleep in, but he was allowed no rest. 'I was terrified,' he says. 'A village woman spent the whole night running back and forth outside my hut, screaming at the top of her voice. She sounded mad, as if the devil himself was inside her. She didn't stop until dawn. It wasn't just the noise that kept me awake – her bloodcurdling screams gave me the shivers. I was cowering inside my hut listening to her padding around just outside the door.'

Michel discovered in the morning that the panicked woman had been conversing with the spirits of the forest, asking them what this interloper was doing in the village and whether his intentions were benign or evil. But his troubles did not end there, for at dawn he was summoned to see the village chief, who welcomed him by ranting angrily at him in Bijagó, a language Michel does not speak. The tirade lasted over an hour. 'I asked my companion what the chief wanted and whether I was being taken prisoner,' he says, his fears echoing those of the eighteenth-century explorer Mungo Park, who during his voyage to the Niger was regularly held captive by village chiefs. Park had to buy his freedom with his dwindling store of provisions, but Michel had not come similarly equipped. 'The chief wanted palm wine or rum in return for his hospitality in putting me up for the night, but I didn't have anything to give him. I didn't even take pencils or paper with me in case they would think I was spying for the government. They are afraid of the government because it tries to tax them.' He finally placated the chief by giving him some francs, which could be used at a later date to buy rum in Bubaque, and was allowed to go on his way. 'It's very traditional in these islands,' he sighs, exhausted and unused to such irruptions in his life, 'very traditional.'

The following day, Christmas Day, we spend on the beach. A short walk from the dock, down a rough path through low bush, a curve of white sand sheltered by nodding palm trees stretches below a red, jungle-covered cliff. Clumps of mangrove dot the shore. Dolphins frolic in the waveless sea. A few hundred yards across lies another island, deserted. A gaudily painted fishing canoe works the channels between the sandbars as a light breeze disperses the heat from a watery sun. There is no sound.

As so often in West Africa, however, ugliness lurks amid the beauty. At first we have the beach to ourselves, shared only with a heron standing haughty in the shallows. But we are soon joined by a group of young boys. They are barefoot, dressed in rags, and they cluster around us, pulling playfully at the legs of small brown crabs and chattering cheerfully to each other about the *brancos*. When I pull out my binoculars to look at an overflying palm-nut vulture, three of them run in front of me and pose, thinking that I am wielding a camera. After some minutes I notice that one of the boys is quieter than the others. Like them he sits on the sand watching us, but he doesn't laugh with them or join them in torturing crabs. His face is darker, more serious, for he is sick, with a hacking cough which convulses his small body. His ribs are clearly visible under his taut skin, and his upper arms are thinner than his shoulders and elbows when they should be thicker. He wears only a pair of dusty shorts. The skin on his legs and arms is badly chapped, resembling the scales of a dried fish.

After a while the boy moves to sit huddled in front of us, his arms folded around his chest. It is a hot day, but we realise that he has moved from the shade of a palm tree to a patch of sunlight, for warmth. He sits shivering, his silence broken by violent coughing tremors. The other boys ignore him until after a few minutes sitting there alone he stands up and, without speaking, walks into the snake-infested bush behind the beach. He bends over and vomits the bilious yellow liquid that indicates malaria, Guinea-Bissau's biggest killer. He looks round to check that I am not watching. I turn away, ashamed.

The other boys notice our concern and at last wander over to him. Ebru asks one of them to take him home to his mother. He obeys and, putting his arm around his friend's shoulders, leads him up the path away from the beach. As they walk slowly away I am surprised to find tears in my eyes, and guiltily relieved that I am not completely inured to poverty's cruelty.

12

That evening we celebrate Christmas with Michel at a provisions store owned by his cousin, Mame. The brick-built store, a small, one-room rectangular block with a raised floor, sells bread, tinned food, candles, bottles of Portuguese wine, beer, soap, onions, garlic and the Maggi cooking stock that has become ubiquitous in West Africa. Its owner also cooks excellent Senegalese fish and rice dishes, which we devour sitting at a little wooden table on her tiny veranda, overlooking the main dirt street of Bubaque village.

Mame is a large, serious woman with shiny, clear brown skin and distrustful, distracted eyes that seem always to be looking at something others cannot see. Her mother was Bijagó and her father a Serrer from Senegal. Born in the islands, she returned here twenty years ago after her first marriage broke down. She is not a happy woman. In the past, she explains, women here were powerful. According to Bijagó custom the first human being was a woman, and island society was organised on matrilineal lines. Women had a hand in all aspects of life. They owned the houses, cultivated the land, and chose their husbands; they sat on and occasionally headed the councils of elders which made vital community decisions about where and when to farm and whether to go to war; priestesses played an important role in spiritual matters, and had the power to punish errant kings and chiefs. The fiercest women even took part in slave raids.

That has all changed now, laments Mame. Women do all the work but receive no appreciation for it from their menfolk. As well as shouldering responsibility for domestic duties and child rearing, they are expected to farm, fish, or earn money to feed their family. 'Men spend their time drinking and sitting around chatting, while their wives tire themselves with work,' Mame says. She looks over crossly at Michel for agreement, which he delivers with an obedient nod.

Mame's first marriage was doomed from the start. Serrer tradition dictates that girls must marry a cousin chosen for them by their father. Mame was fourteen, the selected cousin in his thirties. 'I had five children with him over nine years, but I was miserable. He was no good. He drank, did nothing around the house, and as soon as I'd had children he lost interest in me.' Her words echo those of Maria in Bissau. Eventually, like Maria, she left the man, but this infuriated her family (of which her husband was also part) and she is convinced that they turned to sorcery to punish her. 'I fell sick soon after I left my husband and I couldn't get rid of the sickness,' she says, bending forwards in her chair and peeling a small onion in preparation for dinner. 'It went on and on. The family had cursed me. I had to get away.' Leaving her children with her mother, she travelled through Mali to Niger, Burkina Faso and the Ivory Coast in the hope that distance from the source of the curse would cure her. A few months after she left, however, her mother died – long-term plans in this part of the world are so often thwarted - and she had to return to Senegal. She tried to explain herself to the Bijagó side of the family, her mother's side, but they were deaf to her pleading. Only by performing a series of costly sacrifices, they told her, would she be able to cleanse herself of her sin and slough off the curse.

It was at this point that she met her second husband, Raoul, a Béninois who already had several children from previous marriages. A devotee of the Celestial Church of Christ, a small sect founded by a carpenter in Benin in 1947 after a revelation in a forest clearing, Raoul told Mame that if she joined the sect she would no longer have to worry about the curse (here again was Christianity's promise to set Africans free). Mame was not convinced about the church, but she fell for Raoul and it was not long before they married. They departed for Bubaque, leaving their children dispersed among her sisters in Senegal, and set up a small guesthouse to service the island's fledgling tourist trade.

'For a long time we worked well together. We worked hard. He looked after guests and ran the bar and I did the cooking for the restaurant and the cleaning.' She pauses and gets up to wash a knife in a bucket of water next to the shop, her movements heavy and ponderous. The jovial Michel, who is listening sympathetically to a tale he has heard many times before, orders a bottle of red wine and insists we each have a glass. The shop sees a steady flow of customers, who emerge from the thick surrounding darkness to buy beer for the festivities; Mame banters good-naturedly but firmly with the many who try, in vain, to haggle the price down.

'Everything was going well,' she continues, 'until one day Raoul said he was leaving for Togo to buy merchandise. He didn't come back for nearly three years. He didn't call me or write to me once. We'd had a son together, who was born with a serious heart problem. He had to stay in Senegal because the hospitals are better there. I sent money every month, and whenever the tourist season here finished I went to visit him. Raoul did nothing.' She is speaking loudly now, still angry two years after the event. 'He only phoned when he heard our son was in a coma in hospital. He waited until then to make contact!' Mame hung up on him.

The boy died. Soon after, Raoul appeared in Bubaque. 'He didn't even say sorry. He said he'd been ill so he couldn't get in touch. For three years!' She refused to let him into the guest-house, but one of her daughters begged her not to leave him in the street and she relented. They slept in separate rooms for a while, but Mame's rage did not abate and she moved out, to the shop where we now sit. 'I had to start again with nothing,' she says, 'no husband, no business, no money, no home.'

She sleeps on a string bed inside her store. The shop is so cramped that during opening hours she has to stand the bed on its side against the wall to allow customers to enter. She works from dawn until after midnight, trying to get back on her feet, and sends money to Senegal to pay for her children's schooling and lodging. Every day when she goes to the market she walks past the old guesthouse, which lies empty and untended. Raoul sits outside it all day, drinking and playing chequers with friends. Mame never greets him, though he makes regular attempts to persuade her to come back. 'He knows the guest-house doesn't work without me,' she says. 'He doesn't know how to cook or clean. Guests leave after one night because it's so dirty.' This at least is a small satisfaction, but the real shock for Raoul, she believes, will come later. 'He gives nothing to his children. Children don't ask you to bring them into the world - it's your choice. You bring them, so you must do everything you can to help their development. One day he'll need his children, but they will know he has neglected them.'

I ask her if she plans to find another husband. She wants an older man now, she replies without hesitation, her ideas of romantic love long since jettisoned. 'You need a man who will be a partner. You do your work and he does his. I want someone who is responsible.' Michel takes a swig of wine and smiles sadly, fully aware of female suffering. When our food is served we eat in silence. Mame does not eat with us. She sits watching the dark street, frowning at things we cannot see and from time to time emitting sharp, angry sighs, like a geyser that is about to erupt.

13

On hearing that I am writing a book, Michel is keen to tell me about his work as a conservationist. One morning he takes me down to Bubaque's small market and shows me a stall selling shark fins. The dried, yellowing fins, shaped like breaking waves, are laid out flat on a plastic sheet on the ground. Traditionally, sharks were thought by the Bijagó to have special powers, and they are still represented in local dances and on masks, but Chinese demand for their body parts for use in soup has proved irresistible to the islanders, and the revered fish are now under threat.

The average Guinean would have to work for two months to earn what he can make from selling just one kilo of fins, so when shark dealers come calling from Senegal and Guinea-Conakry it is hard to refuse their business. Once a shark is caught, its fins are sliced off and its body thrown back into the sea, where if not already dead, it bleeds to death or is eaten by other sharks. A number of species have already become extinct in Bijagó waters. Others will die out soon if the fin trade continues. 'The trade is unbalancing marine ecosystems,' Michel says. 'But it's not just sharks - many fish species are in danger because of overfishing by local people and by foreign boats which plunder our seas.' (For the past two weeks, he tells me, the Guinean government has been holding in custody a trawlerful of Spanish fishermen who exceeded their quotas.) As well as thinning out the food reserves available to the Bijagó people, the depletion of fish stocks is likely to harm tourism, for the majority of overseas visitors to the islands are European sea anglers in search of tarpon and other large game fish. 'What will people turn to when the fish run out?' Michel asks, frowning and turning his palms skyward.

He already knows the answer to his question, but is unwilling to elucidate. There is one subject that nobody in the Bijagós wants to discuss. It is the islands' dirty secret. Mention it and even the most garrulous clam up. They look at the floor, inspect their fingernails, and shift uneasily in their seats. Then they hastily change the subject - it is far too dangerous to talk.

The story begins on a hazy afternoon in 2005, when a fisherman on a beach near Quinhamel on the mainland spots a strange object floating in the shallows. On closer inspection he sees that it is a white brick, tightly wrapped in transparent rubber. Intrigued, he wades in to retrieve it. Soon after, he sees another of these bricks, washed up further along the beach. He shows his unusual catch to his fellow fishermen, and together they puzzle over its purpose. They rip open one of the packages, and find that the bricks crumble when rubbed. After some deliberation they conclude that it must be fertiliser. Dozens of packets of fertiliser are bobbing in the surf! The fish-starved sea has yielded up a rare bounty: respite for struggling farmers, a tonic for the parched soil, the promise – for once – of a rich harvest.

The fishermen gather up the packages and, like warriors bringing back the spoils of victory, convey them to their village. The villagers crowd around, singing and dancing. This year they will eat! Their children will grow strong! Maybe – is it possible? – their infants will all survive the year. They give thanks to the ancestors. Some daub their faces with the white powder. They go out into the fields and scatter the precious crumbs.

Instead of thriving, however, their crops wither and die. A few villagers, moreover, are behaving strangely, as if possessed. Have they been cursed? Has the treacherous ocean tricked them? The villagers' hope quickly turns to bleak despair; now it will be more difficult than ever to feed their families. They are still despondent several days later, when two mysterious, white-faced strangers appear among the huts. Like the wandering gypsy Melquíades in Macondo, they emerge from the forest bearing gifts. Colombians (like Melquíades), they offer the villagers huge sums of money in exchange for the remaining white bricks and their silence. The packages, it turns out, contained not fertiliser but cocaine, for the Colombians had chosen Guinea-Bissau as a staging post on the cocaine route to Europe. The white bricks came from a ship that had sunk at the end of its ocean crossing, its intended destination the Bijagós archipelago. As in Macondo, nothing in the islands, perhaps nothing in the country, would ever be the same again.

The Bijagós lie at the end of the shortest transatlantic crossing from South America. The eighty islands, thick with jungle but largely devoid of inhabitants, are an ideal venue for illicit activity, and in particular for smuggling. The Colombians use small boats and specially fitted planes to import large consignments of cocaine from their homeland. Then, having broken up the packages into smaller, more easily portable loads, they despatch the drugs by sea or across the Sahara to the lucrative markets of Western Europe.

Geography is not the only attraction; the traffickers also prey on the country's poverty. Were you in possession of the Guinean government's entire annual budget, you could afford to purchase no more than a couple of tons of cocaine – less than is landed on the islands every month. With the coffers so threadbare, public servants' salaries are paltry, and the Colombians do not need to part with a large share of their profits to buy official acquiescence. Even if it had the motivation to fight the trade, however, the government lacks the means. It cannot support an effective police force, army or navy. The country has no prisons, the air force no aircraft, the navy no ships. Compared with the heavily policed cocaine channels through the Caribbean to the United States, the route through Guinea-Bissau is a cakewalk. The South Americans have free rein.

Some Guineans are benefiting from the trade. Drug mules from the Bijagós who make it to Europe, many of them former fishermen, not only grow wealthy themselves; they also send a proportion of their profits to relatives back home (despite the global recession, remittances from overseas have soared since the drug traffickers arrived). The powerful are also reaping rich rewards. Like wreckers swarming over a treasure-laden galleon, Guinea-Bissau's politicians, army and police have been scrambling for a share of the loot. It is rumoured that a former president transported cocaine in briefcases to Europe, taking advantage of his immunity from customs searches. Others have grown rich by providing security to the Colombians, by helping them elude arrest, or merely by looking the other way. The capital, Bissau, is in the midst of a minor building boom: smart new villas are springing up, with gardens, iron gates and security guards - all funded, according to local people, by drug money.

But these benefits have come at a cost. The global illegality of cocaine dooms those involved in its distribution to subterfuge. The trade therefore becomes a magnet for the devious, the unscrupulous and the violent. By making drugs illegal to avert social problems at home, Western governments deflect the challenge of dealing with them onto developing countries. Battles for control of the industry have torn apart Colombia and rocked northern Mexico, and as European consumers blithely powder their noses, Guinea-Bissau, too, has suffered its first cocaine casualties. Drug addiction is on the rise (a well-known dealer lives next to the mission in Bissau; the Christians have tried in vain to persuade him to forsake his evil ways); politicians and journalists who speak out against the traffickers have faced threats and intimidation; and the contest over access to the trade has turned violent: blood feuds have broken out between police groups, army chiefs have been assassinated or kidnapped, and coups d'état, after a decade of stability, have muscled their way back onto the political scene. The people of Guinea-Bissau, meanwhile, are caught in the crossfire - what appeared to be a lifeline has turned out to be a noose.

The airstrip on Bubaque, appropriately, is a thin white line cut through the bush and hemmed in on both sides by dense forest.

It sees no daytime traffic, but on Christmas night and for several nights thereafter we are woken in the early hours of the morning by the drone of small planes passing overhead. After a few seconds the noise grows quieter and then stops. On some nights there are two or three such interruptions. Occasionally the sound from the motor abates but does not fall silent, as the aircraft slows before continuing on its journey. These latter planes do not land, but drop their cargo over the sea and call in small motorboats to retrieve it. The traffickers are continually devising ways to elude European Union patrols, and regular use of Bubaque's airstrip has become unsafe. The air drops are a new tactic, and we hear too of a visit by a group of South Americans to Canhabaque, to stake out that island's suitability as a staging post. They poked around for a while, asking locals if there is an airstrip (there is not) or a forest clearing (there is) where they can land small jets or helicopters, ostensibly for flying in tourists. The islanders – poor and hungry - are in no position to resist.

14

It can be hard to get at the truth in West Africa. For any single event, there are multiple versions of how, why, when and where it happened. Even something as momentous as the death of a president can take months, perhaps years, to unravel. Sometimes, a definitive version of the story never takes root, and discussion and rumour, unsated, must move on reluctantly to their next assignment.

João Bernardo Vieira, alias Nino, President of Guinea-Bissau for twenty-three of its thirty-five years as an independent nation, died sometime in March 2009. We know this because photographs of his bloody corpse were posted on the internet a few days later. Until their publication, unconfirmed rumours of the assassination had been swirling around the country like a dust storm. As it went on its way, dancing through villages and towns, the storm picked up scraps of information. Nino was shot! No, he was hacked to death by machetes! He was shot *and* hacked to death. He was killed in his palace – no, in his house! The story whirls around the streets and compounds, up the rivers, over the rice fields, in and out of the cashew trees, growing, swelling, changing shape and picking up speed as it advances.

Was the president even dead at all? No, it is impossible! Nino is invincible, immortal, he has special powers to ward off enemies. Did he not defeat the Portuguese in the south almost single-handedly? Had he not already survived half a dozen, a dozen, a hundred attempts on his life? The dust storm changes direction, its progress slows as the consensus grows that Vieira is still alive and merely wounded, that soon he will address the nation and reassure the people.

With the release of the pictures, however, the Chinese whispers ratchet up again. They become a cacophony of specu-lation, theory and reportage of varying authority. Not everybody, of course, has seen the pictures. Even the capital has only a handful of internet points; the rest of the country has to rely on second, third, fourth-hand information from friends or relatives who have seen the photos, or who know someone who has seen them or claims to have seen them. Nino is dead, that much is certain (the pictures were released to prove this), but was he shot, dismembered, decapitated, or a combination of all of these? Who took the photos? How did his killers breach his defences? Who, most important, ordered his death?

I have seen the photos, with my own eyes. I am not relying on second-hand sources, merely on the honesty of the photographer and of the morgue attendants who stand by the corpse. The pictures are macabre. They show the bloated body of the former president lying on cold white tiles, like a dead seal on snow. His cheeks are puffed out, his swollen eyelids closed. His torso is covered in the little red gashes of gunshot wounds, as if a clumsy tailor in trying to undo a tacking stitch has torn the material away with the thread. But it is on the head that the killers really went to work. Contrary to some rumours the head is still in place, but the scalp is rutted on top with a deep, bloody crater. Huge, red, viscous lacerations snake outwards from this crater like molten lava - the killers appear to have been digging for his brain, desperate to ensure his annihilation, to make certain that he could not plot a terrible revenge.

Three years after the murder, nobody has been arrested. A hasty and perfunctory investigation turned up no leads. The new government, wary of fuelling further instability, is keen to move on, to leave old wounds unopened. But this is tropical Africa. In this climate old wounds do not heal, they fester. And we are talking about the death of the president! Of the dominant figure of the past four decades! It cannot just be brushed under the carpet. And so the speculation, the rumour, the suspicion continues. Still no one knows what happened.

A few facts have settled, like a sheet unfurled over a meadow, and become widely accepted. On the evening of the first day of March, 2009, the head of the army, General Tagme Na Waie, was killed by a bomb that exploded under the stairs in the military headquarters in Bissau. Tagme was a Balante, Nino a Pepel. The Balante, one of the country's largest ethnic groups, have dominated the army since the War of Independence. Nino himself was a hero of that war – he was such a brave fighter, they say, that when he walked through a village even the monkeys clapped. But the Balante's grip on the armed forces rankled with him, and his enmity with Tagme was well known. He may have held Tagme responsible for an earlier attempt on his life, which he only survived thanks to his supernatural powers, and may have plotted the general's murder in revenge.

But wait! We are straying from the facts, allowing ourselves to wander! The dust storm of speculation has swept us up! We must remain grounded, and keep a hold on the elusive truth. We must be guided by what is known, not by what is conjectured.

What is known is that on the morning after Tagme's death, armed men (soldiers? police? hitmen? who knows!) broke into, or negotiated their way into Nino Vieira's house. Were they supporters of the general, who had promised that if anything happened to their leader they would come for the president? Were they Colombian or Venezuelan drug traffickers or their representatives, who had come to punish Nino for his failure to pay them for a two-million (or two-billion) dollar consignment of cocaine? Were they from a police or army faction which needed the president out of the way in order to establish a foothold in the narcotics trade? Each of these – and other renderings besides - is possible, each believed by many to be true.

Given his legendary pugnacity (which would have been with him from birth: members of his clan are said to fight like hyenas), it is likely that Nino put up a struggle. Indeed, it is now widely accepted that it took both machetes and bullets to fell him. The photographs support this story, but what of another story: that he disappeared when his killers arrived? That he became invisible, vanished, only reappearing when the intruders had pummelled his wife almost to death? While this would tally with his reputation for supernatural powers, where does it leave Nino's image as a hero, a warrior?

Again, however, we are straying into the realms of hypothesis, allowing ourselves to be carried off by gusts of hearsay. We must not be diverted; we must not let ourselves drift away from the facts. All we know for certain is that some time after the arrival of his attackers, the president's mutilated corpse was photographed in a morgue. The country's two most powerful figures were dead.

The figure of João Bernardo Vieira is a difficult one to pin down. This heavy-set, jowly bull of a man bestrode his country's political scene for nearly four decades, but beyond its borders little is known of him. Guinea-Bissau is a small, poor, forgotten country. No spotlight is ever shone on it, and Vieira has escaped the scrutiny to which other African leaders have been subjected. Dig around a little, however, and a disturbing picture emerges. While the world's attention was elsewhere, it seems, Nino was busy pillaging his nation. Like the more notorious post-colonial dictators – Mobutu, Abacha, the madman Idi Amin – he treated his land as his personal fiefdom, helping himself to its riches and brutally squashing anyone who dared to stand in his way.

'Nino destroyed everything,' Eduardo Gomes had told me back in Bafatá. When Vieira ousted Luiz Cabral from the presidency six years after independence (Amílcar's corrupt, incompetent half-brother had taken over the PAIGC after its founder's assassination), Gomes had had high hopes. He had distrusted the Cabrals, believing they wanted to make his country a colony of Cape Verde, and saw Nino as a patriot who would have Guinea-Bissau's interests at heart. Nino, however, had other ideas. 'He governed for himself,' Eduardo complained, 'he didn't want to help his people.' The old man, who endured years of exile and imprisonment at the hands of the colonists, then delivered the fatal blow to Nino's memory. In a voice no louder than a murmur, as if he was still unsure, nearly a year after Vieira's death, that such things could be freely uttered, he said: 'He was even worse than the Portuguese.'

Little good came of Nino's twenty-three years as president. His trajectory in power, indeed, brings to mind the catastrophic reign of Plato's archetypal tyrant, described with such relish in the *Republic*. Like that despot, Nino came to power as a protector, full of smiles, saluting everyone he met and distributing land to the people (Eduardo Gomes was one of many who fell for his charms). He promised a renewed focus on agriculture and an end to corruption, but despite massive injections of foreign aid his reign was an economic disaster. Public sector salaries went unpaid for months, sometimes years; infrastructure was not maintained, much less improved; food production slumped; poverty deepened: Guinea-Bissau was even poorer when he died than when he had taken office.

His political legacy was no healthier. Like Plato's tyrant, once he had tasted power he turned from protector into wolf. Having promised democracy on his accession, it took him eleven years to legalise other political parties. He was ruthless in suppressing opposition. Potential rivals were either executed or disappeared; the government was hollowed out, its best men removed. Jimi, a high-ranking United Nations staffer I met in Bissau after we returned from the islands, told me: 'Many of Nino's opponents just vanished. He was an evil man.'

Plato's dictator was 'always stirring up some war or other, in order that the people may require a leader.' Nino, true to the archetype, triggered his country's civil war in the late 1990s when he fired the head of the military, Ansumane Mane, on suspicion of arming rebels in neighbouring Senegal. When an independent inquiry found that it was Vieira's own men who had supplied the weapons (by which time the war had claimed six thousand lives and shrunk the economy by a quarter), he was forced to flee into exile in Portugal.

On his return, he quickly made up for lost time. He welcomed South American drug dealers, turning Guinea-Bissau into what the United Nations has labelled 'the world's first narco-state.' He and his cronies grew rich on the proceeds of the trade. He bought houses in Belgium and Portugal and stashed millions of dollars in foreign bank accounts. It was rumoured that he himself took advantage of trips to Europe to transport large quantities of cocaine. Like drug dealers elsewhere, Nino's vehicle of choice was a Hummer with blacked out windows.

But despite his calamitous record, he clung to power. How did he do it? How did a man who was feared and hated by most of his people, who had no support among the military (the entire army turned against him during the civil war), and who had so many enemies in high places maintain such a grip on the country? For Guineans, there is only one possible answer. Street traders, hotel workers, a policeman and Jimi the United Nations man all told me the same thing: Nino had special powers. He was protected by some unseen but impregnable force. He could reverse the course of a bullet aimed at his heart. He could make himself invisible. He could conjure the death of opponents from thousands of miles away (it was the sudden death of Ansumane Mane that paved the way for his return from exile). How else could he have survived for so long, they ask. Many of his subjects believed he was immortal.

To nurture and replenish his powers, Nino drew on the darkest of methods. It is said that after he fled to Portugal during the civil war, ten clay pots were found in his abandoned palace, each one containing a human head. Allegations are hard to prove, of course, but it is widely believed, and not just by the scurrilous, that the heads were the fruits of human sacrifice. In a final, eerie reminder of Plato's tyrant, who 'tasted the entrails' of human victims, Vieira, it is said, would drag his quarry deep into the forest and offer them up to the spirits. He would then devour their hearts.

As well as stamping out his enemies, Vieira also intimidated those close to him. He officially had two wives, but his libido was legendary. He took special pleasure in seducing the wives of his colleagues; if the cuckold found out and confronted him or reported the discovery to others, Nino would have him killed. A well-connected doctor working in our district in Bissau told me about a friend of his who ran a state-owned company. The friend was close to Vieira, having helped him garner votes among the Mandingo people in the east. One day he returned home for lunch to find the president's bodyguards stationed outside his house. They told him they had orders to let nobody pass. 'But this is my house, my wife is in there,' the man pleaded. 'If you try to pass we will shoot you,' replied one of the bodyguards calmly. The man left, but he talked, outraged at the betrayal. A few days later he was found in his office with a gun in his hand and a bullet in his head. Vieira said it was suicide, that his friend had shot himself after an argument with his wife. 'But why would he kill himself?' asked the doctor with a chuckle, amazed that anyone would think of peddling such a story in such a macho society. 'Why didn't he kill his wife?'

Nino's luck – or his magic powers – eventually ran out. 'The strongest,' wrote Rousseau, 'is never strong enough to be always the master, unless he transforms strength into right and obedience into duty.' Nino never achieved this transformation. He relied on force and fear; as a fighter, from the clan who fight like hyenas, he knew nothing else. 'He had to die like that,' said the mild-mannered Jimi. 'If you live by violence you will die by violence.' It is hard to find anyone who disagrees. Jimi said he knew nobody – nobody! – who mourned the president's passing; Guineans are curious to know why Nino died and who killed him, but the belief that the world is a better place without him is universal.

15

We head back to the mission in Bissau, where the assault continues. The Americans and Guineans chip away tirelessly at our defences. The Bible, of course, is their chief weapon. They quote from it a litany of passages that they believe prove Jesus' divine parentage. Dan prints out an article from the internet which claims that there was only a one in several trillion chance (he gives a precise number) of Old Testament predictions about the virgin birth coming true. He lays it before me on the kitchen table as if he has found a diary entry in which I confess to something I have always denied. 'How can you doubt Christ's divinity when there is so much proof?' he asks. When, frustrated, I wonder aloud how such a figure can be arrived at when there has been at most one virgin birth since the dawn of time (making it, for now, a one-in-infinity chance), he moves on, unshaken, to another piece of evidence.

Dan converted at the age of nineteen. There are Guinean missionaries who were even younger when they were re-born. Missionaries' children (who are quiet and serious and well behaved but appear somehow otherworldly and icy) are born into fundamentalism. Their whole lives will be given to Christ. Prayer, Bible-reading and proselytising will occupy their days and dominate their thoughts: all else is frippery. Christianity offers Africans freedom from the old ancestral ties, but in the hands of the missionaries this freedom comes at a price. Submission to the ancestors is replaced by submission to Christ ('deny yourself, and take up your *casanke*,' Jesus commanded his followers in Tony's Sarakole Bible). The old chains are replaced by new ones, a new master usurps the old; African converts are once again enslaved.

But what if the missionaries are wrong? What if there is no God, or if eternal life can be attained without devoting your life to Jesus? All their efforts, all their sacrifice, will be wasted. Their whole lives will have been redundant, their existence no more useful to themselves or humanity than that of one who dedicates his days to lotteries or games of chance.

There is, of course, another possibility, more disturbing in its implications: that the missionaries may be right. Among them are intelligent people, who like Dan and Lalas will have weighed carefully the arguments for and against their chosen path. Who can be sure that they are wrong, that the rest of us have a monopoly on the truth? It may be that they alone will make it to heaven while everybody else burns in hell. The missionaries' persistent attacks do not convert me to their creed, but they sow doubts. While Ebru is repelled by their message and appalled at their use of terror as a recruiting tool, I wonder and waver, my mind perhaps made less certain by exposure to West Africa's whirl of fantastic stories. I borrow Dan's Bible, realising as well as he does that this must be how it starts, how they begin to win over African converts (it occurs to me that this – the fear of hell, doubt, investigation - is how Dan himself started). I realise too that unlike Guineans I have had the benefit of many years at school and university, and yet still the missionaries have penetrated my defences. With no education and with their critical faculties less honed, Guineans, trapped in a maelstrom of Christianity, animism, Islam and Westernisation and not knowing which of these gods to follow, are much more vulnerable to their arguments.

Reading Dan's Bible, Christ's admonishments on hell surprise me with their stridency. 'He that believeth in the Son shall have everlasting life,' he said, 'and he that does not obey the Son shall not see life; but the wrath of God abideth on him.' The wrath of God leads to eternal damnation in a 'furnace of fire,' where there will be 'wailing and gnashing of teeth.' I had forgotten these strictures, and had come to believe that hell was a human invention, designed by the powerful to frighten, dominate and sell pardons to the masses. But here was Jesus, no friend of the powerful, spelling out the grisly fate of those who shunned his message. Belief in the biblical Jesus, it seemed, was not possible without belief in hell; by urging Guineans to give up everything for Christ and warning them of the consequences should they desist, the missionaries were merely echoing their master's call.

After a few days of this we leave again, this time for the south, a quiet, remote part of the country near the border with Guinea. It is a land of dark forests and languid rivers. Men still hunt for food, with bush rat, squirrel, monkey and snake supplementing rice and fruit in the local diet. The poor condition of the roads makes it difficult to take produce to market to sell for cash, and the economy, unchanged for centuries, is based on barter and exchange (rice for cashews, for instance, or fruit for fish, or thatching a house in return for digging a well). Modernity has barely touched the region: a passing car draws crowds.

Our passing car *contains* a crowd. The Peugeot seven-seater, or *sept places*, is the most luxurious form of public transport in this part of West Africa. An estate car modified to incorporate a third row of seats where the boot should be, it is designed to seat seven passengers and a driver. Journeys, which follow fixed routes, begin when the vehicle is full. There are regular stops to take on and offload passengers and produce (often the slowing vehicle will be assailed by packs of baying, desperate-looking women who stream out of the forest and plead with the passengers to buy the onions, potatoes or cakes they carry in buckets or crates on their heads). When a top-up of fuel is required and a petrol station located, the engine is left running and a plastic funnel placed in the filler hole. An attendant holds a square of gauze over the opening of the funnel and pours in the fuel from a glass bottle.

If you are seated in the front or middle row of the car, and provided you are not averse to hard seats, chickens pecking at your ankles, clouds of red dust billowing in through un-closable windows, or droplets of the driver's frequently-expelled spittle blowing back and spattering your face, your journey is fairly comfortable. For those seated in the back, however, life is more difficult. Nobody is eager to bring up the rear; those ensconced further forward will turn down hefty bribes to swap places with you. Three people can squeeze into the back row, but none has the luxury of movement. Shifting from one buttock to the other to avoid contracting haemorrhoids, for example, is impossible, for there is no room to either side. Your legs, moreover, are bent double in front of you, since the seat is raised only a few inches above the floor and that floor is cluttered with jerrycans, machetes, holdalls and sometimes live goats. You can extend your legs by edging two or three centimetres backwards, but this will leave your head jammed up against the low metal roof, a position quickly rendered disagreeable by the bumpy, potholed roads.

Those in the back row, then, are guaranteed a joyless ride, but even the front and middle rows are only comfortable if the driver sticks to the seven-passenger limit. Often, he cannot resist the temptation to wedge a few more in to each row, turning the *sept places* into a *neuf* or *dix places*. This is snug, but it is not the worst of all possible worlds. On our way to the south, our driver takes on sixteen passengers and three chickens. Some passengers are forced to stand up, contort their bodies like the trunks of olive trees, and lean over the middle row from the back row and the front row from the middle. Ebru and I, seated, find our heads nestled in armpits, our shoulders used as armrests. Neighbours' elbows act as safety belts. Nobody complains as our conveyance fills up – when there are fourteen people in a car designed for seven and built for five, a couple more bodies do not make a significant difference.

Our driver, the source of our discomfort, is a willowy Muslim man in a thick black robe and white skullcap. He is nervous. Sweat streams down his long hooked nose from under his cap and drips onto his lap. He grips the steering wheel tightly, as if he might fall through the floor if he lets go, and hunches over it to be closer to the road surface in front. His anxiety is well-founded, for in his hands the Peugeot, normally a placid old hack, becomes a wild and uncontrollable brute. Whenever the driver takes his right hand off the steering wheel to change gear, his left hand moves instinctively in the opposite direction, as if to compensate. This causes the car to veer sharply across the road and the passengers to gasp in alarm. He regains the wheel just in time to stop us ploughing into the forest; that there are so few cars in the south, and therefore very little oncoming traffic, is our salvation.

Sometimes the loss of control is deliberate. When the car reaches the top of a hill, the driver, sweat now pouring in torrents from his brow, switches off the ignition to allow us to descend with the aid of gravity rather than costly petrol. As we career downhill, hurtling through villages and hoping that the press of other bodies will cushion us in the likely event of a crash, terrified children and animals scatter from the road like sparks from an anvil.

Towards the end of the three-hour journey, a rotund, stern-looking woman in the back row asks the driver to stop to let her and her three chickens out. 'Where?' he asks. 'At the mango tree,' she replies. The road is lined on both sides, as far as the eye can see, with mango trees. 'Which one?' asks the hapless driver, gripping the wheel and staring intently at the tarmac. 'That one there, straight ahead,' the woman says crossly, clicking her tongue at his stupidity. At this point, none of the driver's options is straightforward; bewildered, he keeps driving. 'This one!' the woman shrieks after a few seconds. 'Stop!' We screech to a halt and the woman climbs out with her chickens, still clicking her tongue. The number of passengers is down to a more manageable fifteen.

16

Eventually we reach Buba. Once the most important town in the south, it is now no more than a village. Its long, sloping main street, bathed in watery sunlight, is silent, undisturbed by the noise of motor cars or mopeds. A market leads off down a narrow lane, but most of its stalls are empty of goods and they peter out after twenty yards. There is a bureau de change for the occasional traveller crossing to or from Guinea, but it rarely has any money. The village baker seldom has any bread, nor the egg seller eggs (our fellow *sept places* passengers stocked up on provisions before we left Bissau). There is nothing to do, so nobody does anything. People lie on benches or shop counters, dozing in the intense, cloying heat. Groups of men sit about, drinking green tea. Even the river which runs past the foot of the main street, the ambitiously named Rio Grande, cannot muster the energy to flow, instead merely filling up and emptying out with the tide. Signs of life are faint.

We slip into the slow routine. From our guesthouse down by the river we wander up into town, pausing from time to time in the shade of a tree to look at a pig or vulture, or simply to escape the fierce sun. Two young children relieve us of an empty plastic water bottle (nothing here is wasted). Under a large mango tree a girl lies face down on a bench asleep while her friend sells us a bunch of bananas. A stray dog scents a morsel of bread we have found and follows us sadly along until it is shooed away by protective locals throwing stones. When the tide is high enough, I take a swim in the sluggish river. Crabs scuttle off as I squelch across the muddy shore. A red and black gonelek bird flits among the mangroves. By the forested far bank, boys in dugout canoes slap paddles onto the water to frighten fish towards their nets. The heat is suffocating, and the cool, brackish water comes as a relief.

The tranquillity of the Rio Grande today hides a turbulent

and troubled past. In the sixteenth century the surrounding region was the site of intense slaving activity, with three thousand captives exported from the jungle each year. It was not unusual to see twenty or thirty ships stationed in the river's calm waters, waiting to be filled with human cargo. For it is here that the Atlantic slave trade begins.

Guineans first encounter their future nemesis in 1446, when Pepel villagers looking out to sea espy what they take to be a flock of giant white sea birds gliding south towards them, skimming the surface of the still ocean. The villagers gaze on in wonder, but as the creatures draw nearer their awe quickly turns to consternation. The white shapes, they realise, are not wings but sails - the sails of large ships bearing rapidly down on them. Panicked, they sound the alarm and take cover in the bush. As the ships reach the shore they watch in horror as dozens of men, their faces as ghostly white as the sails, stream out and wade through the shallows towards the beach.

Repeated invasions by marauding tribes from the interior have made the coastal people hostile to outsiders, and they treat this new maritime threat seriously. As the white men reach dry land, the villagers gather their spears and charge. Battle is joined on the sand, but the intruders have more men and more weapons and they overwhelm their assailants, killing the bravest and taking several others captive. While the survivors flee into the bush, their unfortunate kin are shackled and ferried out to the waiting ships. This tiny crop of men and women are the first victims of a European hunger for cheap slave labour that will engulf the whole of West Africa, swallowing up over nine million lives and spitting out and leaving for dead the three million who are too weak to survive the Atlantic crossing. Taking advantage of their initial economic and technological superiority, for four centuries the strong will plunder the weak and ensure that Africans remain a few paces behind, permanently exploitable, permanently on the wrong side of the balance of power.

The marauders took their captives home with them, to Lagos in Portugal, where a witness saw the wretched cargo being unloaded. 'Some kept their heads low, their faces bathed in tears,' he reported. 'Others struck their faces with the palms of their hands, throwing themselves at full length upon the ground...And though we could not understand the words of their language, the sound of it right well accorded with the measure of their sadness.'

The sponsor of that first voyage was the Portuguese prince, Henry, known to history as Henry the Navigator. Austere and humble in his personal life - he wore a hair shirt and abjured alcohol and womanising - the prince had expansive plans for his country. He had first sent naval expeditions southwards in a vain search for Prester John, the fabled Christian priest-king of central Africa, but his later forays had different motives. His country had recently occupied the Cape Verde islands and it had plans to farm them; for this it needed labour, and none came cheaper than slaves.

Happily for the devout Henry, the Catholic Church blessed his endeavours. Medieval European Christianity held that the enslavement of non-Christians was justified as a means of saving their souls. Pope Nicholas V issued a papal bull that gave Portugal the right to 'capture, vanquish and subdue Saracens, pagans and unbelievers, and to reduce their persons to perpetual slavery.' The legitimacy this conferred emboldened Prince Henry, and the pontifical injunction to 'convert the captives to his use and profit' encouraged him to step up his activity and increase his investment in the new venture.

He began by sponsoring direct raids on African villages. The English pirates Drake and Hawkins joined in, 'going every day on shore to take the inhabitants, with burning and spoiling their towns.' (John Hawkins's coat of arms displayed a slave in chains; both he and Drake would later be made knights of the realm. As an Englishman brought up on tales of these men's heroism, one is uncomfortably reminded of a line from a song, *You Can't Blame the Youth*, by the reggae musician Peter Tosh. 'You teach the youth about the pirate Hawkins, and you said he was a very great man,' the Jamaican sang.)

But these early raids were costly for the slavers - Africans never failed to put up a fight and dozens of Portuguese were killed. After Columbus's discovery of the Americas triggered an explosion in the demand for slave labour – there were now large profits to be made from selling captives to the Spanish, who having wiped out the natives of the New World were seeking a fresh supply of manpower to grow sugar in the Caribbean and mine South America's gold – Henry the Navigator's successors realised that a more efficient system would be needed ('You teach the youth about Christopher Columbus, and you said he was a very great man,' sang Tosh, who in 1987 fell victim to Jamaica's murder epidemic, his native land still bearing the scars of the slave trade).

The Portuguese turned to Africans to do their dirty work. They formed business relationships with chiefs, offering them European merchandise – guns, knives, looking glasses, beads - in exchange for men, women and children. The chiefs could have refused these gifts - their counterparts further south in Gabon never allowed the Portuguese to establish a foothold in their country - but instead they chose cooperation; the lure of the white man's wares proved irresistible.

The chiefs' choice, like the spark that starts a bush fire, would give rise to a vast international industry. Over the next four hundred years millions of Africans would be harvested, checked for defects, flat-packed into container ships and exported across the Atlantic. Purchased in Africa for rum and guns, the slaves were exchanged in the Americas for sugar, which was shipped back across the ocean and sold to sweet-toothed Europeans. At each stop in this triangular trade, huge profits were made.

For the ordinary African, excluded from these machinations,

the chiefs' choice is the first act in a long nightmare. Until that moment it is only the white man he has had to fear. This is peril enough: the slaver-turned-clergyman John Newton is asked by one captive if his shoes are made from 'Black Skin', and rumours are rife that the white man captures the black for the purpose of eating him. But when his own people become slavers too, the African finds himself in even greater danger. Who can he trust now? To whom can he turn for help now that the chief entrusted to protect him has turned from gamekeeper to poacher? Nowhere is safe; at no moment – day or night – can he drop his guard. The old certainties – tribal loyalty, community, the dependability of chiefs – have evaporated. Now only his closest family can be relied upon; his world, once so stable, has become a Hobbesian horror of all against all.

The chiefs begin by selling the slaves they have acquired in war. When this supply dries up they start new wars, raiding neighbouring villages along the coast and venturing inland to plunder from other tribes (travelling in the interior in the late eighteenth century, Mungo Park passes numerous burnt out villages, emptied of their inhabitants by itinerant bands of professional slavers). While the chiefs are rounding up their victims, Portuguese boats 'hover like vultures in every river,' waiting to ferry the captives out to the larger slave ships anchored at sea - for tens of thousands of West Africans, the banks of Buba's Rio Grande are the last they will ever see of their continent.

Park makes his way back to the coast with a caravan, or coffle, of slaves. They march twenty miles a day for two months under the searing tropical sun, 'tied together by their necks with the thongs of a bullock's hide.' Many of the slaves are 'ill-conditioned.' When one becomes too sick to continue, he is replaced by a young girl from the village they are passing through. Park, who records that a prime female slave costs the equivalent of twelve muskets or ten elephant tusks, looks on with pity as the girl is readied for her journey. 'The poor girl was ignorant of her fate until all the bundles were tied up in the morning and the coffle ready to depart,' he writes. 'Never was a face of serenity more suddenly changed to one of the deepest distress; the terror she manifested on having the load put upon her head and the rope fastened around her neck, and the sorrow with which she bade adieu to her companions were truly affecting.'

The people of the Bijagós islands are among the most feared slave raiders. At first the Europeans attempt to take them captive, but they prove impossible to control and foment frequent rebellions on slave ships and plantations. Many of those who are exported commit suicide in the belief that their spirits will return home. The slavers soon realise that perseverance is futile, and begin to enlist them instead as allies. The islanders, lured by Portuguese rewards of rum, brandy and weapons, prove willing accomplices.

The Bijagó have a reputation as able and ruthless warriors. As boat-builders, sailors and swimmers, they are unmatched in West Africa; their seventy-foot war canoes can hold several dozen fighters and travel on the open sea. Historically, the Bijagó's warmongering has mainly been directed against each other - battles between islands have waxed and waned over the centuries - but after the arrival of the Portuguese this infighting is put on hold, as the islanders turn their attention to slave raids on the mainland.

The raiders' targets have little hope of escape. In the dead of night, daubed in coal, red ochre and clay and with their heads bedecked in feathers, detachments of twenty or thirty Bijagó warriors take to their boats and paddle swiftly over the calm sea towards the river mouths of the continent. They leave the canoes in the lee of the banks, and move stealthily through the forest towards their sleeping quarry. Upon arriving at an unfortunate village they surround it, while a few envoys work their way silently down its lanes, setting fire to each house. The villagers emerge from their blazing homes dazed and panicked, only realising that they are under attack when they see that their neighbours' houses, too, are in flames. Most surrender immediately, terrified by their attackers' reputation. Those who try to escape are hacked to death.

War is not the only source of slaves; looting one's own people proves equally profitable. The chiefs dip into their own tribes, even their own villages, to satisfy the Europeans' demands. They sell off criminals, and distort local laws to encompass a wider array of crimes. Enslavement becomes the default punishment for even the pettiest of misdemeanours. If you fall from a tree and die, your whole family can be sold into slavery for cursing you. Debtors who are late repaying loans are dispatched to the waiting ships. Accused criminals are made to drink poisonous red water: those who vomit are pronounced guilty and handed over to the slavers; those who manage to swallow the water are deemed not guilty, but instead die of poisoning.

The Europeans prey on African poverty. Their depredations set in motion a vicious spiral whereby the slave trade reduces food production; reduced food production increases hunger; and hunger leaves the people more vulnerable to slave raids. Agriculture is assailed from all sides. Since strangers can no longer be trusted, trade in food stops, forcing everyone to fend for himself. But to protect family members from marauding slavers (who do not shrink from stuffing stray children into sacks, never to be seen again), cultivation of crops must be moved nearer to home, away from the most fertile land. This makes it harder to grow enough to eat. As the raids intensify, moreover, energy, time and money must be diverted from agriculture to defence. Farmers spend what little they have not on seeds and livestock but on guns and spears. Fortifying villages becomes more urgent than filling granaries - the Balante reinforce their settlements with watchtowers, moats and spiked walls; other tribes build impenetrable compounds with two-foot high entrances and labyrinthine tunnel systems protecting the main living quarters. With the slavers targeting the best of the farmers - the strongest, most productive men and women – food supplies shrivel. Hunger seeps across the land, presenting easy pickings for the raiders. Mungo Park sees people voluntarily offering themselves as slaves 'to avoid a greater calamity.' Parents sell their children because they can no longer feed them. Slave ships fill up just by offering food.

At the time of the slave trade, less than a quarter of a million people lived in the area that is now Guinea-Bissau. During the eighty years when slaving there was at its most intense, nearly two hundred thousand men, women and children were seized and dispatched across the Atlantic. Their journey was hellish. John Newton reported that the captives would be crammed into ships like books upon a shelf. 'I have known them so close that the shelf would not, easily, contain one more,' he wrote. 'The poor creatures, thus cramped for want of room, are likewise in irons, for the most part both hands and feet, and two together, which makes it difficult for them to turn or move, to attempt either to rise or lie down without hurting themselves or each other.' One in seven of those taken did not survive these conditions. Countless others perished during the journey to the ocean.

But it was not just the captives themselves who suffered: slavery also shattered the lives of those left behind. Although the trade ended in the middle of the nineteenth century, its destabilising effects on the societies of West Africa are still perceptible today. Trust was shattered: people living in areas gorged on by the slave trade remain less trusting of their neighbours, and even of family members, than those in areas that were left unscathed. The trade upended social structures, too: the institutions that had evolved over millennia to help West Africans cope with their harsh environment – chiefdom, the administration of justice, the community, the tribe – were all corrupted, sometimes beyond repair. Social upheaval and the breakdown of trust have proved an explosive combination. Over a century after the end of the trade, the regions from which slaves were plundered are less stable – more liable to erupt into civil conflict, more prone to coups d'état - than any other part of the continent.

They are also poorer. Before slavery, the countries whose people would fill the slave ships were among the richest in Africa; today they are the poorest. The subversion of trust contributed to this impoverishment. Without trust it is impossible to do business: buyers who doubt sellers are reluctant to purchase their products, lend to them, invest in them or employ them; sellers who distrust buyers are unwilling to extend them credit or work for them. Businesses must therefore remain small to survive, and commerce limited to minor transactions. The trade also depleted the region's manpower. By targeting working adults and teenagers it robbed West Africa of its brightest prospects, of those who would have driven their economies forward and shepherded them into the modern era. Agriculture withered. Large swathes of the land were emptied, cutting off the exchange of goods and ideas. Manufacturing, whose profitability could not match that of slavery, never got off the ground.

The psychological impacts were no less crippling. 'The people are gentle when they have no communication with Europeans,' wrote Newton, 'but the intercourse of the Europeans has rather had a bad than good influence upon their morals.' The trade debased both rulers and ruled. Dangling their wares before African eyes, the slavers nurtured a fatal greed for their worthless but exotic trinkets. The desire to acquire usurped the old community values; chiefs who had been revered and often loved were exposed as gluttonous and venal, and their people's faith in them as foolish. Leaders' tastes were imitated by their subjects, and imported cloth, jewellery and liquor came to be preferred to the produce of Africa. The European had proved himself a superior manufacturer and a wilier businessman (one eighteenth-century Sierra Leonean chief aspired not just to the products of Europe but the guile, admitting he 'wished to be rogue as good as white man'). Honour and duty had given way to seedy compromise, and from that point on the black man would view himself as inferior to the white. 'This was the greatest damage done to the Negro by slavery,' observed the Trinidadian writer VS Naipaul. 'It set him the ideals of white civilisation and made him despise every other.'

17

Our guesthouse in Buba is the property of Gabi, a large, peroxide-blonde Romanian, and her diminutive Guinean husband Cassama. They met while Cassama was studying economics in Romania during the Cold War (his country's socialist government was loosely allied to Russia), and returned to his homeland after they married.

West Africa has softened their communist leanings. On our second night we are surprised by the arrival of Wade, Katie and their two young children. Wade and Katie are American evangelists who work at the mission in Bissau. We had had dinner with them once at their house, and they had spent the evening regaling us with tales of Wade's extraordinary healing abilities (we had listened politely, wondering which of us was furthest from sanity; seeing them now in the guesthouse as we arrive back from a swim in the river, Ebru conjectures, only half in jest, that they might be pursuing us).

Before moving to the Guinean capital they had lived in a mud house in Kolda, the fly-blown Senegalese border town we had passed through on our way to Bafatá. There, they told us with wonder in their eyes, a local Muslim family had appeared one day on their doorstep and presented them with their three-year-old daughter, who had been having regular and alarming seizures. The parents believed she was possessed by evil spirits, but Muslim and animist holy men had failed to cure her, and they were bringing her to these strange white Christians as a last resort.

Wade, a giant of a man who towers over his petite blonde wife, took the girl in his arms. He noticed that she was wearing a pendant containing Islamic script, and instructed the parents to remove it. Then he prayed over her. The girl's seizures never returned. Her parents paraded her around the town with joy, singing the praises of the Christian miracle workers. 'But it wasn't us who cured her,' the devout Katie told us, 'it was Jesus. We love Jesus so much.'

On arriving at the guesthouse in Buba, Wade provides another demonstration of Christ's munificence. He asks Gabi if she has any ailments, and she tells him she has had a splitting headache for the last week. Wade places his hands on her head and prays. The headache immediately clears. 'It was a terribly painful headache,' Gabi tells me a couple of days later, speaking Portuguese with a lugubrious Romanian accent. 'I'd tried aspirin and other medicines but they made no difference. I couldn't get rid of it. The American offered to try to heal me, and I had nothing to lose so I let him try. I haven't had any pain since.'

Gabi, who is as assertive and garrulous as her husband Cassama is mild and quiet, renounced Christianity as a teenager and, swapping gods, became a committed communist. She is in no doubt, however, that it is to Wade's healing powers that she owes the disappearance of her headache. She realises that this is difficult for Europeans like us to accept, but her three decades in West Africa have made her less certain about how the world works. 'You might not believe any of these things now,' she tells us, 'but if you stay here long enough, you will.' They are words we will have frequent cause to remember.

In an ideal world, Buba would be a good starting point for the next stage of our journey, to Sierra Leone. If the roads were passable and safe and one could find reliable public transport, it would be possible to head south to the border with Guinea, along the coast to its capital, Conakry, and then south-east towards Freetown, the capital of Sierra Leone. Unfortunately, travel in this part of the world is never so simple. The road to the border, Gabi tells us, is atrocious, littered with large potholes and in parts completely fallen away. The road on the other side is worse. Cassama warns us, too, that the notorious corruption of officials on the Guineén side might double or treble the cost of the trip.

Since these obstacles deter all but the most desperate from using the route, travelling by public transport would involve many hours, perhaps many days, of waiting for vehicles to fill up.

The above are minor impediments, however, compared with those placed in our way by the regional security situation. The military government in Guinea has been massacring opponents and preparing for civil war. Both the French and British governments advise strongly against all visits to the country, and Guinéens in Senegal and Bissau have given us similar counsel. Our alternatives are limited. There are no flights or ships from Guinea-Bissau to Sierra Leone, and the much longer overland route which bypasses Guinea takes you instead through the Ivory Coast and Liberia, both of which are themselves recovering from civil wars and are also on European governments' travel blacklists. This leaves heading north by *sept places* to Gambia, or to Dakar in Senegal, and then flying south, back over Guinea-Bissau and Guinea, as the most feasible solution (although even this route means braving West African airlines, nearly all of which are banned from European airspace due to safety concerns).

The traveller wishing to reach Gambia or Dakar from Guinea-Bissau must first negotiate the Casamance in Senegal, which borders Guinea-Bissau to the north. The decades-old rebellion in this region means that it too has been placed on Western governments' lists of no-go areas, and coming down from Dakar at the beginning of our trip we had avoided the most volatile districts by circumnavigating Gambia and entering Guinea-Bissau in the east. The prospect of retracing those same, gruelling steps fills us with gloom (even the normally cautious Ebru talks of taking instead the shorter, more direct route), and the length of the trip and the poor condition of the roads mean that it too is not without hazards. The shorter route north traverses rebel country, where in the preceding weeks there have been several deadly skirmishes between separatists and soldiers. It is an option that two months ago we would not have considered, but now, accustomed as we are to having a looser grip on our destinies, it is this path that we decide on.

18

Gabi's husband Cassama joins us for the *sept places* journey back to Bissau, where we will pick up onward transport to Senegal. He is taking the guesthouse's generator to be repaired (we have spent the last few nights with just candle and moonlight for illumination). The *sept places* has only nine passengers, but there is a problem with the engine, which cuts out ten minutes into the journey. Fortunately we are at the top of a hill, and a push by two of the passengers is all that is required to restart the vehicle. Fifteen minutes later it cuts out again, and then again shortly after that (on this last occasion, one of the pushers has to run back to retrieve a pistol that has fallen out of his pocket and clattered unnervingly onto the hard surface of the road). The fourth time the engine stalls, the combined pushing power of all six of the male passengers is deployed in vain, as the ignition stubbornly refuses to ignite. No further progress is possible.

There is no alternative but to wait. While the driver pokes hopefully at the engine, the passengers wander across the road and sit on the ground in the shade of a ponderous, deep-green mango tree, the dried-out forest at our backs. What we are waiting for is unclear. The few cars that pass all stop to offer help, but since nobody knows what is wrong, we wave them on. The minutes pass, then the hours; nobody complains. After a while the driver hitches a ride to the nearest town, twenty miles away, presumably to find help. Under the mango tree, the men smoke cigarettes, the women chat. An older passenger lies down in the dust and falls asleep. From time to time someone gets up to go and have a look at the engine, and then saunters back to us, nothing to report. All around is silence - it is too hot even for birds to sing, and as noon approaches the trickle of passing vehicles dries up, the occasional scurrying monkey now the only sign of life. Heat haze liquefies the surface of the long, straight road, turning it into a steaming grey broth. It is good weather for waiting.

After some time, a car approaches and drops off our driver and a mechanic. They set to work, but give up after a few minutes, stumped. We wait some more. Fortunately, our driver has also found a rope on his expedition. When eventually a crowded minibus comes past and stops to offer assistance, the two vehicles are tied together. The *sept places* passengers get up from the shade of the mango tree, shrug, and climb back into the car as if nothing has happened. We are towed off to the nearby town, where we change to a trustier conveyance.

This is not the end of our travails, however, for as we approach Bissau we are stopped at an army *controle*, or checkpoint. These are ubiquitous in West Africa. On the outskirts of almost every major town and many minor ones, you will find a small group of soldiers sitting under a makeshift wood and straw shelter, ordering vehicles passing into and out of the town to stop. Their raison d'être is not always obvious. In areas where there is unrest, such as the Casamance in Senegal, they seek weapons and the drugs that are often sold to purchase them. If they are lucky, they will stumble across a rebel fighter (although savvy passengers can avoid checkpoints by trekking in a wide arc through the bush on foot before rejoining their car further on, out of sight of the soldiers). In more peaceful regions, while their ostensible purpose is to ensure that drivers have the correct papers and their passengers' identity cards, the soldiers' principal objective is to extract bribes to supplement their meagre salaries. Most often it is the drivers who pay the bribes - even if their documents are in order, it is seldom difficult for the soldiers to find something amiss with their vehicles - but sometimes passengers are asked to get out of the car and present the contents of their baggage.

This is one such occasion. Our fellow travellers have little to show, but one soldier, a tall and fierce-looking man in wraparound shades, takes an interest in the *brancos'* rucksacks.

He points at them with his pistol, and asks us to empty them onto two small chairs. The other passengers are indignant that he is picking on the foreigners – 'guests in our country' – but we remain outwardly calm as we unpack our bags, knowing that any expressions of anger or frustration will increase our risk of arrest or extortion.

Once we are halfway through, the chairs piled high with clothes, underwear and books, the soldier tires of the charade and orders us to be on our way. The nether reaches of our bags, where any illegal objects are most likely to be hidden, remain undisturbed. Cassama and the other passengers, who have been standing by us to ensure we make it through the *controle* intact, mutter angrily about the soldier's venality, and amid much huffing and puffing we pile back into the car and continue on our way.

The soldiers' vigilance is unusual. On our outward journey from Bissau to Buba we had avoided a bag check by mentioning the name of the Manchester United manager Sir Alex Ferguson to a football-loving cadet. Since then, however, the game had changed, for in the intervening days the country's numerous checkpoints had failed to halt the passage into the capital of one of its most wanted men. Rear-Admiral José Americo Bubo Na Tchuto, the former head of the Guinean navy, had spent two years in Gambia, having fled Guinea-Bissau in fear of his life after a failed attempt to oust Nino Vieira in a coup. With Nino dead, Admiral Bubo, weary of exile, had decided to return home. Leaving Gambia in a dugout canoe, he had made his way through the waterways and forests of his homeland, walked into the United Nations building in Bissau, and demanded refugee status. Although Bubo was widely suspected of being involved in the drug trade through the Bijagós - as head of the navy he was perfectly placed to grab a slice of the action, and he was renowned for being generous with the rewards that came with his position - the United Nations, constitutionally bound to grant him asylum, had refused the government's requests to hand him over for trial. (He would only be freed several months later, when a group of renegade soldiers took him under their "protection" and made him the figurehead for their own coup attempt. Within weeks of his release, and despite the United States labelling him a "drug kingpin" and banning American citizens from doing business with him, Bubo was reappointed as navy chief.) Those staffing Guinea-Bissau's checkpoints, meanwhile, chastened by their failure to catch the fugitive but oblivious to accusations of shutting the stable door after the horse had bolted, were now putting on a display of relative efficiency.

As we finally near Bissau, seven hours into our three-hour journey, Cassama, who has been quiet and pensive throughout, places his hand gently on my forearm and asks me my views on Wade's healing powers. A trained economist and committed communist, Cassama is torn between scepticism and wonder at the sudden cure of his wife's headache. If you stay here long enough, you will believe in these things, Gabi had told me. Her husband's old beliefs were seeping back in, jostling aside the scientific view of the world he had brought back with him from Romania. He asks me very respectfully whether, as an educated writer, I can think of a rational explanation for Gabi's rapid recovery. Conscious that the profession of traditional healing might not have survived for so long if nobody had ever felt better after visiting a medicine man, I remind him of the placebo effect that is so apparent in clinical trials, and of the healing powers of positive thinking; nor, I add, can coincidence be ruled out. He nods, but is unconvinced. 'You don't seem sure,' he says, accurately diagnosing my doubts. 'I'm not,' I find myself answering. 'It could have been Jesus, too.'

Interlude: Senegal

In Bissau we stop briefly at the mission to bid farewell to Dan, Lalas and the other fundamentalists. Dan says he will miss us. He has enjoyed our nightly routine of dinner, card games, a mug of Portuguese red wine (smuggled into the hostel) and discussions about religion. He has been glad, too, of the opportunity to hear about different lives, to talk about things other than the problems of the local people who visit his clinic every day. Now, he tells us, he will return to his old routine - morning prayers, the clinic, Bible reading and then bed. Leaving him to plough his lonely furrow, we head for the transport park and climb into a *sept places* bound for Senegal.

You can learn a lot about a country by leaving it. Although itself one of the world's poorest nations, Senegal seems affluent compared with Guinea-Bissau. We see things in Ziguinchor, the old riverfront trading post that is the capital of the Casamance region, that we have not seen in months. We see buildings of two, three, even four storeys. We see market stalls displaying piles of food rather than mere scraps. We see factories, cash machines, newspapers, bookshops. People in boats wear lifejackets. There are tourists, and the incessant hassle from hustlers that accompanies them. Most amazing of all, there is electricity. You press a switch and a light comes on. Fans turn instead of lying dormant. There are streetlights, so you do not need a torch to pick your way between the potholes at night. Food is stored in refrigerators, drinks are iced. Guinea-Bissau, back in the Dark Ages, has none of these things.

Ziguinchor was used for most of its existence as a slave trading port, but these days, surrounded by roadblocks and watched over by low-flying army helicopters, it is an oasis of peace in a turbulent region. The town is frequented by newly-retired recreational sailors from France, who moor their yachts in the slow-flowing river and buzz over its surface in motorised rubber dinghies, visiting other boats or touching down in the town for a morning coffee and croissant or an evening aperitif.

The sailors are accompanied by their African wives or girlfriends. The nineteenth-century explorer Richard Burton, translator of the Kama Sutra and the Arabian Nights, described the women of the Casamance, the Diola, as 'wild, half-naked pagans,' but today they are beautifully dressed and graceful, the fairest of them labelled admiringly as "gazelles". They are understandably popular with aging Frenchmen, with whose affluence young African men cannot compete. As these greying, overweight white men in shorts and bulging T-shirts parade their beautiful young partners down Ziguinchor's streets, the boys of the town look on impotently.

After a few days living like colonials, our lazy days punctuated by long lunches and sundowners by the river, we board the overnight ferry to Dakar. We arrive in the capital just as the sun is climbing above the tower blocks of downtown, and after elbowing our way through the crowd thronging the dock take a taxi to a three-room hotel in one of the city's residential districts. The hotel is run by David, a bearded, heavy-drinking chef from Birmingham who claims to be fifty-eight but looks a decade older. When we had first arrived in Dakar at the beginning of our trip, we had stayed in a nearby guesthouse and stumbled across the poolside bar of David's establishment while seeking respite from the chaotic streets outside. At that time he had been running it in partnership with Gilles, a melancholy Frenchman with a Salvador Dalí moustache whose wife had recently left him because she could no longer tolerate Dakar's heat, dirt and disorder (she had turned to drink, and managed to escape back to Europe before it consumed her).

The hotel had doubled as a brothel, frequented by rich Senegalese businessmen and their mistresses and by declining Frenchmen saved from solitude by young African *gazelles*. The three musty rooms, reached via a spiral metal staircase climbing from the back of the restaurant, resemble those of an old Parisian bordello, with high ceilings, four-poster beds and large baths with heavy antique brass taps. Since few Senegalese can afford to spend a night here and tourists prefer to stay in the city centre, Gilles had let the rooms out on an hourly basis to couples, to help balance the books.

The hotel's restaurant seldom had any customers, so David's shift in the kitchen finished early and he would spend the rest of the evening drinking. We had spent a few nights sitting with him by the bar before we left the city. Although he speaks French so fluently that he sometimes struggles to find the right word in his mother tongue, he had not met anyone from his homeland since his arrival in Dakar a few months earlier and was delighted to discover we were from Britain. When we told him we were heading to Guinea-Bissau, which has a reputation in Senegal for instability and violence, he had been worried for our safety, and he is relieved to see us on our return.

Gilles is no longer there, he tells us: he has decamped to a downtown bar, leaving David to manage the place by himself. He says he has cleaned it up and that it no longer operates as a brothel, and offers us a discounted room. 'I'll be glad of some company,' he adds by way of explanation - we are the hotel's only guests. Every night for almost a week, we sit at the bar over Gazelle beers (the gazelle seemingly signifying all that is good in these parts), and David, in his slow Brummie drawl, talks.

Like many expatriates of a certain age, he has a lot to talk about. His wife left him some years ago while he was running a restaurant in Paris. Since then he has been wandering the world. He worked in Qatar and then Saudi Arabia, where he cooked for the royal family. He hated the Saudis - 'a nasty, rude race' - but liked the lifestyle and the salary until Al Qaeda began to target Westerners and he was forced to leave. He went to South Africa, where a friend had promised him a job. When he arrived, the friend was nowhere to be seen. He was stranded. His hotel room, where he kept his cash, was burgled. He ended up sleeping in a park, where he was robbed of his few remaining possessions. He hates South Africans now, too.

After a few weeks in Cape Town, he had a lucky break and met a Frenchman who owned a restaurant in Dakar. Impressed by David's wealth of experience (before Paris and the Gulf he had run a bistrot in central London, and he speaks enthusiastically and knowledgeably about food), the Frenchman paid for him to fly to Senegal and put him up in a small flat above his restaurant. Then, as so often happens here, David was derailed by events beyond his control. An adverse reaction to a yellow fever vaccine crippled his legs and left him barely able to walk. Dakar's doctors were unable to ascertain what was wrong, but predicted a lengthy recovery period. Eventually his sponsor lost patience, and this latter-day Mungo Park was stranded again. 'I was very lucky to meet Gilles,' he says, tired but resilient. 'I don't know what I'd have done otherwise – I was running out of options.'

He likes Senegal so far. 'The women are beautiful,' he swoons in a drunken slur. 'I love women. I like hunting for them, but I need my legs to get better first!' He laughs a big, slow laugh and strokes his bushy grey beard in appreciation of his frankness. He tells us he has big plans for the hotel and restaurant. He is changing the menu, refurbishing the rooms and lowering prices. But he is not a well man. He walks unsteadily, often with the aid of a stick. He wonders if he should go back to Britain for treatment. He is frustrated about his health, unable to adjust to the loss of mobility, the sudden and possibly irreversible lurch towards old age. He rails against his bad luck and takes refuge in drink.

On our first visit to Dakar we had been unimpressed by the city. It had seemed menacing and impersonal, its reputation for crime made real to us when we were threatened with violence by a downtown hustler. But on our second visit we view it differently. The Senegalese capital is a light, airy city by the sea. With its shady avenues, bustling street markets, and bright, dusty outlying districts it is a happy blend of Mediterranean France, sub-Saharan Africa and the coastal cities of Morocco and Algeria. Coming from Guinea-Bissau we are struck by Dakar's modernity, evident not just in its smart shopping malls and patisseries, its extensive public transport system and its multiracial population but also in the sight of young men and women performing stretching exercises and short sprints on the city's beaches, as if in preparation for a race or match. This impression of organised leisure, of purpose and planning and self-improvement, is absent in Bissau, whose all-enveloping torpor is interrupted only very occasionally by an impromptu game of street football.

It is easy to be lulled by Dakar's attractions, to relax and become too confident in one's ability to thrive in the West African city, but an unnerving episode soon reminds us of the dangers of dropping your guard. One afternoon we are awoken from a siesta by a knock at the door of our room. We ignore it, but when we go downstairs later the receptionist, a young Senegalese, tells us that a man has been in asking for me, claiming to have met me that morning. I have spoken to nobody all day, but the receptionist insists that the visitor, who said he would come back in the evening, had asked for me by name.

I think no more of it, assuming it is either a case of mistaken identity or an effort to extract money, but Ebru is worried, and unbeknown to me spends the next hour puzzling over who the man could be. Finally an answer comes to her. 'You wrote that article this morning didn't you?' she asks, sounding panicked. I clutch my forehead in alarm. Earlier that day I had published on the internet a short update about the drug trade in Guinea-Bissau. Although I had thought it safer to wait until we were in Senegal before writing it, the report contained little that was new, and the readership of the website to which I posted is small, numbering in the tens of thousands. That the article might be read by the traffickers was unlikely, that it would prompt them to hunt me down almost inconceivable. To find me, moreover, they would have had to ask for me by name in every hotel in Dakar, and all within a few hours of the offending report appearing.

I should have had no cause for concern. Back in England I had published several pieces on the same subject, on the internet and in magazines, and the idea that they might put me at risk would have seemed preposterous. Here, however, your mind works differently. Here, the steady bombardment of your mental and physical defences – by the heat, by other people, by the pathogen-tipped arrows hostile nature flings at you - eventually has an effect. You begin to see things that are not there, to overlook the obvious, to seek answers in the realm of what back home in rational Europe you would have seen as the fanciful, the magical, the impossible.

As the minutes pass in the turbulent wake of Ebru's epiphany, we both grow increasingly certain that the man who had come to the hotel intended to kill me. How else could he know my name? How else could he have found me unless he had the support of the South Americans' all-seeing organisational machine? I marshal arguments to feed my paranoia. Have the traffickers not already threatened journalists in West Africa? Have they not killed dozens of prying hacks in Colombia, Mexico and Venezuela? It occurs to me that neither their new airdrop tactic nor their staking out of Canhabaque is common knowledge, and that this might be valuable information for those in charge of European Union patrols. Might the traffickers think I was an EU spy? Eliminating me would cost them nothing. The Senegalese police would not protect me, and there would be so little chance of them catching the killer that it would barely be worth paying them off. Acquiring the services of a local hitman, moreover, would cost no more than a few dollars - perhaps the equivalent of a line of cocaine. A shot to the head or a knife to the throat in a hotel room or an unlit street would send a cheap but resonant message to other would-be sleuths.

As evening approaches, our fears coagulate. What is most likely a case of mistaken identity or a pure coincidence has morphed in our minds into a cold blooded murder plot. The man had said he would come back after six, but as dusk falls there is no sign of him. This provides only momentary comfort, before we realise he is more likely to complete his task in the dead of night. We debate whether it would be safer to sleep elsewhere, and decide to consider our options over a beer at the poolside bar. We are the only drinkers. Night has fallen. The humidity and fly-filled darkness feel more cloying than ever. A faint underwater light fills the small swimming pool with a spectral glow. Under the thatched roof of the little bar, open on three sides, we sit and think.

The bargirl serves us beers, oblivious to the tempests raging in our heads. Rather than calming each other, my suggestions feed Ebru's fears, her suspicions tauten my nerves. We tumble together, locked in a mutually destructive embrace like skydivers fatally entangled in each other's straps. Then, while pondering our next move, we are suddenly confronted with a new crisis. While we have been immersed in discussion a man has materialised at the bar. He has taken a seat behind the shorter section of the L-shaped counter, facing us. Unlike the hitman we have been imagining, who is huge and powerful, this specimen is thin and wiry. Some of his front teeth are missing. Dressed in a grubby brown calf-length gown, he gives off an air of seediness and, to our fear-tinted eyes, stop-at-nothing desperation.

He orders a beer and takes out a packet of Marlboro. Judging by his appearance, he should be unable to afford either. Where did he get the money? Why is he here, alone, tonight, in a bar whose few customers are almost exclusively European? Is this the man who came for us earlier? Is he here to warn us or to eliminate us? Granted, he looks more like a petty criminal than a murderer, but we decide that a petty criminal – cheap, anonymous and unlikely to be missed if he has to be disposed of - would be the perfect conduit for the South Americans' plans. Besides, we reason, you do not need brawn to shoot someone at two yards: all you need is courage, coolness, and hunger.

While he sips calmly at his beer, the assassin looks down repeatedly at his mobile phone and taps messages into it. What do the messages say? That he has found us? That he can kill us now if they give the word? Or is he arranging a getaway or final-ising payment? All the thrillers we have ever seen hurtle through our heads like a news ticker on speed. The man glances up at us every few seconds, so frequently he could be painting our portrait, as if to make sure we do not escape. Ebru tells me later that she was convinced at that moment that this was the end, that he would pull out a gun and put a bullet in my head, maybe in both our heads. Maybe in the poor, oblivious bargirl's head, too.

We decide to leave, flight our only hope. As we walk away from the bar towards the busy street outside, I look back. He is watching us carefully. To throw him off our scent, we turn left out of the gate, cross the road and then turn right, back on ourselves. We walk a couple of hundred yards until we reach the darkest stretch of pavement, and stop to hail a taxi. This time Ebru looks back, and is horrified to see the man emerging from the hotel gate. He glances around and turns left. We have managed to trick him, but it is at this moment that I too am sure they are after my blood. Until now I have been worried, but at the same time hopeful that it is all a delusion. Now I am convinced it is real. Tension and fear tighten my throat. We jump in a taxi and head for the guesthouse where we had stayed on our first visit. Fortunately they have a room.

The guesthouse is a one-storey building in a small compound. The compound is entered through a solid metal door. A passageway between this door and the building leads to a dusty yard, in the corner of which a wretched goat is tied to a tree, being fattened up in preparation for having its throat slit during the great Muslim festival of Tabaski later in the year. Our room lies directly opposite the metal door. A wooden shutter blocks our view. We leave it closed, as added protection (there is no glass). We lock ourselves in, switch off the light and fan, and await our fate. Sweat pours off us in torrents. My hands are shaking. We can barely raise a whisper. If anyone comes for us, we agree, we will either jump out of the window and run or, if they station a man on the gate, hide under the beds and pray to Dan's God.

We know that if we get through the night we will have only a few hours of daylight to negotiate in the morning before our flight to Sierra Leone. But it is not yet midnight, and the hours of darkness stretch interminably, mercilessly, ahead of us. Every noise we hear rattles our brains. Cars passing outside are taken for convoys of drug barons. When a phone rings it jangles my nerves as if I were one of those old cartoon alarm clocks. Each knock at the metal door has us cowering by the window, trying to peer through the vents in the shutter. We cannot go on. We reach a point where we would prefer to give ourselves up, to run out into the waiting hail of bullets, than continue to endure this dread.

We walk out into the yard like condemned criminals, resigned to our fate, expecting the gunman to walk in through the metal door at any moment. There is only one other guest, a cheery German named Mikhail who is researching a radio programme on what African philosophy can teach the West. We sit with him in the dusty yard and he listens amused to our story. He seems unconvinced that our fears are justified, and even volunteers to accompany us out of the guesthouse to buy cigarettes (we ran out hours ago). We warn him of the dangers inherent in such a mission, but he is undeterred. He points out a black cat in the road and asks joshingly if this alarms me, since black cats are thought unlucky in West Africa (many of them are indeed ill-starred, for their skins are used by witch doctors as protective charms; it is rare to see one alive). His humour relaxes us a little, and we continue chatting with him back in the guesthouse yard, cigarettes safely bought. We hope he will sit with us all night, but are aware that he has work to do, and that soon we will be alone again with our terrors.

When he finally takes his leave, we return to our room. Exhausted, we fall into a fitful sleep, illustrated by dreams of falling. Then, suddenly, after what seems like just a few minutes, we are woken by a loud banging at the metal door. We leap out of bed and take our stations by the window, immediately wide awake and ready. It is three o'clock. The young man who looks after the guesthouse opens the door. We hear talking, not in French but in a guttural, harsh-sounding African language, probably Wolof. Voices are raised. We huddle close together, certain our time has come. I can feel Ebru's fear mingling with my own, as if she is plugged into me and pumping volts into my veins. We strain to hear or see what is happening, but the talking at the gate has stopped and there is only silence. Have they gagged or killed the caretaker, or bought him off? Has he told them where we are hiding? We hear footsteps moving down the passage, and then, joyously, the sound of a woman's voice. Relief floods over us, for we know that our assassin was unaccompanied. The intruders are nothing more sinister than guests arriving off the night flight from Paris. We are spared. Perhaps it was all just a paranoid delusion. Perhaps it was West Africa toying with us, keeping us on our toes, pushing us to the edge before drawing back and saving us for another day.

We collapse back into bed, and sleep until dawn. Nothing else happens. We walk back towards David's hotel, checking over our shoulders from time to time but feeling reprieved. On the opposite side of the main road, by a hospital which sits under a permanent cloud of scavenging black kites, we pause, checking for signs of a break-in. There are two large men in sunglasses on either side of the hotel gate and a jeep with blacked-out windows

parked on the pavement nearby. Too weary to panic, we wait
nervously for a few minutes - although we think it unlikely that
anything will happen in broad daylight on a busy road, our
pursuers are ruthless and brutal, so you cannot be too careful.
Eventually the jeep drives off. One of the men by the gate boards
a bus and is carried out of our lives. A few minutes later the other
man walks away. We cross the road and steal back into the hotel,
past the empty bar and up to our room. David is still in a
drunken sleep, unaware of our absence. The previous day's
visitor has not returned, and the mystery of how he knew my
name remains unsolved (I begin to wonder if it was the receptionist who mentioned my name, which the visitor, who may
have been a hustler, jumped on as proof that he knew me, but am
still left with the question of why he did not come back). We pack
our bags quickly, leave a note for David, whom we hope to see
again when we come back from Sierra Leone, and take a taxi to
the airport.

Sierra Leone

19

Lungi International Airport is located just ten miles from Freetown, the capital of Sierra Leone. This is less convenient than it sounds. Most of the ten miles are liquid, for between airport and town lies the gaping mouth of the Sierra Leone River. The river has no bridges, and there is of course no tunnel, but it is not an insurmountable obstacle, or at least not quite.

The new arrival has several options, none of which is without risk. For the well heeled there is a privately-run helicopter service, which drops you by the beach in the smartest part of Freetown. The choppers are not always expertly flown, however, nor assiduously maintained, and they frequently crash. A safer but slower option is a hovercraft, but this is only feasible during the dry months, when the sea is calm, and it is not unheard of for the vessel to run out of fuel en route (on one recent occasion a clumsy attempt to refuel amid the waves resulted in an on-board fire and a mass jumping of ship). Slower still is the ferry crossing. The boat is a rusting hulk whose best days were spent long ago plying the tranquil waters around Greece. It has no life jackets, and several of its predecessors have sunk, but compared with the alternatives it has a reassuring solidity, and it is also much the cheapest choice.

We head from the airport to the ferry terminal in a taxi full of women. I sit in the front talking football with the English-speaking driver. Behind me, one of the women apologises to Ebru for conversing in Temne with her companions. The atmosphere is jolly and relaxed, a welcome change from our nervous days in Dakar. The driver is confident we will make it to the dock in time for the last daylight ferry. If not, we will have to wait three hours for the next one, and will arrive in the city at midnight. A daylight arrival would be preferable - we do not have accommodation booked and downtown Freetown has a reputation for crime - but West Africa has by now dismantled most of our defences and we are less concerned by this than we might have been at the beginning of our trip.

We arrive at the dock as the ferry is leaving, and settle down in an outdoor café to await its return. The air is warm and humid. Reggae music blares from the café's speakers as dusk falls rapidly over the broad river. On the far bank through the gloaming we can make out a few buildings nestling below the looming hills of the Freetown peninsula, whose resemblance to resting lions inspired the country's name. The buildings are soon extinguished by the darkness, however, leaving us to concentrate instead on fending off a siege.

Our small plastic table is not the only one in the café, but since it is the only one at which white people are sitting it attracts a disproportionate degree of attention. Hawkers, hustlers and beggars parade past, taking turns at trying to sell us their wares or tug at our heartstrings. A few are bold enough to pull up a chair: a teenage boy in a fake Chelsea football shirt sits down and sells us a SIM card for our mobile phone; another offers us watches (although timepieces in this laid-back part of the world serve a purely decorative purpose); beggars in various states of disrepair ask us gloomily for a few leones or pounds. Amid the other tables a comedian gesticulates wildly as each of his jokes reaches its apparently hilarious climax; at the end of his act, which has been delivered entirely in Temne, he cheekily asks Ebru and me for a tip, which draws another laugh from the appreciative audience.

The ferry arrives half an hour late. Seeing the colour of our skin, the man at the ticket desk sells us a first-class ticket without asking our preference, so we climb up to the deluxe lounge and slump onto a cockroach-covered bench by the window. We look out across the river. There are a few specks of light on the far bank, but nothing resembling a city. Unlike Guinea-Bissau, Sierra

Leone has a state electricity company, but the grid is not far-reaching and its output is fitful. While reservoirs in the hills above the capital provide electricity during and just after the rainy season, no provision is made for the dry months. As in Guinea-Bissau, therefore, nightfall at this time of year sees most of the country cloaked in darkness.

The first-class lounge boasts a television and two fans. Although we sit next to one of the fans it is nevertheless swelteringly hot, the air so damp you feel you could drink it. In one corner of the room a boy sells pirate DVDs; in another is a small bar. Most of the passengers ignore both, transfixed instead by the television, which is blasting out a Nigerian comedy programme at full volume. The passengers laugh raucously, shaking their heads at the characters' stupidity and commenting knowingly to each other about what is likely to happen next. Everybody seems to know one another, drawn together by mirth - it is as if we have landed in someone's drawing room, where a huge extended family has gathered for an evening of companionship and entertainment.

In search of fresher air I wander outside, to where a narrow gangway leads back to the second-class area. I lean over the railings and look out at the calm black sea. The gangway is crowded with gold prospectors and dealers (Sierra Leone is better known for its diamonds, but in a global recession it is gold that provides the safe haven for frightened investors). I meet, separately, a Sierra Leonean who has flown in from London, a Ghanaian and a Guinean. All are here to buy or dig for gold. A millennium ago the Persian geographer Ibn al-Faqih wrote in his *Concise Book of Lands* that in the West African kingdom of Ghana, 'gold grows in the sand as carrots do, and is plucked at sunrise.' From that time until the seventeenth century West Africa was the principal source of the world's gold. It is still a significant supplier today, but production in Sierra Leone is not yet well developed. The men on the boat are the pioneers, hoping to carve their fortunes out of the festering jungle. They are purposeful and serious, knowing that there could not be a better time to be in this place, doing this job. They are anxious, too, in a hurry to stake their claims before the bigger mining companies get wind of the treasure trove. 'One day everyone will be here,' says the Sierra Leonean from London. 'People don't realise how much gold there is in this country.'

We reach the dock and prepare ourselves for the inevitable scrum. A crowd of hustlers descends, offering to carry our luggage or find us a taxi. After a few minutes of haggling we climb into a jeep and head for the centre of Freetown. Although it is approaching midnight, the streets of the East End near the dock are full of life. We pass rows of candlelit market stalls spilling out onto the road. Between them drift lithe girls in wraparound skirts and young men in basketball shirts. Hip hop music thuds from dark drinking holes constructed of wire mesh and corrugated iron. Groups of youths sit on the steps of rickety, wooden-slatted houses, coolly eyeing the passersby. As our taxi rolls slowly through, encased in traffic, hawkers surround us, proffering their wares. We can choose from a range of goods - chewing gum, bananas, knives, mobile phone cases, Barack Obama or Osama bin Laden T-shirts, smoked fish in transparent polythene bags, school text books, pirate DVDs, even wigs – but we content ourselves with a couple of sachets of water, to replace some of the sweat that has been pouring off our faces like rain down a window.

When we reach downtown Freetown the traffic and the commerce thin out. This part of the ride takes us back in time through Sierra Leone's modern history, like a cinema reel in reverse. We pass bombed out buildings destroyed during the 1990s civil war, then the grand law courts built by the British colonisers, their portal guarded by Greek gods, and finally the ancient Cotton Tree in whose shade the first returned slaves gathered to thank the Lord for their safe arrival and chart a course for their new lives.

Freetown owes its existence to the slave trade, or more precisely to its abolition. After the American War of Independence, thousands of former slaves who had fled their plantations and fought on the British side sailed to England to demand compensation. Receiving none, many turned to begging and petty crime to make ends meet. To rid the country of this growing menace, the British abolitionist Granville Sharp proposed establishing a settlement for freed slaves on the West African coast, from whence they and their ancestors had originally been pillaged. Such a settlement, he prophesied, would be home to 'the freest and happiest people on earth.' The site selected for his utopia was Sierra Leone, and in 1787 the British bought a parcel of land from a local chief and deposited three hundred "black poor" on a muddy beach in the mouth of the great river.

This first attempt at settlement was not a success. Within a hundred days a third of the new arrivals had died, and a local ruler evicted the remainder soon after, following a dispute over ownership of the land. The colony disintegrated, the survivors fleeing into the bush after the chief set fire to their homes. The old Temne name for the area, which meant "the place of wailers", began to seem appropriate.

The abolitionists tried again five years later, shipping in over a thousand freed slaves from Nova Scotia. This time, with the help of forceful British military assistance against hostile local chiefs, the settlers managed to gain a foothold. Their numbers quickly multiplied. Slavery was collapsing under the weight of its own contradictions. For centuries, the widely accepted argument that Africans were no better than animals had given the industry moral legitimacy (the clergyman Newton wrote to his wife that the black man was incapable of love). But to many of slavery's exponents the humanity of their captives was painfully apparent, and momentum built rapidly once influ-

ential individuals turned against the trade. Mungo Park encapsu-
lated these dilemmas. Although he befriended slavers and never
condemned their activities, the explorer was so often treated
kindly by slaves that he could not but feel empathy for them. One
evening, as he was sitting under a tree chewing straws, 'an old
female slave passing by with a bucket on her head asked me if I
had got my dinner...My boy told her that the king's people had
robbed me of all my money. On hearing this, the good old
woman, with a look of unaffected benevolence, immediately took
the basket from her head, and showing me that it contained
groundnuts presented me with a few handfuls.' The woman
walked away before Park could thank her.

Such tales inspired the abolitionist movement ('Am I not a
man and a brother?' asked the black figure on the popular anti-
slavery medallions produced by Josiah Wedgwood). The moral
case put forward by Granville Sharp, William Wilberforce and,
after many years growing rich on the trade, John Newton helped
convince the British crown to put a stop to it. But moral qualms
were not the only consideration; slavery was also beset by
economic contradictions. Slaves had no incentive to work hard
bar the threat of violence, and supervising hundreds of reluctant
captives was burdensome and costly. Keeping them healthy,
moreover, was impossible - death rates among slaves were
stratospheric, with some reports putting them at fifty percent per
year. Indolence and ill health had a devastating effect on productivity. 'The work done by freemen,' observed Adam Smith,
'comes cheaper in the end than that performed by slaves.' Slaves
were neither willing nor able to produce the quantities of sugar
and precious metals expected of them, and it became clear to the
British that there were more efficient ways to farm and mine.

Britain passed the Abolition of the Slave Trade Act in 1807 and
took over Sierra Leone as a colony a year later. Ending the trade
at home, however, risked rendering British territories uncompet-
itive in the short term relative to those of countries that continued

slaving. The Royal Navy therefore took to patrolling the coast of West Africa, seizing Portuguese, French and Dutch slave ships and unchaining their human cargo. By 1850, this "preventative squadron" had deposited fifty thousand freed slaves onto Sierra Leone's muddy shore. The settlers passed through Freetown's Freedom Arch, on which an inscription they could not read reminded them that they had been 'Freed from slavery by British valour and philanthropy.' They came from far and wide, speaking hundreds of different languages and with a variety of grisly histories. A third had been captured in war, another third kidnapped, and the remainder sold by relatives or chiefs. To this ragtag, traumatised group was entrusted the construction of a new country, and a new way of living.

20

Our taxi takes us to a cheap hotel above a building materials shop in the middle of town. The dim, generator-powered neon sign jutting out from its long first-floor balcony is the only light on the otherwise pitch-dark street. We climb the stairs to the dingy lobby. The receptionist, a young woman, is slouched asleep across the counter, behind a blue metal grille. She seems annoyed that we have disturbed her, but gets up to show us to a room before sloping off down the corridor back to her slumber.

The large, square room is sparsely furnished and tawdrily decorated, with a purple tiled floor, peeling pale blue walls, and scarlet curtains covering a long window which gives onto the communal balcony. It is lit by a single bulb hanging limply from the ceiling beside a dusty fan. In one corner is a table with a metal chair, and there is a hard, wooden double bed with a thin mattress and a superfluous blanket. In the small bathroom, a shower drains through a hole in the middle of the floor. The lodging compares unfavourably with Freetown's more famous but recently demolished City Hotel, where Graham Greene set *The Heart of the Matter*, but it is at least clean and central.

The next morning dawns cool and bright. In a few hours we will learn that the dawn is false, and that debilitating tropical heat is Freetown's true condition (Greene described 'an impression of heat and damp'), but for now it is pleasant to walk around and explore.

The grid of streets that makes up central Freetown renders navigation easy. Movement, on the other hand, is difficult, for the city is full up. Hemmed in on three sides by water and on the other by hills, it has been unable to cope with rapid urbanisation and is visibly bursting at the seams. There are people everywhere, their ramshackle tin homes spilling down river banks, oozing up the sides of hills, and tumbling down to the edge of the sea. Not an inch is wasted. Market traders occupy pavements, roads, bridges, churchyards, stairwells, roundabout islands, alleys two feet wide and petrol station forecourts. They display their wares on the ground, on walls, on fences, tree trunks, telegraph poles, lampposts, even on parked cars. Walking the streets is full of hazards. On the pavements you trip over people and merchandise. Forced onto the road you must negotiate the dense stream of traffic, dodging wing-mirrors like a matador. The noise emitted by traders, car horns, DVD shacks, lorries, motorbikes, minibuses and radios is cacophonous. All the time, too, you are assailed by hawkers, beggars, raving madmen and moneychangers. The experience is intense, the claustrophobia heightened by the tall buildings that loom over the streets, trapping the heat and noise and dust and smells of smoked fish, sweat and petrol in a frenzied, chaotic swirl.

We wade through, like forest hunters driving a path through thick undergrowth, and take refuge at a street corner coffee trolley down by the old Government Wharf. After the turbulence of the city the still ocean beyond is a picture of calm. Gulls and kites wheel silently above it. Small, brightly-painted fishing boats work the shallows. Further out a container ship lies at anchor, waiting to dock. We order Nescafés. The coffee trolley belongs to Basheru, a quiet young Guinéen with a clipped goatee beard and a white apron. He came to Freetown a year ago after the military coup in his homeland, convinced that the ensuing instability would limit his opportunities to earn a living, if it did not lead to outright civil war. With his meagre savings he set up as a petty trader, and sold second-hand radios from a table in the street until the police destroyed all his stock one day because he had not bought a license and could not afford the necessary bribes. He picked himself up, bought some wood, and had a trolley made. He bought a license so the police would not disturb him, tried out a few different locations before settling on this corner in a relatively peaceful part of town, and learned the coffee seller's trade.

Making coffee is a skilled craft, lovingly performed. First, Nescafé powder and sickly sweet condensed milk are tipped into a small plastic cup. Water is then added from a metal kettle that has been boiling on a stove in the trolley's innards. To cool and mix the coffee, Basheru takes an empty cup in his left hand, raises the full cup in his right hand to a great height, and pours the scalding liquid between them. He then pours it back. He repeats this process several times, unhurriedly. Only when he is certain that it has cooled to the right temperature for drinking does he hand us the finished product. We stand in the shade of the trolley's wooden canopy, sipping at the hot, sweet brew, and catch our breath.

I ask Basheru about the experience of arriving in a big foreign city with little money and few contacts. 'It was exciting at first,' he says. 'I came from a village in northern Guinea, where there wasn't much to do. Having all these people around, and all these cars and all this bustle was fun.' As time passed, however, the novelty wore off; city life became a grind. 'The excitement has gone now. I feel lonely sometimes. I miss my family and friends. Here nobody knows you.' Like the new urbanites in Bissau, Basheru is finding the transition to modernity tough. He is scraping a living, but after sending money to his parents – his father was paralysed by a stroke five years ago and can no longer work - he has nothing left, and therefore little hope of advancement. He asks me about life in England, whether it would be possible for him to obtain a visa and find a job. I begin to tell him how hard it is for Africans to get into Britain when suddenly a moneychanger who has been standing nearby and listening to our conversation interrupts aggressively. 'You colonised us and stayed here for a hundred years,' he spits, 'and now you don't let us into your country.' Basheru is embarrassed and mutters a rebuke to the man in Krio, but I tell him not to worry about it. I have no answer to the reproach; life's cards, I am reminded, have fallen in my favour, not theirs.

The moneychanger and Basheru are not alone in wanting to escape Sierra Leone. Back in Guinea-Bissau, Joka and Tino had talked vaguely of moving to Europe and knew a handful of people who had already left. Here in Freetown, however, was a much more intense yearning. Here, as the moneychanger's tone attested, there was urgency, desperation, anger; during our stay in the capital we would be asked on a daily basis for help with acquiring visas or to act as sponsors or guarantors for would-be migrants to Britain – seldom would a conversation finish without such a request being made. Nor is the restlessness limited to street traders. An opinion survey carried out early in 2010 asked people in one hundred and fifty countries whether they would emigrate or stay at home if there was free migration in the world. Fifty-six percent of Sierra Leoneans – a higher proportion than any other nationality - said they would emigrate.

Compared with the slow, gentle existence of those who have moved to Bissau, life in Freetown is brutal. When Basheru and his fellow migrants moved here, forced off the land by the population explosion or in search of peace or their own little slice of modernity, they plunged immediately into a vortex. There was nothing to help them settle in. There was no housing, so they had to construct tiny corrugated-iron shacks in already-crowded slums. There was no education – only one in three Sierra Leoneans can read and write – so they could not learn the skills they needed to carve out a career. And there was no health care, so they often fell sick – the country has just one hundred doctors ministering to five million people; life expectancy is forty years.

There was nobody, finally, to cushion the fall. Basheru's loneliness is symptomatic of a wider sense of alienation in the mushrooming West African city. Back in the village you had an identity. People knew you, greeted you, helped you out, talked to you. You belonged to a family, a clan, a close-knit community; you had a name, you were somebody. In Bissau, where villages were transplanted to the city and families and tribes stuck together, new arrivals still have this comfort. Freetown too was once like this. Freed slaves settled with their compatriots: Wolof from Senegal founded the Leicester district, the Congolese Congo Cross; Yoruba from Nigeria settled the modern-day East End near the ferry terminal. But the population boom landed in the middle of this patchwork like a boulder dropped on a tiled floor. In Bissau there is space - the city seeps back unhindered from the coast like water over a floodplain – but Freetown's growth is constrained by its hills, the ocean and the surrounding river estuaries. New migrants do not have the luxury of building communities and sticking together: they must set up home wherever they can find room. They are on their own, surrounded by strangers. No longer of the village and unable to find a niche in the city, they are confused, dislocated, no longer knowing who they are.

The pressure on young West Africans, and particularly on young men, is acute, for although they aspire to modernity and its promises of freedom and control, they cannot ignore the exigencies of old. Like their ancestors before them they are expected to set up a home, marry at least one wife, and accumulate children and other dependents. Until they pass these tests, society will not see them as adults. Those who must continue to rely on others to supply them with food, money, shelter or work – be they more successful relatives, or patrons encountered through some other stroke of serendipity – cannot earn respect, and cannot become men. It was pressures such as these that forced many young men to the cities in the first place, for the population boom had made it impossible for them to achieve their goals in the village. But the city is no panacea. As their countries have grown poorer, young West Africans are having to wait ever longer to attain adulthood. There are men aged twenty, thirty, even forty who are still seen by society as children. Their elders, born at a more propitious time, have sequestered their nations' treasures, and there is nothing left for the younger generation.

Back in Dakar, Lamin, the caretaker of our guesthouse, who had moved to the city from the interior to make his living but remained unmarried in his thirties, had complained that he could not find a wife because he was considered too poor (at the guesthouse he slept on the ground outside, behind the metal door of the yard, a parka jacket with a fur collar his only defence against the night-time cold). 'Girls only want to marry men with money,' he said, 'but I can't afford a house or a car, so they're not interested in me. If you don't have money they don't see you as a man.' Today's young men, far from fulfilling their duty of gathering dependents, are instead condemned, perhaps forever, to reliance on others. They are stuck in a cruel trap: their poverty means they cannot break free of their dependency, and without breaking free it is impossible for them to amass dependents of their own and complete the transition to adulthood.

Many look abroad for escape, and the target of their wanderlust is the West. Just as their ancestors, the chiefs and bandits who sold their fellow men to lay their hands on European goods, were drawn irresistibly to what the white man had to offer, so are many of today's young Africans defenceless against the West's allure. Europe and America not only possess abundance (the growing economies of Arabia and Asia might offer equally promising opportunities to escape the dependency trap, but few talk of moving east); they also symbolise modernity and change. Guineans have been shielded from Westernisation by their country's remoteness, and by the lack of electricity which renders televisions, cinemas and computers redundant. Urban Sierra Leoneans, by contrast, are bombarded with Western images. Freetown is replete with generator-powered DVD shacks showing the latest American films and pop videos; mobile phone companies promote their appliances as emblems of the modern lifestyle; foreign aid workers ply the streets in Land Cruisers; and politicians, as eager as the chiefs of old to adopt the airs and attitudes of the West, parade through the capital in German cars, Italian suits and American sunglasses.

Young West Africans want a part of this. Dazed and made rootless by their move to the city, they see the Western as an identity worth aspiring to. The West represents the new, not the old, the chance to lead rather than follow, the future to Africa's past. Only by moving to Europe or America, they believe, will they have the opportunity to rise up, to become someone again, not just to be respected at home but to take their place in the modern world. And so they make plans to leave. The words of a young Freetown market trader, who is intent on following his older brother to Britain, are typical. 'If you don't have a nice car and a house,' he tells me, 'people here don't think you're serious. But if you stay here you can work for twenty years and you can't even buy a bicycle.'

After leaving Basheru we walk across town, past the bat-filled Cotton Tree, its grey trunk folded like an elephant's skin, past lines of rickety clapboard Creole houses (the style of the buildings brought back by freed slaves from the North American plantations), past the old Maroon church whose roof timbers were torn from slave ships, and down into the Kroo Bay slum.

Originally settled by Kroo from neighbouring Liberia, who migrated here to work on British sea liners in the early twentieth century, the slum is now home to a mishmash of peoples from all parts of Sierra Leone. The Kroo have been joined by Temne, Limba, Mende and Fula. There are Christians, Muslims and animists; numerous different languages are spoken. Only the age of the inhabitants is relatively homogenous: four in five are below the age of thirty, well over half younger than twenty.

Ryszard Kapuscinski hailed slums as 'the highest achievement of human imagination, ingenuity, and fantasy.' Using nothing but tyres, corrugated iron, old car doors and bits of wire and wood, the Kroo Bay residents have constructed a small miracle spilling down the hill from the Cotton Tree to the sea. The walls of their tiny houses, fittingly known as *pan-bodis*, are made of patched-together sheets of rusted zinc or iron. Windows have been cut out and covered with wood or metal shutters. The corrugated-iron roofs, held down against the wind by tyres, are propped up by wooden poles dug into the hard mud outside (on a few of the roofs there are satellite dishes). There is neither a brick nor a layer of cement to be seen.

The narrow alleys between the closely-packed houses are unpaved. They wind down the slopes of the settlement like dried-up mountain watercourses. We pick our way down to the bottom, where a sluggish brown stream gathers up its final dregs of filth before depositing them into the sea, and find a shack selling cold drinks. A skinny old man sitting on a bench inside moves up to let us sit. We are soon joined by a group of teenage boys, while a huddle of younger children gathers outside in the sun to watch the foreigners. The old man, Edward, is a veteran of the British merchant navy. He has been to Bristol and Liverpool, he tells us proudly, but is angry with the British because the pension he is owed after many decades of service has not been paid. He and his former colleagues have complained to the authorities, but are still awaiting news.

Neither Edward nor the teenagers are happy with conditions in the slum. Fewer than six hundred of its eleven thousand residents have running water in their homes. None has a toilet - four public pit latrines serve the entire population – and there are no defences against the regular rainy season floods. The global economic crisis and rising food prices, meanwhile, have hit the slum hard. A micro-lending organisation which operates in the area has seen its profits halve in the past year as default rates on loans have tripled. Jobs are harder to come by than ever. Relations between the small group of Muslims and Christians in our soft drink shack appear friendly, but slums are not always so harmonious. Living in close proximity to strangers under conditions of such stress can strain neighbourly bonds. A number of studies have found that slum dwellers are less trusting of others than are their rural cousins, and as the competition for scarce resources intensifies, distrust sometimes boils over into violence. Slums have been a tinderbox for civil strife in Africa, and many of the fighters in Sierra Leone's civil war came from settlements like this one. Edward warns us darkly that the increasing difficulty of life in Kroo Bay means continued peace here cannot be guaranteed. The teenagers around us nod in agreement. 'We should be shitting four or five times a week,' the old seaman adds bitterly, rising to leave, 'but nowadays we only shit once or twice.'

21

In the evenings downtown Freetown empties of its daytime worker crowd. The few cafés and restaurants close, and the only options for dinner are streetside food stalls. These, as I would soon discover, can be perilous to health, but the range of dishes available is wide enough that one will not quickly tire of what is on offer. On the street around the corner from our hotel, well-fed women sell fish balls, smoked fish, fried fish, boiled cassava, fried plantains, green-leaf stew with rice, haricot beans, cold spaghetti in tomato sauce, meat kebabs on skewers, corn on the cob, egg mayonnaise rolls (the eggshells cracked by knuckles), or just plain bread and butter. Each woman brings only small quantities of her signature dish, and stays until she sells out or runs out of the fuel needed to keep it hot.

We alight on a stand specialising in grilled chicken legs. The rotund woman behind it tips hot pepper powder onto the limbs of our choosing and stuffs them into the bread rolls we have bought from her neighbour. We are standing there munching, watching the crowded, dimly-lit street and listening to the music blaring from the DVD shack opposite, when one of the market traders on the long row of streetside stalls calls us over and offers us a seat beside him on his bench. His name is Musa, and he is an unlicensed seller of medicines. Short and stocky, with a large bald head and a full, slightly plump face, he sits under a broad umbrella behind a table covered in packets of pills, lit by a small oil-lamp. A second generation Freetonian, whose parents moved here from Makeni in the interior in search of work, he lives out in the East End with his mother, two sisters and his wife. His elder brother, who lives in New Jersey, built the house for them. Musa is trying to get in touch with this brother to ask for help in obtaining a green card so that he too can emigrate to the States, but his brother has gone quiet and is not returning his calls. Musa thinks his sister-in-law must be jealous, and is poisoning her husband against his family, but he is not giving up and says he will keep calling until he gets through.

The life of an unlicensed medicine seller can be hazardous. Musa claims his pills are all genuine. 'There are lots of fake drugs out there,' he says. 'We are poor. But mine are the real thing. I buy them directly from a pharmacist.' This does not protect him from regular police round-ups, however. Sometimes they just fine him or take his medicines. 'They take them and sell them back to the pharmacists,' he says, a wry smile breaking across his normally guarded and expressionless face. On other occasions they lock him and his fellow illegal traders in prison for the night, 'to teach us a lesson.' The message goes unheeded. 'I've been doing this for twenty years. How else can I make a living?' he asks. These days most of the boxes on his table have had their contents removed, so that if the police swoop they will go away empty-handed. The pills are hidden in plastic bags at Musa's feet.

I ask him how much he has taken that day (a working day that began at eight in the morning and will finish towards midnight). Forty thousand leones, he replies - around eight dollars - but he is not sure how much is profit because he often sells his drugs at a reduced price. 'People are poor,' he explains, rubbing his bald head. 'You have to be reasonable.' His most profitable item is Venegra, a Viagra imitation popular with young men. He sells it by the pill for at least double what he paid for it. Mindful of the slow but steady spread of HIV/AIDS across West Africa, I ask him if he sells many condoms. He shakes his head, and then asks me whether I 'believe in' AIDS. Many people here do not, he says. While we are sitting, a teenage boy comes up and shyly asks for one of the pills. Musa chuckles conspiratorially as he walks away. 'The boy is too young,' he sniggers. 'He's not strong enough to satisfy his woman!'

Musa's own private life is complicated. A devout Muslim who leaves his stall only when it is time to pray in the mosque (he briefly tries to convert us, but we have had our fill of proselytising so the attempt is short-lived), he sees it as his duty, if he can afford it, to have four wives. 'If he has four wives, a man won't go out into the market and fornicate with ten women,' he reasons. His first wife divorced him after they had had three children, and he then had a few years on his own before his family found him a second bride from Makeni, with whom he had a son. The woman does not love him, however. 'She doesn't like living in the city and she doesn't treat me with respect. When I go home at night she doesn't even greet me. She only smiles at me when I give her money.' (His words echo Lamin's complaint about Senegalese women.) If he makes it to the United States, Musa plans to leave his wife here and send her money. He hopes she will eventually find another man, and that he will earn enough to acquire a new brood.

We sit with him for a couple of hours, shooting the breeze and watching the bustling night-time street life, the dark, slow-moving silhouettes framed by the oily light like shadow play puppets. On the other side of the road a crowd of teenagers has gathered outside the DVD seller's shack, gazing raptly at a pop video. Musa is worried by a cough I have picked up, perhaps caused by the dust and the fumes from his oil-lamp. He picks up one of his packets and urges me to take a pill with some water. I am impressed that he instantly knows which of his plethora of medicines I need. 'Yes, I have been here since 1990,' he declares. 'I have accumulated vast knowledge.' His doubts about HIV reduce my confidence in his prescription, but thinking it would be impolite to refuse I take the offered pill anyway.

Before we leave, Musa introduces us to his neighbouring stallholders and to his pretty daughter who comes round asking him for money and us to take her to England. One of his neighbours, another medicine man, is having an affair with a married woman. He is married himself and is terrified of his wife, so if his mistress is present when his wife comes to visit his stall, Musa covers up for him, pretending that it is he and not his friend who has 'got some business' with the mistress. Another of the street traders takes the opportunity to thank me for Britain's intervention in his country's civil war. 'We love the British. They saved our country. British taxpayers spent their money to stop our war. We love Mr. Tony Blair.' He and Musa insist on walking us the hundred yards back to our hotel, to make sure we arrive home safely - they tell us the night-time streets are too dangerous for us to walk alone (throughout our stay, our sleep will be interrupted at enervatingly frequent intervals by raging, murderous-sounding altercations in the darkness outside).

22

I have been reluctant to ask people about the civil war. My own grandfather, a Second World War bomber pilot saved from almost certain death when he contracted tuberculosis and was invalided out, would not discuss his experiences even half a century after it ended. Sierra Leone's conflict finished just a decade ago, and I had expected the wounds still to be raw.

But many Sierra Leoneans are keen to talk about it, and they often raise the subject themselves. It is as if they have not yet made sense of what happened, and hope through conversation and discussion to unravel its complexities and, eventually, to put it to rest. The war was one of Africa's longest, most brutal and most lethal. It is difficult to comprehend a conflict with no victors, whose main targets were innocent civilians, and whose worst atrocities were perpetrated by children, a war in which combatants devoured their enemies' hearts, raped their sisters, and gambled on the sex of unborn babies before ripping open the mothers' stomachs to find out who had won the bet. How can anyone make sense of this? How can a country come to terms with such horrors, and its wounds heal sufficiently to move on?

Perhaps, despite the best efforts of historians, psychologists, sociologists and anthropologists, some of these episodes will never be explained, but to begin to understand why the war started you need to look back. The roots of the catastrophe grow deep. They reach back in time, through the near-anarchical chaos of the late 1980s to the cold-blooded kleptocracy of the Siaka Stevens era, and then further back, through the population explosion to the ecstasy of independence and, before that, the stasis of British rule. They go back too to the discovery of diamonds in 1930, while the longest roots of all burrow through the centuries, to the slave trade, whose abolition left such a disparate mass of traumatised and untrusting souls on Freetown's steamy shores.

By the time war broke out in 1991, Sierra Leone's was a society riddled with divisions. City against country, east against west, rich against poor, young against old - the cracks were there for all to see, and like a shattered pane of glass still clinging to its frame, it would only take the lightest of blows to send the whole thing crashing down.

Antagonism between Freetown and the rest of the country had been kindled by the British. To deflect their subjects' thoughts from the injustice of foreign occupation, the colonisers deployed the traditional divide-and-rule strategy of empire and focused resources on the capital at the expense of the hinterland. In the former they invested in infrastructure and industry; in the latter they left development to weak and penniless chiefs and charged a hated annual tax on each house which provoked the bloody Hut Tax Revolt of 1898. Freetonians looked down on their rural cousins, whom they referred to as "aborigines"; country-dwellers resented the relative prosperity of the capital. Thus opened the first of the nation's great rifts, sundering city from country, urbanite from peasant.

The departure of the British created a second, much more important divide, with the rich and powerful on one side pitted against the poor and voiceless on the other. When the colonisers withdrew they left a power vacuum. As in Guinea-Bissau, the authority of traditional chiefs had been weakened by the slave trade: those who became involved in slave raiding forfeited trust; those who tried but failed to protect their people forfeited respect. Colonialism further eroded their standing. The British permitted chiefs to govern their communities, but they kept them on a tight leash. They put them on the colony's payroll, making them answerable not to their own people but to the colonial government, and undermined their authority by retaining the right to override their decisions.

Before they left, the British rushed to place Sierra Leoneans in positions of power and responsibility. But with the abasement of the chiefs and the absence of any other Africans with more than the most rudimentary education, those they appointed were unfit for office. The ability to govern, unneeded for so many years, had evaporated. 'The fact is that the colonised does not govern,' observed the Tunisian writer Albert Memmi. 'Being kept away from power, he ends up by losing both interest and feeling for control...How could such a long absence from government give rise to skill?' A former British Foreign Secretary shared these concerns, comparing the granting of independence to 'giving a child of ten a latch-key, a bank account and a shotgun.' But Britain ignored such qualms. It announced that the handover ceremony would mark 'the fulfilment in Sierra Leone of the United Kingdom's policy in its dependencies of working in partnership with the local people to build up new nations, capable of making their own way in the world...As the people have gained political experience, more and more authority has been transferred to them until now the territory has a very large measure of responsibility for its own affairs.'

Sierra Leone's post-colonial rulers, cleansed by five hundred years of history of any notion that leaders should be public-spirited, were less interested in building up a new nation than in cornering its treasures. The two major political parties that had materialised in the lead up to independence – the Sierra Leone People's Party, which drew its support from the rural classes of the south and east, and the All People's Congress, which repre-sented northerners and the Freetown elites – engaged in a protracted battle for the national coffers. Their country was bursting with minerals – gold, bauxite, titanium, platinum, iron ore and, above all, diamonds were oozing out of the ground. After a series of coups and counter-coups, a small band of men under All People's Congress leader Siaka Stevens emerged at the top of this glittering pile. They quickly set to plunder.

Sierra Leone is a classic example of what economists call the "resource curse". If its bounteous mineral reserves had been effectively harnessed, it would be rich. Instead, it is one of the poorest countries in the world. What went wrong? How did so much wealth go to waste? The same could be asked of many other African countries. Congo, Angola, Nigeria and Zimbabwe are all abundant in minerals but mired in poverty and conflict. None has managed to convert its assets into sustained and widespread prosperity; to each could be applied the old Sierra Leonean joke, where in response to the angels' protest that giving Sierra Leone such copious natural resources is unfair on all the other countries, God interrupts Creation to reply: 'Don't worry. Just wait and see the people I've put there.'

The resource curse has plagued Africa for five hundred years. From the fifteenth to the nineteenth centuries the value of its main natural commodity, slaves, dwarfed that of everything else it produced. Some Africans prospered from the slave trade, but the long-term costs were enormous. In the nineteenth and twentieth centuries the spotlight switched to minerals. The European colonisers' scramble for Africa was in large part a struggle for its resources. When the Europeans left, a series of wars broke out. Many of these wars had minerals at their heart. Slaves in the eighteenth century gave way to oil, gold and diamonds in the twentieth. These gifts proved to be white elephants, distorting economies, corrupting politics and destabilising societies - most developing countries, like the successful but resource-scarce Asian tiger economies, would have been better off without them.

Once the resource curse falls on a country, like a deadly virus it spreads rapidly, crippling its host's every organ, paralysing its every function. First to suffer are farming and manufacturing. The profits from diamonds (or oil or gold) far outweigh those achievable through agriculture or industry, and it makes economic sense to allow mineral extraction to become the dominant productive activity. Often it becomes the sole productive activity. Diamonds give a country's leaders more wealth than they ever dreamed of, so they no longer need to worry about other parts of the economy. Minerals become the only way to make a living; everything else is left to rot. As other, more labour-intensive sectors collapse, the majority of the population has no work (the decline of Sierra Leonean agriculture was swift: twenty years after discovering its precious stones, the country had gone from exporting rice to importing it). A chasm opens up, between the rich few with access to mineral wealth, and the poor masses who are shut out.

The masses have no outlet for their frustrations, no way of redressing the balance. While they are growing rich on diamond exports the leaders of a resource-cursed country do not need to agonise over what their subjects think of them. Governments in countries lacking in valuable minerals depend on taxes to keep them in business; without them, ministers would not be paid and the machinery of government could not function. For taxes to be paid, the state must count on at least some degree of support from its citizens, and is to some degree answerable to them - if it ignores their needs entirely, citizens will use non-payment of tax as a bargaining chip. But in diamond-rich economies, governments need nothing from their people; profits from the gems are more than sufficient to keep the leaders in luxury, and their subjects, lacking any leverage over them, have no way of agitating peacefully for a fair share of the pie.

Facing no pressure to govern, the leaders can focus their energies on protecting their bounty. They know that it is coveted by others, that since there is no alternative route to prosperity the ambitious, those who desire power and wealth for themselves, will soon hone in on the mineral trade. These enemies are desperate; they will do anything to seize control. The stakes are high: if the losers are lucky, they will be condemned to scratching a meagre living in the dust like everybody else; if they are less fortunate, they will face imprisonment or execution at the hands of the victors ('when you lose power in Africa, they come after you,' reflects Musa during one of our evening chats).

The leaders must therefore take extreme measures to extinguish the threat and close off the would-be usurpers' options. Siaka Stevens had political rivals hanged for invented crimes; other malcontents were hunted down and tortured by the young thugs of his private "Red Shirt" militia. He banned opposition parties, so that power could not be wrested through the ballot box, and purged adherents of the Sierra Leone People's Party (so fearful was the dictator of the SLPP-supporting Mende people that he ripped up the railway line connecting the diamond fields of their eastern stronghold to the coast in the belief that it gave them too much control over the nation's wealth). Finally, like the British before him, Stevens closed off channels for dissent by silencing the media and hollowing out state institutions. The Truth and Reconciliation Commission, which was set up in the aftermath of war to investigate its causes, was damning in its indictment. 'The judiciary was subordinated to the executive,' it reported. 'Parliament did little more than rubber-stamp, the civil service became a redundant state machine, and the army and police force became vectors of violence against the very people they were established to protect.'

The brooding, stern-faced Stevens ruled Sierra Leone for two decades. That he retired of his own volition, without being murdered or forced to flee into exile, is perhaps the greatest testament to his power. Almost unique among African dictators, he died in his sleep, at home in the country he had tyrannised. In his wake he left a nation fizzing with tension, a divided society, festering with mutinous intent.

23

In its discussion of the causes of the civil war, the Truth and Reconciliation Commission reported that 'Siaka Stevens's government sustained itself through corruption, nepotism and the plundering of state assets. These practices were replicated at regional and local levels.' When the dictator stepped down, this corrupt status quo could no longer hold. His retirement left Sierra Leone on the brink of chaos - the resentments that he had both nurtured and smothered could no longer be contained. The country was ripe for upheaval.

For revolution, however, you need revolutionaries, people who despite their lack of means are desperate enough and angry enough to risk their lives for change. Step forward Sierra Leone's crowded-out young men. Forced off the land by the population explosion and with nothing to do in the towns and cities, the fruits of modernisation had remained tantalisingly beyond their grasp. Their leaders' ill-gotten wealth had been rubbed in their faces; women, repelled by their poverty, spurned their advances (unwittingly digging their own graves); and their failure to set up on their own and complete the transition to adulthood meant the elders they had venerated showed them none of the respect they craved.

The young men grew sullen and resentful, their bitterness slowly curdling into rage. But there was no means of voicing their frustration: all the channels had been blocked. They could not make use of the ballot box, the courts or the media; peaceful demonstrations were crushed; and chiefs no longer had the authority or the will to respond to their concerns. Sierra Leone's young were like caged bears tormented to the point of insanity by their keepers, ready to burst out in a murderous fury as soon as they were released.

All that was needed was somebody to unlock the gate. While Siaka Stevens was raping his country, next door in Liberia an ambitious young government official had been plotting his own rise to power. Charles Taylor, a light-skinned, smartly dressed descendant of slaves, had returned from studying in America to seek his fortune back home. His family traced its lineage to the founders of modern Liberia, to the first heroic settlers who defied disease, climate and hostile local tribes to establish a new country, and Taylor saw it as his birthright to lead his nation as his forefathers had. Confident, businesslike and a fluent English speaker, he found a job in charge of purchasing for the Liberian government. Although this did not give him the status he craved, the position allowed him access to the national purse and to bribes from salesmen, and he spent his time embezzling public funds and drumming up support for a future bid for power.

He quickly grew rich, but was unsatisfied. Taylor dreamt of opulence on a grand scale, like leaders in other parts of Africa. To acquire such dizzying wealth, he would need to broaden his horizons - his own little country's scant resources would never sate his hunger. He cast around for alternatives, and his gaze soon alighted on his neighbour. As he stood on the Liberian hills and peered over the border, Sierra Leone's diamonds glinted at him in the sun, mocking him, tormenting him. He knew that if he could lay his hands on the stones he would have all the wealth he needed, enough both to fulfil his personal requirements and fund his planned assault on his government. He knew, too, that as long as Stevens was in power the diamonds would remain out of reach, for the dictator would never surrender the source of his fortune. But Taylor was a patient man, a cold-blooded schemer. Knowing that his rival was aging and would one day have to let go, he was content to bide his time and wait for his opening.

Stevens kept a lid on his nation's simmering tensions. His security forces and network of spies snuffed out rebellion while it was still a half-formed thought in plucky minds; anyone who slipped through the net was either killed or dispatched into exile. When he retired, however, the country unravelled. Supporters of the Sierra Leone People's Party in the south and east saw their opportunity and began to agitate for change; young people more openly vented their anger at the wealth stolen by the corrupt elders (a final great rift opened up, between the generations); and the rural poor, downtrodden for centuries and with no weapons but their stifled rage, began to hunt around for a means of cutting the Freetown elites down to size.

No sooner had the dictator left the stage than his government began to crumble. Stevens's successor, Joseph Saidu Momoh, lacked his predecessor's ruthlessness and was ill equipped to keep the peace. The economic state of emergency he declared failed to stop the economy collapsing; corruption continued to eat away at dwindling public funds; and although he released political prisoners and allowed opposition groups to form political parties, Momoh refused to let them challenge his grip on power by holding elections.

Frustration grew, and the new president's task was made more difficult by military unrest. Siaka Stevens, fearful of coups, had deliberately weakened the army, reducing its numbers, cutting its supply of weapons and ammunition, slashing wages and allowing soldiers to go hungry. Like many leaders of resource-cursed nations, he was more concerned by the threat from within than any foreign enemy, and he directed the bulk of his resources to internal repression. The favoured status he accorded to his well-armed, well-funded Special Security Division (popularly known as Siaka Stevens's Dogs) engendered great resentment among regular soldiers. The army was left debilitated and embittered, in no state to perform its role as protector of the nation.

Sierra Leone's implosion did not escape the notice of Charles Taylor. The Liberian had spent the last few years on the run. Fired from his government post for embezzling a million dollars, he had fled to America, but was arrested on arrival. While waiting to be deported back home, he somehow escaped prison and went underground (he would later allege at his war crimes trial that the CIA helped him, perhaps as a means of increasing US influence in its former colony). He resurfaced in Libya, in one of Muammar Gaddafi's training camps. The Libyan leader welcomed all sorts, from terrorists to budding dictators to dissidents exiled by Siaka Stevens – anyone willing to spread his socialist revolution across Africa and the Middle East. Huge sums were lavished on his desert training facilities, where the "Brother Leader" drilled home his message and taught his protégés the arts of rebel warfare.

Taylor was less interested in ideology than power, and he spent his time at the camp recruiting soldiers from Liberia and other West African nations. Never lacking in self-belief, he was plotting an ambitious war on two fronts – one to wrest power from Samuel Doe in Liberia, the other to gain control of the treasures next door. A chance meeting increased his confidence in his plan.

Foday Sankoh, a former Sierra Leone Army officer recently released from a Freetown prison, had found his way to the Libyan desert. With his grey beard and plump cheeks Sankoh had the look of an amiable uncle, but the kindly exterior masked a bitter, vengeful core. He had been jailed for his part in an attempted coup against Stevens, and his hatred of the Sierra Leonean establishment was implacable. A charismatic speaker and a shrewd manipulator of men, he was in Libya, like Taylor, to recruit soldiers. His professed goal was to deliver fairness and equality to his country by bringing down the corrupt elites. In reality he sought vengeance, power and wealth, and was prepared to use the most ruthless methods to obtain them.

The two men had much in common, and they soon struck a deal: Taylor would support Sankoh's rebellion in Sierra Leone; Sankoh would supply Taylor with his longed-for diamonds. Using their revolutionary message to convert impressionable young compatriots to their cause, Taylor formed the National Patriotic Front of Liberia, Sankoh the Revolutionary United Front of Sierra Leone. Together, the two rebel armies would be responsible for a quarter of a million deaths.

By the end of the 1980s the new friends were ready to launch their push for power. Taylor, now a fully-fledged warlord, returned to Liberia on Christmas Eve, 1989, with a force of several hundred men. He declared war on the president, the inept, corrupt dictator Samuel Doe. His men quickly gained notoriety for their brutality. They rampaged towards the capital, Monrovia, cutting off limbs, eating the flesh of their enemies, and enslaving and torturing women and children. Within a year they had unseated Doe (a home video appeared on the streets showing the dictator's ears being sliced off with a knife as he pleaded for mercy, minutes before bleeding to death). But Taylor's work was not complete, for his army had split into factions, triggering a new civil war that would last a further six years. In 1996 a peace accord was signed, and Taylor ran for election under the campaign slogan: 'He killed my ma, he killed my pa, but I will vote for him.' Having cowed voters into submission in the run-up to the polls, and with his opponents crippled by seven years of terror, he won the ballot and became president, finally attaining his goal.

Sankoh's own campaign had begun in 1991. Sierra Leone was coming apart, its decades-old divisions widening into chasms. With Siaka Stevens off the scene and the national army reduced to an ineffective husk, Sankoh seized his opportunity. A combined RUF and NPFL force invaded from the Liberian border in the east, vowing to overthrow the government. They headed first for the diamond fields. Mayhem enveloped the land.

24

'The war started ten miles from our village,' says Alex, a former RUF fighter we meet in a Freetown restaurant. 'Some rebels came in a group. We had heard rumours but we couldn't believe it was really war. They were recruiting young men.' Alex was in his early teens. He fled with his brothers and sisters, his cousins and his grandmother to an abandoned farmhouse in the bush. 'We hid there for three days but we were running out of food, so I had to go back to the village with my cousin. It was then that they captured me.'

The RUF's recruitment drive did not stop in the Libyan camps. Throughout the eleven years of the conflict they cajoled, bullied and bludgeoned young men and women into joining their ranks. A few of those who enlisted were inspired by revolutionary goals, believing that the RUF would clean up their country's mess, but most had narrower motivations. Some joined up because the rebel army offered them an identity, something to belong to, others in order, by looting, to get something to eat. The most ambitious were driven by the desire to improve their standing in society, to become adults by amassing dependents – in this case, troops – and exercising power (the bravest fighters and the most successful pillagers garnered the most followers).

Not all recruits were so willing, however. Large numbers were abducted or forced at gunpoint to join up. 'They wanted to instil fear in the population,' Alex continues, 'so they had to kill people. They brought captives from neighbouring villages and executed them in front of you. They told you the same thing would happen to you if you refused to join them. In every village they executed ten or fifteen people. Some of my friends, cousins and playmates were killed before my eyes. It was the most painful thing I've ever experienced.'

Sankoh took his lead from Charles Taylor's recruitment strategy. He targeted children aged between ten and fourteen.

Boys were abducted as fighters or porters, girls as sex slaves or "bush wives". He ensured his soldiers' loyalty by forcing them, on pain of death, to rape their mothers and sisters, to murder their fathers, to hack off the hands and lips of baby brothers. This served a triple purpose: it made it impossible for the boy soldiers to return to their communities; it traumatised them, making them more reliant on their new family, the RUF; and it inured them to violence – after you have murdered your parents it is much easier to kill strangers.

Alex is in Freetown on a short visit from America, where he now lives. A fit-looking, laid back man in an open-necked white shirt and dark trousers, he˜ is the image of the successful, Westernised exile. He has been sitting with friends in the restaurant, but on hearing I am writing a book has come over to tell us about his war. His eyes are slightly awry, and after he describes his capture it becomes clear why. 'My left eye is blind,' he says. 'From birth?' I ask, guessing the answer already. He shakes his head: the rebels inflicted harsh punishments on those who tried to escape their clutches.

So he signed up. Had he resisted further he would have been killed. He was given a job. 'Only very few of us were literate,' he says, 'so they made me secretary. I had to write communiqués telling villages we would be coming for them the next day.' He moved with the insurgents around the country. Most of their battles were assaults on civilian settlements, with not an enemy soldier in sight. Pumped full of hashish and heroin (Taylor sent drugs and weapons from Liberia), they ran riot. Anything that moved was hacked to pieces. Eyes were gouged out like shelled peas. Amputation and rape became official RUF policy, visited with particular relish on the elders who had failed to respect the rebels and the women who had spurned them. Deranged games were invented. In one, captives were forced to choose from a handful of scraps of paper. On each was written a punishment – rape, the slicing off of your lips or ears, the amputation of a limb of your choice, or some other mutilation. The scrap you chose determined your fate. A Canadian envoy to the country summed up the modus operandi in a report to his government: 'the rebels have two calling cards: dead civilians, and hundreds of living civilians with their hands, feet, ears or genitals crudely amputated.'

Alex eventually made it to Freetown; from there, relatives helped him flee to the United States, where he was granted asylum (he declines to tell me how he escaped the RUF's grip). He goes back to his village in the east whenever he visits his homeland. Ebru asks him if the community is recovering. 'It is,' he replies, 'but there are still many problems. People don't understand how to resolve disputes by dialogue. They always want to use violence.' As an outsider who has seen the world, he is a respected figure in the village, and he spends hours every evening mediating disputes. 'I try to encourage dialogue,' he says, 'but it's not easy. They have been through terrible things.'

While the war was raging in the rest of the country, for a long time Freetown remained unscathed. It was not until six years into the conflict that the violence finally reached the capital, but when it did breach the city's defences, it was as if the end of days had come.

In May 1997, the latest in a series of post-Stevens coups d'état brought to power the Armed Forces Revolutionary Council (or as some weary students renamed it, Another Fucking Revolutionary Council). This was not just another government, however, but a depraved, mutant group of junior Sierra Leone Army soldiers who were bent on subjecting the country they had hijacked to a reign of terror. Instead of fighting the RUF rebels, the AFRC formed an alliance with them. Together they created the "People's Army", a renegade band of drugged-up, homicidal thugs which sowed chaos across the land. The alliance – the national government! - took over the diamond fields and used child slaves to mine them. Its soldiers burned down large swathes of the capital, and set up roadblocks at which anyone who refused to give them food or money was shot. Mutilation, extortion and public beatings became epidemic. The country was brought to its knees.

After a few months, horrified governments elsewhere in West Africa stepped in. A well-armed force was mobilised, consisting mainly of Nigerian soldiers and South African mercenaries, and the AFRC junta was ejected from Freetown. But this merely displaced the problem. Furious at having lost its hold on power, the People's Army launched a new campaign of terror – "Operation No Living Thing". Like an enraged hydra breathing death on anyone who came near it, it went on the rampage against civilians in the countryside, hacking, raping and pillaging its way through villages. 'The AFRC demonstrated a specialisation in the practice of amputations in the period from 1998 to 1999,' says the report of the Truth and Reconciliation Commission. Daughters were raped in front of their fathers. Hot iron poles were thrust up vaginas. Victims' heads were skewered, Kurtz-style, onto stakes.

On 6 January 1999, a date that has now become a symbol of infamy, the war reached its nadir. The People's Army had regrouped and worked its way back to the capital. It was there to take revenge on the civilians who had rejected its rule, on the journalists, writers and intellectuals who had criticised its abuses, and on the political establishment that had conspired to unseat it from power. It was there, in short, to punish Freetonians for their lack of respect, and in its quest to achieve this goal, nothing was beyond the pale.

The rebel leaders had planned the attack for months. They had smuggled weapons and men into the city to await the arrival of the main body of troops. When the troops arrived, high on drugs and seething with rage, everything was in place to inflict the maximum damage. 'They came through the East End, cutting, cutting,' says Musa. He and his neighbours fled west, but when Nigerian forces based in the western districts tried to fight back, the rebels used the fleeing civilian crowds and captive villagers they had brought with them from the interior as human shields. They opened up the prisons, tortured people in their hospital beds, threw children into burning houses, and mass raped students at the College of Nursing. Alfred, the owner of a downtown bar where we sometimes spend the hot afternoons, shows me a row of burnt-out buildings on his street. 'They overran the city,' he says. 'People I knew went over to their side so they could loot and get money. You didn't know who was a rebel and who was a government soldier. You couldn't leave your house - we didn't even go near the windows for fear of being seen and shot.'

At Congo Cross, the old Congolese settlement, the Nigerians halted the rebel tide. Joseph, a young human rights worker we meet in a café, was in the area at the time. 'I was hiding in King Edward church,' he says. 'I was frightened because I was expecting the rebels to take the power station next door, but after a long gunfight the Nigerians fought them off.' The rebels retreated from the city. 'After a few days things settled down,' Joseph continues, 'and I came into the centre of town. I saw a pile of corpses outside Connaught Hospital mortuary. I hope nobody ever has to see that again.' By the time the People's Army was driven out of Freetown, six thousand people had been killed and tens of thousands raped or abducted.

In the aftermath of the invasion the Nigerians and the Sierra Leone Army sought out any rebels who had stayed behind. Many of the city's surviving inhabitants joined in the hunt. 'There was mob justice,' says Alfred. 'The Nigerians and the SLA executed anyone they suspected of collaborating with the rebels. I saw a young boy shot dead a yard away from where I stood. There were gangs of civilians roaming the streets. People were burned alive with tyres around their necks. Some were decapitated. The

Nigerians let it happen because the RUF had killed so many of their men.' As he spoke, I remembered a young man back in the Kroo Bay slum, who had shown me a large dark scar on his upper arm where there had once been a tattoo. He explained that the Nigerians had had a policy of executing people with tattoos, which they took as evidence of rebel sympathies. He had pressed a hot iron to his arm to remove the markings.

The war rumbled on for three more years, through a series of failed peace agreements (one of which, to general incredulity, made Foday Sankoh Minister of Mineral Resources), until the British military intervention which saw Sankoh arrested and the remaining RUF leadership putting down their weapons. Nobody won the war; few emerged with credit. A Special Court that was set up at great cost to rake over the embers convicted just a handful of combatants. Sankoh died in custody, Charles Taylor was sent to The Hague to be tried for his crimes. A broken country, meanwhile, remained unhealed; Sierra Leone had taken a giant step backwards on the long road out of poverty.

25

Musa's street, where we often sit with him in the evenings, is abuzz with movement and energy. There are shacks and tables on both sides, with only a narrow space left for cars and the packed *poda poda* minibuses that are the cheapest form of intra-city transport. Hawkers weave among the traffic in the semi-darkness with trays of fruit or smoked fish balanced on their heads. Enterprising amputees in wheelchairs cling to the backs of buses, hitching a hairy free ride. Madmen stride past looking vexed. The usual crowd is gathered outside the DVD seller's shack, watching pale-skinned African-American women dancing on a beach in bikinis. The fumes from exhausts and oil lamps cloak the scene in a sooty haze.

One evening Musa tells us about juju. Juju means different things in different parts of West Africa, but when Sierra Leoneans talk about it they are talking about sorcery, and specifically about the ability to improve your own life or damage someone else's by means of magic. Musa guides us through its tenebrous alleys. 'Juju is very powerful,' he begins. 'It can even kill people. People who are envious of your wife or your money or who want revenge on you for something use it as a way to harm you.' Musa believes his own father, who died in mysterious circumstances twelve years ago, was a victim of juju, visited on him by a jealous rival. He has never been to his grave. 'I am afraid,' he explains. 'They might do the same thing to me if I go there.'

Those wishing to engage a juju man or woman to deliver a curse can choose from a menu of spells. 'You can pay a witch doctor to send your enemy crazy,' Musa says. 'You see all these mad people walking around? It's because of juju. Or if you want to kill someone the sorcerer will call down a fly from the air and tell it to land on the arm of your enemy. The fly can travel hundreds of miles. It lands on your enemy's arm and when he slaps it to kill it' - he smacks his own forearm hard to demonstrate - 'his arm starts to rot.' The putrefaction then spreads to the whole body. The victim's only hope is to find an even more powerful medicine man to stop the rot. 'I have seen these things with my own eyes,' Musa assures me, sensing my scepticism.

'Another juju,' he goes on, warming to his theme and seemingly oblivious to what practitioners of his religion in other parts of the world might think of such heresies, 'is when the witch doctor takes a mirror and calls up the image of the person you want to curse. When the face appears in the mirror, the witch doctor strikes it with his knuckles and the person dies.' I ask him if his own medicines would help if one were cursed in this way. He shakes his head gravely. 'You need to find a strong witch who will give you protection,' he says.

Juju explains many things. Musa tells us about his first child, a daughter, who was born to a girl he was with in his teens. The baby would not breastfeed, so he consulted a sorcerer. It transpired that, for reasons that are not clear, the mother had talked to a stone. Within seven days the devil had taken possession of her ('a woman must never talk to a stone,' Musa warns Ebru darkly), and thereafter the spooked baby was too afraid to approach. The sorcerer cast out the demon, and the baby's mother went on to have five children with another man, but the exorcism came too late for Musa's daughter, who died the following day.

Child deaths are usually blamed on juju. While the American Christians in Bissau weakly attributed such tragedies to the repercussions of original sin, for most West Africans witchcraft is the likeliest culprit. The children of those who, like Musa's girlfriend, contravene taboos or fail to observe religious rituals are especially vulnerable. The ancestral spirits will protect you against juju, but only if you pay them sufficient homage and give them regular offerings of palm wine and rice, and only if you abide by their rules. Sometimes these rules demand almost superhuman forbearance. In Guinea-Bissau, for example, women must not cry out during childbirth for fear of angering the ancestors or attracting evil spirits. If a mother fails to keep silent and allows a demon to enter her child, the possessed infant will come back again and again to haunt her, dying young each time (Guinean children whose predecessors have all perished are given the Kriolu name, Mortu, meaning Death, to avoid tempting fate).

For some Sierra Leoneans, juju provides an explanation for the civil war. The 1990s, they say, was the decade God slept. Juju, on the other hand, was wide awake. Rebels and government soldiers used *gris gris* – pendants filled with earth or animal bones or scraps of scribbled-on paper - to protect themselves from harm. Witches were dispatched into the skies to locate enemy positions. Spells diverted the course of bullets or froze them in mid-air. The atrocities of the war, too, could be put down to juju, to the fulfilment of curses inflicted on their victims. Families were cursed by other families, villages by other villages, tribes by other tribes. Perhaps the whole country was cursed, the war a punishment for its rejection of community values and embrace of individualism, corruption and greed. Perhaps the orgy of violence was a resurgence of the biblical flood, which the society had to suffer to pay for its sins. How else, after all, to account for what happened? In a world with a God – and no Sierra Leonean doubts His existence – how else could such things be allowed? 'Juju is the work of the devil,' a young Christian told us over coffee at Basheru's one day. The country had let the devil in, and he had duly sown chaos; in an inexplicable universe, juju, like religion, is a way of making sense of life and death.

26

It is not only the uneducated who believe in the power of juju; even the most Westernised Sierra Leoneans cannot quite shake it off. Jim, a Christian who works in our hotel (his exact role, like that of most of his colleagues, is unclear) is reading business studies at one of the country's top universities. Bright, and fluent in English, his ambition is to work in America when he leaves college. While we sit one night on the hotel balcony, overlooking the dark but still-busy street, I ask him what he thinks of juju.

'I don't believe in it because I am Christian,' he answers emphatically. 'I only believe in God.' But this is not the end of it. When I dig a little deeper he admits the existence of juju, but says that God is a mightier force (West Africans, it seems, have a different concept of belief: everything exists, but some things are more powerful than others). 'I have seen juju work for people,' he acknowledges, 'but it is not as strong as the Lord. If you go to church you will be protected.' Religion is his defence against magic. It occurs to me that he might have chosen Christianity to escape the spell of juju, but that Jesus has not lived up to his side of the missionaries' deal. Jim is still haunted by the old ways. Juju, like a dead star whose light can still be seen, remains a part of his life, and he must continue - albeit now with the help of his new god - to watch his back.

Another Christian, Joseph, the smartly dressed, fresh-faced young human rights worker who had so narrowly survived the AFRC invasion of Freetown, is a member of the capital's Westernised elite. He was educated in the best schools, obtained a degree in political science, has travelled abroad, and his work gives him regular contact with godless Europeans. But he too is wary of witchcraft. One afternoon, over a beer in a downtown restaurant frequented by aid workers, government officials and foreign businessmen sweating in suits, he tells us the story of his driver, Abubakar, whose wife was recently shot in the leg by a witch gun.

Witch guns are the juju device *du jour*. Made of wood or metal and covered in cowrie shells or some other adornment (neither the shape nor the decoration seems to matter, and many of the guns are invisible to the human eye), they are a devastatingly effective tool for felling your enemies. The process, Joseph tells us, is straightforward. You approach one of the city's "herbalists", who can be found outside the Law Courts or at the enigmatically-named Upgun Turntable roundabout deep in the East End, and, having paid a small fee, show him or her a photograph of your target. The herbalist takes a shot, and although there is no obvious sign of a bullet nor any crack of gunfire, the victim, who may be many miles away, falls down and dies. 'There are many of these killings all over the country, even in Freetown,' says Joseph, wide-eyed. 'They have escalated since the war.' (Witch guns' power is taken seriously – we read in the newspaper one day that a herbalist has been arrested and is being tried in court for using one.)

Abubakar's wife was shot in the leg and wounded; her attacker, who has not yet been identified, seemingly wanted only to hurt her rather than kill her. When I respond with my habitual but ever more hesitant scepticism, Joseph calls his driver on his mobile phone and asks him to join us. Abubakar, who has been sitting in the car waiting, comes in and confirms the story. He and his wife had to seek the help of another herbalist to cure her, he says. Joseph went along too - although he believes in juju, he had doubted the effectiveness of witch guns and wanted to see it for himself.

The herbalist, who is famous in the capital for his great healing powers, was brought to the house where Abu's wife, unable to walk, was lying in bed. He took out a razor blade and cut a little cross in her thigh. Blood came gushing out. Unperturbed, the herbalist bent down and put his mouth to the cut. He sucked out ninety-two small metal bullets, sealed the wound with his lips, and the woman was cured. Abu, a devout Muslim, has kept the bullets in case anyone doubts the story. When I suggest that they might already have been in the herbalist's mouth before he performed his miracle, Joseph is indignant. 'How could you hide ninety-two bullets in your mouth?' he asks. Abu nods sagely in agreement.

Although I am unpersuaded by Joseph's response, there remains the incontrovertible fact, attested to by both him and his driver, that Abu's wife was sick when the herbalist arrived at her house and healed by the time he left. As I am mulling over this story the words of the Romanian woman come back to me: If you are here long enough, you will believe, she had said in her haunting Eastern European tones. A shudder shoots up my spine, my rationalistic view of the world having taken yet another hit.

In the Nigerian writer Wole Soyinka's play, *Death and the King's Horseman*, British colonial officials attempt to abolish a local custom that decrees that when a chief dies, his equerry must commit suicide in order to accompany him to the heavens. Their efforts run up against a wall of silent refusal. 'You think you've stamped it out,' complains Pilkings, the frustrated British District Commissioner, 'but it's always lurking under the surface somewhere.' Jim, Joseph and Abubakar embody West Africa's tussle between the modern and the traditional. Many West Africans are embarrassed by and struggle with this dichotomy – Jim only reluctantly admits the existence of juju, and several others I speak to shyly preface their fantastic tales by saying, 'you people don't believe these things.' But Joseph and Abu are comfortable living in both worlds. That magic may exist in an era of mobile phones, the internet and the jet plane does not disorientate them. That their city, with its office blocks, banks and paved roads, is surrounded by sacred forests where drums rumble and spirits whisper in the trees does not seem to them remarkable. The new and the old both have their place. Unlike so many of their contemporaries, whose rush to modernity demands complete rejection of the traditional, Joseph and Abu have adjusted to this compression of time, to Africa as it is, not as it was or as it will be. As I reflect on our conversation, it strikes me that it is this elusive ability to reconcile themselves to the present that gives these two young men, perhaps more than anyone else I have met on the trip, the aura of people who are at ease with their lives.

27

After a few weeks in Freetown, we decide to make for the diamond mining areas in the east. In West Africa, however, decisions are for the optimist; nothing can be taken for granted, least of all the reliability of transport. A realist would adopt a less cavalier mindset. Rather than rashly "deciding" to head for the diamond fields, he would resolve instead to establish whether such a journey was a remote possibility: whether the government bus was likely to be in the vicinity of the capital that morning, whether its schedule was the same as the previous day or week, whether its driver had turned up for work, and whether the vehicle was in reasonable working order and had taken on a sufficient quantity of fuel. These conditions satisfied, the realist would then plan for spending the day sitting in the bus, with movement a bonus and arrival at the desired destination at the desired time an extreme longshot. Finally, aware that contingency plans are at least as likely to be called upon as the original, the realist would make provisions for spending that night and several nights after it in the town from which he intended to depart.

Naively, we draw up no such fall-back plans. Awaking at five, we check out of our hotel and lug our bags through the darkness to the government bus station, a bare hangar at the bottom of our street. The bus will leave at seven, but the station master has told us to arrive by six to make sure of a seat. We present ourselves obediently at the ticket window just before the deadline: we are the first to arrive, and the first to acquire tickets. The bus is nowhere to be seen. We settle down on our bags to await departure in an hour. Dawn breaks slowly and the metal roof of the hangar begins to heat up. In the street outside, market stall-holders set up shop for the day. A girl in a long wraparound skirt walks past bearing a tray of peeled oranges on her head. A group of amputees, legs or feet hacked off in the war, swings by on crutches. A bus station worker chases off a madman in rags who was about to accost us. Three street boys sleep on the ground under a lorry, huddled together like eels on a slab.

The bus trundles in half an hour after its scheduled departure time. We board, along with many others - too many others, it turns out, for the driver's assistant, who proves unable to seat us all. Although our tickets display seat numbers, several passengers sit in the wrong place, and grow angry when the poor boy tries to persuade them to move. Unfathomably, given he must have performed this procedure many times before, he has also made the fatal mistake of allowing the front rows to fill up first. This would not present a problem if there were a clear route to the rear of the bus, but unfortunately for the assistant the aisle seats, which had been propped up against the side seats to keep the passageway clear, have been flopped down into their horizontal positions and occupied. Pandemonium ensues, as new arrivals seated further back are forced to climb over those already in place. Sitting near the front, my head is buffeted by elbows, hips and luggage. Someone stands on my shoulder as he attempts to climb past. There is much shouting and grumbling. Ebru and I, helpless, sit quietly, sweating in the gathering heat.

Eventually, as the chaos threatens to overwhelm him, the assistant decides to go on the offensive, evidently concluding that attack is the best form of defence. He yells at the grumblers in the back, telling them to organise themselves. He yells at passengers who arrive late (the scheduled departure time passed an hour ago but these people, apparently seasoned and experienced travellers, do not seem in a hurry). Finally he yells at the whole bus, telling us all to disembark and start again. This works surprisingly well, and we are soon ready to leave.

But we have reckoned without the driver. A heavy-set, square-faced man whose prominent jaw and forehead guard sly little eyes, he has been sitting in his elevated seat taking no notice of the chaos behind him. Instead he leans out of his window chatting to a woman. He continues his conversation when we are all finally seated. Some of the passengers, already in a high temper, beseech him to set off - we should have left nearly two hours ago - but he ignores them. When they raise their voices in protest he shouts back angrily, ordering them to wait. That there are over fifty passengers crammed into the sweltering bus is of no import to him; all must be kept waiting while he finishes his conversation.

The concept of customer service has yet to make much headway in Sierra Leone. As a general rule, only those running their own businesses show any courtesy to their clientele. Employees, on the other hand, are inefficient at best, lazy and rude at worst. Waitresses fling menus wordlessly onto your table and bring you one glass when you order two drinks; hotel staff treat you as if they are doing you a favour by telling you the room rate (in one instance, we were told to come back the following day to see a room as the receptionist was too busy cooking her lunch); the immigration office gives a husband and wife visa extensions of different durations and then refuses to rectify what it admits was an oversight because it would look 'unprofessional' for us to have so many stamps in our passports; a judge in the law courts interrupts a murder case to take personal calls on his mobile phone; teachers demand bribes to teach; and a Sierra Leonean friend of ours who has flown in from China for an interview at a government ministry is told on arrival that the interviewer has gone abroad for two weeks, so he will have to postpone his return to China and wait.

It is difficult to fire anybody here – an employer who does so knows that he is consigning someone who may be a large family's only breadwinner to abject poverty. Several employers I speak to complain that people take no pride in their work. Fred, a former US marine newly returned to his homeland to set up in business, reports that the architect he contracted to build his house failed to ensure that lines were straight, with the result that the sagging roof already needs replacing just a few months after it was finished. He tells me how hard it is to compel his staff to turn up to work on time – even after repeated reprimands many of them arrive hours late, day after day. A returnee from England says his workers routinely ignore deadlines, and then lie brazenly to cover their backs. And a politician of our acquaintance complains that her housekeeper is stealing from her, but she is reluctant to fire her because the woman is a single mother of three young children and casting her out could be a death sentence.

Spend long enough in the country and the question of why nothing works as it should will inevitably, as the fan above your head stops turning due to yet another power cut, begin to keep you awake at night. Some blame it on colonialism, whose subjects had no incentive to work hard or well because they did not see the fruits of their labour. The radical Martiniquais anti-colonial Frantz Fanon saw professional incompetence as a deliberate act of rebellion. 'How many times,' he asked, 'in Paris, in Aix, in Algiers or in Basse-Terre, have we not heard men from the colonized countries violently protesting against the pretended laziness of the black man? And yet is it not the simple truth that under the colonial regime a fellah who is keen on his work or a Negro who refuses to rest are nothing but pathological cases? The native's laziness is the conscious sabotage of the colonial machine.'

Once the imperialist yoke was lifted, it might have been expected that commitment and quality would regain their importance in Sierra Leoneans' lives, and that the country would thereby take steps at last towards economic development. But the corrupt few who prospered in the post-colonial era displayed little evidence of either commitment or quality - it was obvious to all that their success had nothing to do with merit. In this new world, venality, ruthlessness and sheer good fortune were the most effective levers for advancement; hard work got you nowhere.

Juju may also have played a part in the society's descent to mediocrity. People who reach high rank are assumed to have used witchcraft to help propel them there; those who do not possess special powers and cannot afford to requisition them have little prospect of achieving their objectives. But just as juju can raise you up, it can also cut you down. We hear of a civil servant who died of a heart attack just a week after a long-sought promotion. Everyone who knew the man put his death down to sorcery – a jealous rival must have deployed a curse to bring about his downfall.

Where status and wealth are so precarious and owe so little to your own efforts and abilities, there is little point in striving to get ahead through hard work. Fatalism inevitably sets in, commitment weakens, and quality declines. Musa hints at the deadening effects of juju one evening, when after relating to us some more of its mysteries he strokes his chin ruminatively and says, 'We have witches that fly in the night, but the white man, who doesn't have juju, has planes that fly and big ships that float. We have all this magic, but we are still poor. Why can't we use it to rise up?'

Our bus finally departs two hours behind schedule. About a mile into the journey, however, still in the heart of the city, it breaks down. The driver does not seem surprised, and his assistant immediately starts to examine the fuel pump: it is an old problem that nobody has bothered to address, and the driver has not thought to check the vehicle that morning. When we had broken down in Guinea-Bissau our fellow passengers had remained calm and relaxed throughout, but here tempers fray quickly. Everybody is on edge. A few passengers shout invective at the driver. He ignores them, so they shout at each other instead. Drawn by all the noise, a crowd gathers around the bus, like hyenas surrounding a dying elephant, but after a while the assistant manages to fix the problem and we chug on for another half-mile before again coming to a halt. This time we are close to the bus depot, and the driver, unruffled, wanders off to find a mechanic.

After some minutes of discussion, a few passengers decide to make a representation to the managers of the depot to demand a new bus. Bored, we offer to go with them, and they gratefully accept, reasoning that the managers are more likely to take action if they see white faces. In the depot we find the driver sitting drinking coffee and chatting merrily to colleagues. I expect my companions to fly into a fury, but by now they are resigned to their fate. 'They don't value us, they only value money,' one of them grumbles. The management refuses to put on a new bus, so the mechanics spend three hours fruitlessly fiddling with the engine of our own crippled beast. Eventually we give up; six hours after leaving it, and having travelled perhaps two miles, we find ourselves back at our hotel in Freetown.

28

At the beginning of our trip, I had expected to move around the three countries as an observer, taking notes, forming impressions and generally remaining an outsider, a tourist. In Asia and southern Africa, where I had previously spent long periods, effective public transport systems, well-equipped hotels and visitor facilities, and the presence of numerous other Westerners had made it easy for me to retreat into a comfortable cocoon whenever I had had my fill of the reality outside the gates. There, I had been able to stay above the fray, keeping aloof and only occasionally feeling part of life as it is lived by local people.

But in West Africa such detachment is impossible. You are dragged into the mêlée and forced to become part of it. Your physical and psychological distance is stripped away. Unless you spend all your time in one of the capital's few luxury hotels, even money does not protect you from the visceral nature of the experience; as soon as you venture out into the city or travel around the country, you will be drawn into its exacting ways. Of course, your travails are as nothing compared with what the region's inhabitants have to endure – as a visitor, you have more money and the ever present option of escape – but if you stay here long enough, you will inevitably be confronted by some of the same challenges, and your resilience, like theirs, will be regularly tested.

Crime, for instance, afflicts both locals and foreigners. My mobile phone lasted just a few days in Freetown before it was removed from my pocket (within minutes, Musa, appalled and embarrassed that this had happened to 'a guest in my country,' took me to see a friend of his who led me down a dark alley and sold me another, second-hand phone, possibly also stolen). As the victim of a crime, whether foreign or West African, you have little recourse. Musa and his friend warned me that if I reported the theft, the police would find some way to extort money from me. Back in Dakar, while on the run from phantom hitmen, I had known that the authorities would be more likely to pose a threat than provide protection (those phantoms, of course, were not so different from the evil spirits that fill West Africans with such dread).

Public services are equally threadbare for both visitor and resident. If you fall sick, as I did after three weeks subsisting on Freetown street food, you have nowhere to turn. The nearest functioning hospital is in another country - the wealthy fly to Ghana, Senegal or Europe for all but the most basic treatment - and with reliable transport so scarce you could be long dead by the time you reach it. As my temperature climbed alarmingly between fits of violent vomiting and the worried hotel staff began to pay regular visits to the room to check on my condition, the saintly Ebru's only option was to plaster my head and body with wet towels, ply me with what she hoped was genuine paracetamol (a quarter of drugs sold in developing countries are fake), and pray.

That night we were fortunate. Our hotel had both power and water. This was unusual. Most weeks we had water for a total of twenty-four hours, power for perhaps a third of each day. This is not dangerous, as a health scare or a criminal act might be, but in a climate with regular bouts of ninety percent humidity it is grindingly uncomfortable. Like Sierra Leoneans, most of whose homes have neither electricity nor taps, you must get used to being caked in grime and dust, and used too to long spells at night where without the benefit of a turning fan it is too hot, the air too close, the sheets too damp with sweat to sleep.

Corruption is another blight which affects both visitor and local. The triumphant smile of the woman in the immigration office as she avenged herself for my refusal to give her a bribe by rejecting my request for a visa extension is something all West Africans have to suffer with enervating regularity. When we solved the problem, as any well-connected local would, via a contact at the Ministry of Foreign Affairs, we found a queue of supplicants waiting outside the office of the bureaucrat who was dealing with us. While we sat on a sofa beside her desk waiting for my passport, the petitioners shuffled in disconsolately, one by one, and as they handed in various forms the bureaucrat opened them up to check whether the requisite sweetener had been inserted. She then pulled open her top drawer, which was strewn with high-denomination banknotes, and added the new gift to the pile. It did not seem to matter to her that we were watching.

Some difficulties are more acute for the foreign visitor. The efforts of hawkers and moneychangers ratchet up when they see a white face. 'FRIEND!' they shout, every time you pass. 'Hey white guy! Change money? Banana? Coconut? Egg? You want taxi?' Fending them off is usually painless, sometimes fun if you are in the mood for banter, but after a few months, and when combined with the draining effects of the climate, the constant attention can grow wearying ('you are very exposed,' said the only other tourist we met in Sierra Leone, a browbeaten Austrian who was relieved to be on his way home to a place where solitude and quiet were not alien concepts).

Harder to deal with are the incessant requests for money. These come at you from all sides. Children appear to have been trained to ask for cash as soon as they see a white face. 'Give me money,' they parrot in a monotone, some with hope in their voices, most without. In the countryside it is often difficult to locate the source of these calls, which can come from a hundred yards away or more as a distant child spots a flash of your white skin. Refusing children's demands is relatively easy, for you know that by yielding, and thereby encouraging a belief that reward can be gained without effort, you will be doing them no long-term favours.

Brushing off the advances of adult beggars is more compli-cated. Again you can rationalise by saying to yourself that if you give, the government does not have to, and that in the long run this will harm rather than help the country. But when you look down at your feet and find a sprawled amputee smiling up at you; when you see a man in rags kneeling in the traffic to drink from a hole in the street where an underground water pipe has burst; or when you see a woman victim of the war lying face down on the pavement day after day in the pounding sun, her blank eyes locked in a world of unimaginable horror, it is difficult to think of the future, and difficult to cling to cold reason.

Requests for money from West African friends present different quandaries. I had grown accustomed to these on earlier visits to the region, but as an Englishman brought up to prefer a slow death to asking a friend for financial assistance, I cannot prevent the questions queuing up in my head each time a request is made. Did the supplicant befriend me solely for financial reasons? Does he have any feelings of genuine companionship? How will he react if I refuse or give too little? And what of everyone else we have met – are they too in it for the money and merely awaiting the right moment to ask?

The expectation that Westerners will solve your financial problems can partly be explained by the belief that the white man, so much of whose wealth was built on African minerals and slave labour, owes a debt to the black. There is a sense, too, that relationships here are transactional: I do something for you – join you for a drink, regale you with tales about my country, show you the way to the transport park – and it is only fair that you give something back. But it is also linked to fatalism. As the anthropologist Michael Jackson has observed, if you believe, as most West Africans do, that you have no control over your destiny, then your only hope of rescue from your impossibly straitened circumstances lies in external 'benefactors and saviours.' A Czech woman we met in Freetown, who had spent several years in the interior conducting anthropological research, put it slightly differently. 'People here see you as God sending them a white man,' she said. Perhaps we were seen as an answer to people's prayers, reward for their religious devotion.

In previous visits to poor countries, the misery of their inhabitants had had only a limited effect on me. I had persuaded myself, and was detached enough to be convinced, that allowing it to move me emotionally would serve no purpose; people back home who said they were put off visiting such countries because they 'couldn't handle the poverty' I had shrugged off as blinkered and shallow. The poor were ugly statistics, numbers on a page, with short life expectancies, empty stomachs and no jobs - a problem worth addressing not because I had any acute emotional empathy with the afflicted, but because it defied reason and fairness that an accident of birth should give me so much and them so little.

During our first week or two in West Africa I had carried around a similar attitude, that of the shallow observer. But the ubiquity of individual tragedy here and your close proximity to it make it difficult to sustain such detachment, and my old certainties slowly crumbled. Seeing the boy on the beach in Bubaque, hearing Ibrahima's tale of estrangement and lost opportunity, listening to Maria and Mame's laments for their dead sons, and being confronted with Freetown's unending parade of the sick, the lame and the mad, I began to understand what being unable to 'handle the poverty' meant. It meant vexation at life's unfairness and anger at those who had caused this to happen. It meant a constant dilemma over how to respond. It meant a realisation that the optimistic view of the world you had in middle-class England was a Panglossian delusion. And most of all, it meant guilt. Guilt over your wealth, guilt when you refused to give, guilt that when you gave you did not give everything, and guilt that having had your fill of their destitution you could and one day would fly away to a magical world of comfort and security.

Even the rational argument for not giving to those who ask

for money has flaws. In this respect it is a microcosm of the arguments over the usefulness of foreign aid. In the long-term, the countries of West Africa will be better off if they can steer their own courses without relying on charity from the rich world - this assistance lets governments off the hook and absolves them of the responsibility for developing their countries. Similarly, giving money to beggars reduces the pressure on the political classes to tackle poverty or implement social programs (if nobody gave anything and the streets were wracked by crime or littered with the bodies of those who had starved to death, even the most amoral government might feel compelled to take remedial action). But if you do not give money, and if foreign governments do not help out, millions will suffer today for the sake of possible - and only possible - improvements in the lives of future generations. Donors are therefore caught in a trap: give, and you protect those alive now but impair the prospects of those to come; desist, and you sacrifice today's generations. It is a hard heart that can take the latter path.

West Africans often give to beggars. They also give foreign aid. At the turn of the millennium a village in Mali, one of the world's poorest countries, raised money for a town in Canada, one of its richest, to help it rebuild after being damaged by storms. While we were in Sierra Leone, to many Freetonians' bemusement their government, which cannot afford to feed, educate or house its own people, sent money to earthquake victims in Haiti, explaining that the country needed to play its part as a member of the international community.

It is not only foreigners who must field demands on their pockets: when a West African comes into money family members, friends and neighbours can be quick to pounce. The custom has a long history. In the 1770s the British naturalist Henry Smeathman spent four years in Sierra Leone collecting specimens of flora and fauna (he it was who recommended the country to the British crown as a suitable habitat for freed slaves). As well as observing

nature – he had a particular interest in termites, whose industrious, hierarchical societies he saw as a model for future human
colonies – Smeathman studied how West African society
functioned. He was struck by what he termed the "law of hospitality", whereby 'if there is provision in the country, a man who
wants it only has to find out who has got any, and he must have
his share. If he enters any man's house during his repast, and
gives him the usual salutation, the man must invite him to
partake.' Smeathman believed the law of hospitality discouraged
hard work, since the fruits of one's labour were so quickly
dispersed. 'Whatever abundance a man may get by assiduity,
will be shared by the lazy,' he wrote. 'If an industrious man gets
a spare shirt or utensils he will be teased to death for it...Thus
they seldom calculate for more than the necessaries.'

Little has changed in the intervening centuries. A friend of
ours named Mohammed, who makes a living painting advertising slogans on Freetown houses and walls, tells us that he is
the sole provider for ten people. 'When I get paid,' he complains,
'my mother asks for money for her hospital bills, I have to pay
my brother's school fees, and my neighbour wants money. After
I have paid them all there is not much left, and soon my own son
will have to go to school.' Another Mohammed, who works as a
foreman at a diamond mine, says he tries to avoid his family now
because they always ask him for cash. He once offered his uncle
a job at the mine, but the uncle refused because he preferred to
maintain his status in his village as a mediator of disputes (an
unpaid but prestigious position). Instead he asks his nephew for
handouts. 'People don't want to work for money,' Mohammed
says. 'My family even steal from me while I am sleeping.' Not
long ago he met a girl he wants to marry, but as soon as he
secured the job at the mine the dowry demanded by the girl's
parents doubled. He and his beloved will now have to wait while
he attempts to save the extra funds.

In traditional Africa, sharing everything made sense. In an

environment where the climate, wild animals, disease and the scarcity of food all conspired against you, safety in numbers was a critical survival mechanism. Anyone striking out on his own would face certain death. The old southern African proverb, 'humans are humans because of other humans,' refers not just to the emotional value of friendship and love, but to the literal imperative of pulling together to fight off nature's assaults.

But in a modernising Africa, where nature, although still powerful and frequently lethal, poses a less persistent threat to daily existence - the wild animals have mostly gone and humanity is better protected against disease - the case for collectivism is less clear. If nine members of the mural painter Mohammed's family can get by without working, the group, and by extension the economy as a whole, are unlikely to make significant headway. If something happens to the lone breadwinner, moreover, the family, its safety net pulled from under it, will have nowhere to turn. For the individual, too, the law of hospitality can be more of a burden than a boon. If you are expected to part with all you earn, you yourself cannot rise up. You cannot invest in and expand a business (or hire people who want to work for a living), and you cannot buy what you need to live a comfortable life. The law of hospitality holds you back, prevents you from realising your ambitions, keeps you mired in poverty. Many decide it is better to stagnate. 'I don't want a higher salary,' says Mohammed the diamond miner with a resigned smile. 'It will just be taken by my family and my girlfriend's family.'

After weeks of deliberation, and having weighed up the arguments without reaching any firm conclusions, I settle on a muddled policy of infrequent and fairly random donations of small amounts of leones, peppered with occasional larger, unsolicited gifts to those we have grown especially fond of or who have helped us in some way (these latter handouts make me feel uncomfortably like an angel investor). It is not enough, and I know that I am barely helping my prospects of avoiding Dan's increasingly plausible hell, but there are no easy answers, my budget and sense of generosity are limited, and the policy lies somewhere between my hard-headed certainty of old and the new, more agnostic way of looking at the world with which West Africa is slowly infusing me.

29

After recovering from our first attempt to leave the capital, we make another bid for freedom a few days later, and draw up a tentative plan to visit the city of Bo in the south-east. This time we spurn the government bus and head early in the morning for the "Texaco" transport park in the East End, where a petrol station of that name once stood and which is now a large expanse of rutted dirt dotted with trucks, rusting minibuses, and trusty *sept places*.

The discomfort of transport is a further blight shared by both local people and visitors, although the former are much better at coping with it. Experience helps. An experienced user of Sierra Leonean public transport would be aware that a car or bus that looks full may in fact be empty. Travellers know that vehicles can take hours to fill up, and that they will not leave so long as a cubic inch of space remains vacant. To hasten departure, therefore, and although this guarantees that they will barely have room to breathe, the canny make for the most crowded cars. Drivers, of course, are alert to this tendency, so those who do not yet have a full load employ decoy passengers - young men with nothing better to do who in return for a tiny commission are happy to sprawl across the empty seats or mill about in front of the vehicle - to give off the impression of repleteness. The decoys remain in position until their places are taken by unwary genuine travellers, who like hopeful insects approaching a Venus flytrap are drawn in by the deceit, never to re-emerge.

Although you only fall for this trick once, it can cost you many hours of your life. The system whereby transport never leaves until full, while understandable from the perspective of a driver who might make only one long journey each day, is grossly inefficient for passengers. Those who have the misfortune to be first on board can have no idea when they will reach their destination, and their total journey time can be hours, perhaps even days longer than that of later arrivals. Over time, if you travel often enough, matters will even out and fate will allocate you your fair share of long and short waits - it is perhaps their awareness of this that allows Sierra Leoneans to maintain their equanimity in the face of what to a European seem insufferable delays – but for the infrequent traveller or the short-term visitor, this knowledge offers scant consolation.

This particular wait, we are told as we board a large minibus on which we realise too late that we are the only genuine passengers, will last no more than fifteen minutes. 'You mean an hour, don't you?' I say to our informant, who has been unsuccessfully besieging new arrivals to try to cajole them onto our bus. He laughs, but there is hesitancy in his eyes. I have exposed his white lie and am now inadvertently forcing him into another. 'Let's say one hour,' he replies without confidence.

This is unpromising, but since we have already bought our tickets and are therefore powerless to effect change, we do not dwell on it. We take our seats. Outside, the driver sits in the shade of a hut playing chequers. Hawkers gather around our window and take turns shouting at us. Every ten minutes or so a new passenger boards the bus and slumps down to wait. As the rising sun assumes a position from which it can take aim at us with maximum impact, the temperature soars into the high thirties. Sweat begins to ooze from my neck, back, forehead and armpits, then, less predictably, from my calves, forearms and the backs of my hands. To keep from overheating I try to switch off all bodily functions and sit immobile, spreading my arms and legs as wide as the slowly filling bus will allow. To keep from insanity I lock down mental processes, such as counting the passing minutes or the absent passengers, or devising juju spells to inflict on the chequers-playing bus driver. I slip slowly into a state of numbness.

After perhaps an hour, with the bus half-full, a scruffily dressed middle-aged man with a worn face and tired eyes climbs on board and stands by the empty driver's seat, facing us. He begins to preach, and exhorts us to pray to the Lord (being harangued by religious zealots is another West African experience to which neither visitor nor local is immune). The man lacks charisma, and seems merely to be going through the motions, but he succeeds in persuading some women in the back to sing a hymn with him. 'We thank God for everything,' they yodel sweetly, a gratitude that in our current circumstances we find baffling. After a few verses the preacher decides he has done enough. He collects money from the devout and departs to find another captive audience.

The respite is only temporary, however, for his place is taken soon after by a younger, better-fed man in a sweat-soaked maroon shirt. This one is a Muslim. Unlike his predecessor, he is bursting with energy. He starts yelling at us in a local language. Few are listening, as our bus seems to consist mainly of Christians, but he is unbowed. For what seems an eternity he hurls hellfire and brimstone at us. With each new reprimand he grows more frenzied, his bald head glittering with perspiration, the puddles of sweat on his shirt joining to form lakes as we sink lower into our seats to escape his wrath and evade his spittle. As hawkers and beggars grab at my elbow through the window; as a baby screams and vomits on the floor behind us; as our row fills up and we are compressed so tightly that we must take turns leaning forward to allow our neighbours to sit back; as the sun pelts us with its rays and pools of sweat form at our feet; and as the preacher bellows at us with ever-increasing urgency and volume and the driver continues blithely with his chequers game, I wonder, from my zone of resigned but patient misery, if this is what hell will be like.

After two hours, the driver's assistant climbs on board to switch on the ignition. The decoy passengers give the bus a push and the engine rumbles into life. Hope! Is there to be relief, movement, progress? Are we finally to escape the city's clinging tentacles? Will we at last feel cool air through the window? Alas, not yet. Turning on the ignition, it transpires, is another ploy, designed to show wavering would-be passengers that we will be leaving imminently, and certainly long before any other vehicle they might be sizing up. Come with us, the engine murmurs seductively, purring like a purveyor of potions, and soon you will reach your destination.

The ploy works, and the few remaining spaces are quickly occupied. The driver finishes his game of chequers and takes his place at the helm. The Muslim preacher collects a few leones and disembarks. The door closes, and two and a half hours after our purgatory began, the bus departs. We head out through the busy streets of the East End, but before we can settle down to enjoy being on the road again there is one more test in store. Unseen by us, another Christian charlatan has boarded the bus. Tall and well built and dressed in what appear to be factory overalls covered in Chinese script, he stands at the front and introduces himself as a "pastor" from Ghana. He begins to pray aloud, and after each verse orders us to shout 'Amen!' Receiving only a lacklustre response, he grows angry. 'Louder!' he shrieks. The weary passengers raise the volume slightly, and he goes on. When he has finished praying, he hands out printouts of verses from the Bible, including some that urge patience (God is here today). Then he asks if any of us is ill. About a third of the passengers put up their hands, listing an assortment of maladies, from malaria to backache to stomach pains. 'I will pray for you and cure you,' the pastor promises. 'As surely as I speak God's Word, you will be cured of these sicknesses today.' He looks to the heavens and prays silently.

Finally, he passes round a pile of empty brown envelopes. 'God needs your help today to spread his Word, but one day you will need God's help,' he threatens. When a few hapless passengers insert banknotes into the envelopes, he announces that 'if you ask for money in Ghana people laugh.' 'Probably because Ghanaians are better educated,' I remark to the young man sitting next to Ebru. He smiles and nods in agreement, but the pastor catches me fomenting rebellion and tells the bus to 'give an envelope to the white man.' When I wave it away he retaliates by trying to embarrass me: 'The white man brought us the gospel,' he sneers, 'but now we are bringing it to him.' Once all the envelopes have been handed in he asks the driver to stop and disembarks. The passengers around us grumble forlornly.

After a month in downtown Freetown it feels good to be on the move, to leave behind the cloying, clamouring city and the strains of urban life in Africa. As we roll slowly over the lush, jungle-covered hills to the east of the capital, a sense of release washes over me, a feeling of happy limbo, of having to think neither about the place we have left nor the next destination. As the cool air gently buffets my face, my mind feels clear and free, free to think not of day to day matters but of the journey as a whole, of how it has been and how it will be, of what we have learned and what remains to be worked out. After a while even these thoughts recede, leaving the soothing road to lull us into torpor.

The road, built by the Chinese, is paved and good. With the fume-clogged city behind us the light is glassy and bright. We tumble down the hills through little villages tunnelled out of the forest, their tiny one-room houses made only of mud, straw and wood. Women with tall pestles pound yams in the shade of mango trees. Men sit on stools and stare at the road. Young girls pump determinedly at wells while high above them palm wine tappers cling like woodpeckers to their precious trees, siphoning out the milky liquid which because it needs no additional ingredients to intoxicate you is known by appreciative locals as God's gift to man.

Graham Greene travelled through these villages in the thirties. Comparing them to Freetown and the coast, he remarked on the hinterland's 'greater simplicity,' its 'older more natural culture, and traditions of honesty and hospitality.' Those on the coast, Greene felt, had been corrupted by European influence and, like the author himself, 'lost touch with the primitive source.' Today the old ways are under still greater pressure. A few of the villages we pass are empty, abandoned in the rush to modernity or in the war (there are many gaps where buildings once stood before they were razed by rebels or the army). Those left behind on the land soldier on, battling the hostile elements and hoping for God to send them a white man or a relative who has struck gold. Their way of life is no longer considered desirable. 'The poorest man is a farmer,' says the young man sitting next to Ebru. It is a view most of his peers share.

30

'We have a saying here,' says Ali, 'that the profits from diamonds reach from the tips of your toes to your knees, but the losses reach up to your throat.' He makes as if to strangle himself, drawing curious stares from two young women who have strayed into his cavernous store in the centre of Bo.

Things are bad in the diamond industry. The price of the gems fell by eighty percent in the recent recession, and the ravages of war and the strict certification scheme put in place by the government when the fighting stopped have left miners and traders gasping for air. Many have switched to gold. 'Gold is solid - you can find it everywhere,' Ali sighs. 'Diamonds are risky. I've cut back on diamond trading in the past two years - I'm keeping my head down. I lost a lot of money.' He longs for the good old days, when the Lebanese had free rein to mine and sell the gems wherever, however and to whomever they pleased. 'The government controls everything now. It's much harder to make money.'

Ali, whose mop of thick black hair, deep-set eyes and pallid, slightly sagging cheeks put one in mind of a washed out Italian mafioso, describes himself as a Sierra Leonean of Lebanese descent. A family man in his early fifties, he speaks Arabic to those closest to him, Krio to his neighbours and the customers in his shop, and English with a Krio accent to us ('I spent a year in London in the nineties,' he explains. 'It was so cold I didn't take my jacket off once'). We had entered his general store to buy cream cheese for lunch, pausing on the threshold to allow our eyes to adjust to the gloom, and he had insisted we sit behind his counter with him to chat.

'My parents came here to work,' he begins, pleased to have the opportunity to reflect on his life. 'There was no work in Lebanon. It's the same with all the Lebanese here. We are economic migrants.' For a long time the uprooted community did well -

Siaka Stevens allowed them to monopolise the diamond trade provided they kept him and his cronies in funds, and their links with the global Lebanese diaspora helped them build highly successful export businesses. But the war took a heavy toll. 'Before the war,' Ali says, 'there were a hundred and fifty Lebanese families in Bo. Now most them have gone. There's not enough money in diamonds any more, and the economy is weak. There are only twenty-five families left. Some fled during the war and didn't come back. Others have drifted away since the fighting ended.' He looks straight ahead while he talks, keeping an eye on the doorway and the activity in the street. Although he has good relations with Africans, engaging in a steady banter with customers, suppliers and the many other waifs and strays who drift in and out of his shop, he regrets the decline of the Arab community. 'We still meet at weekends and go out for picnics or go fishing, or play snooker or darts at the old Bo Club, but the gatherings are smaller these days. It's quieter.'

In his store, a large, rectangular, warehouse-like room lit only by the sun that bounces mutedly off the street in front, he sells tinned foods, cleaning materials, soft drinks, sweets, biscuits and numerous other sundries, piled high to the ceiling in boxes from China, Oman, Turkey, Libya and Europe. The boy he employs as his assistant is standing on the pavement outside auctioning a new cooking oil product through a loudspeaker. 'You can't find these foreign goods anywhere else,' Ali says, explaining his business strategy. 'I provide variety. I do wholesale, retail, everything.' He sits behind a wire mesh screen in the corner at the back, looking out through the large entranceway that frames the bright, bustling street. The counter before him is strewn with banknotes, a receipt book, two mobile phones and a calculator. From time to time he scoops up a handful of the notes and counts them while he talks. There is a constant traffic of customers and mysterious "business partners". The local chief, a large, jovial man in a white linen suit, drops by briefly to discuss a construction project they are collaborating on. A shopkeeper fills a wheelbarrow with Ali's exotic foreign goods and takes them away on credit. A market woman comes in and haggles hard over a few boxes of washing powder. Ali banters back good-naturedly, reminding her of the tiny profit he is making at the price and of the wife and five children he has to feed. The woman stomps out theatrically, feigning anger, until he caves in and calls her back.

Our conversation is frequently interrupted by the Arabesque ringtone of one of Ali's mobile phones, or by calls he makes himself. He calls a local immigration officer to ask him to ease the passage into the country of a group of Lebanese friends who are due to arrive the following weekend. Minutes later, the official appears and receives a wad of cash for his troubles. A young Sierra Leonean expatriate visiting from Germany, where Ali helped him to find a job, calls in to say he needs a gold necklace for a lady friend. Ali takes two hundred dollars from the man, makes a phone call, and the deal is done. He gives a few leones to a beggar who drops by, and a few more to an old man who used to walk him to school and now comes in every other day for food money. All day long he is doing deals, oiling wheels, making calls, and taking in and handing out thick bundles of cash.

'I have to do all this because I was swindled by my business partner last year,' he announces suddenly, during a lull in the human traffic. 'He gave me a fake cheque for two hundred thousand dollars for diamonds he was going to sell in Antwerp. He had always paid in cash before, and we had been partners for years so I trusted him. He's Lebanese too,' he adds, surprised to be betrayed by one of his own. He is weighing up his options. Taking out a hit on the man, he has discovered, would cost only a couple of thousand dollars; reporting him to Interpol would be a less direct solution. 'Isn't it dangerous to mess with him?' I ask, mindful of the cold amorality for which the diamond trade is famous. 'I'm more dangerous,' Ali replies.

The partner is now in Mugabe's Zimbabwe, where unlike in

Sierra Leone diamond exporters face neither taxes nor costly certification processes. 'They're making millions down there,' Ali says, becoming animated for the first time, excited by the prospect of a new frontier. 'Finding the diamonds costs nothing, and then they ship them illegally to South Africa and Belgium. Everyone's going there. I'd go myself if I was younger. I'm doing all these things – this shop, construction, gold – because I have no choice after what happened to me last year, but diamonds are my business. I can't do engineering or teaching. I do diamonds.'

He was recently offered a job in the Congo, where he spent a few years in the early nineties (he still uses the old name of Zaire). 'The quality of the diamonds isn't as good as here, but they're much easier to find,' he remembers. He had to refuse the job because the company that offered it to him was run by a Jew. Ali has nothing against working for Jews as long as they pay him well, but the Lebanese Islamic radical movement Hezbollah is less pragmatic. 'They have been taking names of people who work with Jews. The Jew warned me about this so I got in touch with Hezbollah myself.' Naturally, Ali proposed a deal. 'I told them I could work with the Jew and send them half of what I earned. They said they didn't want that sort of money, but it was up to me if I wanted to work with him.' Instead he has embarked on a new project and, unable to resist any longer the lure of the precious stones, is setting up a small diamond mine of his own near Bo. An American partner has joined him in the venture. 'The American wants to use the profits to help this country,' Ali laughs incredulously. 'I told him he can do what he likes with his money - mine's going in my pocket.'

31

After several hours chatting, we take our leave of Ali and wave down a pair of motorbike taxis, known as *okadas*, to take us back to our hotel on the outskirts of town. Okadas ply the streets of Sierra Leone's main cities. Cheap and convenient, they provide a vital income to their pilots, many of whom are former combatants attempting to reintegrate into society. The journeys are often exhilarating. While the helmetless biker weaves his way as rapidly as possible through the traffic, you cling to the seat behind him, trusting that his luck will hold as trucks, animals and pedestrians lurch out into the road in front of you and the bumps in the asphalt jolt you high into the air. Edward, who picks me up outside Ali's store, is well aware of the dangers of his job. 'There are many accidents,' he says. 'Every night when I arrive home safely I thank God. I have had two small crashes in five years, but I've been lucky.' As a passenger, also helmetless, you run similar risks, with the additional worry that you have no control over the fate of your travelling companion. Each okada can carry only one adult passenger, so our policy is for Ebru to board the first bike we flag down while I wait for a second. As she is whisked off, and although I realise that the risk is slight, I can never suppress a shiver as I wonder whether and in what condition I will see her again (asking your riders to go in tandem does not help: on one occasion the bike carrying Ebru had suddenly accelerated away from my side towards a forest, only slowing down when she yelled at its owner to stop; as we watched them disappearing into the distance, even my driver, a veteran okada pilot, had seemed alarmed).

Bo is the beginning of diamond country, at the edge of Sierra Leone's "Wild East". With its wide, dusty streets, flanked by lines of two-storey buildings whose balconies run the length of the upper floor, it resembles a film set for a Western. There are diamond dealerships all over town, most run by Lebanese, many doubling, like Ali's, as stores selling foodstuffs, electrical goods or construction materials. The diamonds are brought in to the town from the nearby mines and sold to dealers from Freetown or Europe. Although the industry is going through a rough patch, there is nevertheless a feeling of excitement as you imagine the life-changing deals being negotiated in musty back offices, out of view of the busy streets.

Bo's position as the gateway to the diamond fields made it a target in the civil war. As rebels rampaged through the surrounding forests, the people of the town, realising that the demoralised, corrupt Sierra Leone Army had no intention of protecting them (some soldiers, indeed, were fighting for the army during the daytime and the rebels at night), took defence into their own hands. Edward takes up the story, shouting above the whirr of his motorbike as I lean over his shoulder to listen. 'It was during the time of the AFRC junta,' he says. 'The army deserted the city so we local boys organised ourselves to fight. We found ammunition and weapons and set up checkpoints every night, looking for RUF or AFRC fighters.' Similar vigilante bands, which came to be known as Civil Defence Forces, were being set up all over the country, often with the support of sympathetic elements within the government who supplied the groups with arms. 'The rebels came to the outskirts with heavy bombardment,' Edward continues. 'But we fought them off. We didn't let them take control of the city.'

The rebels went away to regroup, so those defending Bo brought in reinforcements in the shape of the mysterious Kamajors. The Kamajors and their counterparts in the north of the country, the Tamaboros, were fighting groups linked to the secret societies to which nearly all Sierra Leoneans belong. They traced their lineage to the ancient hunting castes, whose members doubled as village guardians and kept their people safe from the dangers of the forest. Implacably opposed to both the rebels and the army, the Kamajors' use of juju medicines to protect themselves and eliminate their enemies earned them a fearsome reputation. 'They were defending villages but when we asked for help they came to Bo to fight with us,' says Edward. 'They have amazing powers. They have charms so that they will not be hit by bullets. If you are standing behind a Kamajor and he is shot at, his charm will protect you too. I have seen this with my own eyes.' He is not alone. Joseph, the human rights activist we had befriended in Freetown, spent part of the war in Bo. He was there when the Sierra Leone Army ambushed the Kamajors in a field after tricking them into meeting for peace talks. Many were killed ('their charms did not protect them because they must have sinned against Kamajor rules,' Joseph explained, referring to the strict prohibitions against looting and sexual activity during combat), but their commander, who had long been hunted by the SLA, heard about the planned attack at the last minute and 'vanished into thin air.' Joseph, who had been watching through a fence at the edge of the field, observed this miracle himself.

As well as using magic to defend themselves, the Kamajors possessed a frightening array of attack methods. Metamorphosing into birds, they would fly in the night to recon-noitre rebel positions and then, back in human form, sneak up on guards from the depths of the forest and strangle them or slit their throats. They used potions to immobilise or blind their enemies or to give themselves night vision. To reinforce their powers, they drank their victims' blood and ripped out and devoured their hearts and livers. 'They were worse than the rebels,' says Ali during another of our afternoon chats. 'They would bring a human head into my shop, put it on the counter and ask for money to take it away. Then they'd go and play football with it. The rebels never took Bo but the Kamajors were just as bad.'

During our travels we had caught intriguing glimpses of secret society activity. In Bissau we had watched a truckload of boys being taken off into the bush. Wearing nothing but loincloths and painted from head to toe in white chalk, they were celebrating their departure with delirious singing and dancing. In Freetown one morning we had seen a devil from one of the women's secret societies. The size and shape of a human adult, its body was covered by a black raffia gown tied in at the waist by a belt strung with jangling bells. On its head it wore a black, two-faced wooden mask, its lips pursed and narrow eyes staring blankly ahead and behind, and in its right hand it carried a black and red stick. Although the devil was a terrifying sight, a group of young women were jauntily following it, clearly not in the least afraid. As it strode down the middle of the street, female passersby stopped to give it money. Men, on the other hand, scattered for cover as soon as they saw it, for it is said that any man who approaches a female devil will find his genitals swelling up painfully (I too kept my distance).

Stranger still was our brief sighting on the road to Bo of a teenage boy in a white loincloth and headband whose right arm appeared to be covered in blood. He was standing with two others, smiling serenely. We were later told that the boy was a member of the Soko Bana secret society, whose tricks include gouging out initiates' eyes or intestines before reinserting them into the body with no ill effects. The Soko Bana, found mainly in the north of the country, are spoken of with hushed awe, even by Christians. 'They are very powerful, they can do incredible things,' Jim told us in our Freetown hotel, his smile failing to mask his disappointment that such forces can exist in a world ruled by God.

Westerners have been trying to penetrate the mysteries of secret societies since they first set foot on the West African coast. They have had little success. A seventeenth-century Spanish Jesuit friar lamented that the societies have 'such secret rules that to date we have no information about them, and it is almost impossible to find out the secret.' Members who have divulged information to outsiders have often disappeared, presumed dead

– in 1680 a Dutch trader reported that even those who are merely curious might be 'fetched away by the spirits and killed.' Whistleblowing is no less perilous today; Joseph had graduated to a high rank in his own society, but although frank and open about other matters he had refused to tell me any details about this part of his life. 'It is too dangerous,' he explained. 'I can't take the risk.'

In the past hundred years or so a hazy, still incomplete picture has emerged of how the societies operate. The first and most important step is initiation. Every year, or every few years, a group of uninitiated boys or girls are taken from their village by a cadre of masked elders and sequestered for several weeks in the bush. Recruits are usually teenagers, but can be much older. Their departure, like that of the boys we saw in Bissau, is feted with dancing, drumming and singing, and also sometimes with tears – not everyone who disappears into the forest will return.

The details of what happens in the bush are murky. Over the centuries there have been rumours of human sacrifice, or of initiates dressed as leopards emerging from the forest to commit murder, leaving scratch marks on the corpse as a calling card. In the 1930s Graham Greene heard that a young girl had been killed by members of a Gorilla Society; twenty years later, an English colonial official reported that two members of a Baboon Society had been hanged for carrying out a ritual execution. Even today one occasionally hears of such killings, although the authorities are keen to hush them up.

It is usually impossible to confirm these rumours by talking to graduates of the societies, but in Bissau I had met a born-again Christian, Mario, a small, beady-eyed, middle-aged physician whose new faith emboldened him to share with me some of the secrets of his own initiation. 'I'm not afraid any more,' Dr Mario proclaimed as we sat one morning in his herbal medicine clinic. 'I don't believe in those spirits now.'

He recounted his experiences with relish. 'I went into the bush for a month before the rainy season with ten other boys. Every member of my tribe, the Balante, must endure this. Different tribes go at different times, and boys and girls go at different times. Your family send food and clothes with you, but it is the elders who take you and it is their responsibility to bring you back safe.' Recruits' self-preservation abilities are severely tested. I had been told that among some tribes, groups of initiates would disappear into the forest knowing that one of their number, as yet unidentified, was fated not to return alive. 'It is a trial,' explained Dr Mario, who had also heard of this tradition. 'You have to go through it to reach manhood. You learn how to act in society and cope in adversity. For example, so that you will be able to survive in a famine you are forced to eat three-day-old food that might be full of worms. You are beaten with sticks until you obey. Sometimes people fall sick and die, sometimes they are taken by wild animals, sometimes they die after being circumcised.' (Both male and female circumcision take place during the weeks in the bush, with no doctors in attendance and rudimentary tools shared across the whole group.) 'Most people come back though,' the doctor added reassuringly.

The initiation process was a transformative experience for Mario. 'You learn many useful things,' he said. 'You learn to hunt, make traps for animals, identify witches and cast out evil spirits. You learn about farming and about natural medicines, and how to use spells to ward off curses. And you learn social skills, like how to deal with colleagues and friends and how to speak to and respect your elders.' Wrenched from the succour of their family environment, initiates grow up quickly. The difficulty of the experience and the need to withstand it as a group encourage them to put their community first, ahead of themselves and their families; although a brutal ordeal for those forced to undergo it, the period of seclusion is considered vital for community survival. 'When you finish you are delighted to have made it through alive, and to have passed so many difficult tests,' Dr Mario said, his smile, many decades on, still containing a hint of wonder that he had come through intact. 'It is very satisfying. Now you are a man.'

I asked him about ritual murders. Like many others, he had heard about human sacrifices but attributed them to other ethnic groups. He admitted, however, that Balante boys, before they are circumcised, must show that they are ready to be men by stealing from people of other tribes. 'You have to show your bravery. You must steal cows or goats from the Fula or Mandingo. This is dangerous. Sometimes you have to kill people in order to steal from them, but once you have completed the task the women of your village admire you for it. They fall in love with you when you tell them how you accomplished it.'

The work of the secret societies does not end with initiation. Those who graduate to a high rank play a vital role in their communities. They make decisions on the appropriate times for planting and harvesting, rule on disputes, help their fellow alumni to acquire jobs or land, and perform religious ceremonies. When a community is threatened the secret societies organise its defence, and when it is damaged they take charge of repairs. In the wake of Sierra Leone's civil war, when the world was collapsing around them, the societies helped keep communities together, and community members from losing their minds. Male societies rebuilt shattered villages and helped ex-combatants reintegrate into their families. Female societies held cleansing ceremonies for women who had been raped or abducted as sex slaves, bathing the victims in sacred rivers and purifying them by sacrificing animals.

Not all secret societies survived the war, however. The rebels, bent on both overturning the old order and wreaking revenge on the Kamajors who were so closely linked to the societies, targeted the sacred sites and tools with which village elders kept the old flames burning. Shrines, masks, medicine chests and other appurtenances were burned or smashed to pieces. The elders themselves – the upholders of tradition - were also a prime quarry, and they were the slowest to flee when the rebels came calling. As they were hacked to death in their thousands, centuries of secret knowledge - the glue that had held their communities together - went with them to the grave.

32

Bo has no obvious visitor attractions. Its central market, however, nestling in a labyrinth of narrow alleys behind Ali's store, is an impressive sight. On its stalls - wooden tables under corrugated-iron roofs held up by poles - can be found an assortment of foodstuffs, all divided into small piles. Once your eyes adjust to the darkness it is a colourful scene. There are succulent pineapples, yellow tomatoes, sesame seed biscuits, dried chilli peppers, smoked fish, unsmoked fish, gobs of peanut butter, tough white cassava tubers, sheaves of green leaves, black eyed beans and the hard, pouting red or white kola nuts which, used variously as medicine, stimulant, symbol of hospitality, currency, peace offering (white kola) and challenge to war (red), are such a fundamental part of social interaction in this part of the world.

The market is populated almost entirely by women and girls. At one end of it, the alleys open out onto sunlit lanes where the female vendors sit not behind tables but on low stools or stones, their wares laid out before them on the ground on scraps of sack or in baskets or tubs. They compete for business with the many ambulant hawkers who sashay between them, buckets or crates piled high with produce balanced on their heads. Most of the women have children with them, either strapped to their backs, their little legs and arms splayed wide like tree frogs, or sitting near them on the rough ground. One baby boy sits watching the scene from a washing-up tub. Older children run around playing. Their shouts and laughter blend with the voices of their mothers, who cry out their wares in a discordant but sweet sing-song.

Ebru and I sit for a while on a low wall outside a water seller's shop, behind a row of seated vendors. In front of us, a well-built fishwife kneels on the ground. An old woman squats beside her to fill a yellow plastic bag with little shiny fish, presumably to sell on elsewhere. A palm oil seller further along the row is also doing good business, pouring the thick, reddish liquid from a jerrycan into bottles proffered by her customers. Between them a plantain seller crouches amid a jumble of baskets and tubs. The women are stocky, their faces serious and unsmiling. They wear plain vests or blouses over long, flower-patterned calico skirts of green and yellow and purple and blue, which hug their bulging thighs like clingfilm. Scarves matching the skirts are wrapped around their heads. They treat their customers civilly but with slight impatience, as if keen for them to move on so they can make the next sale. 'The market mammies,' said the Ghanaian president Kwame Nkrumah in the 1950s, 'occupy a very important position in this semi-capitalist society of ours.' The women in Bo are fully aware of their standing, and will not gladly suffer loiterers.

Nor will they tolerate anyone who interferes with their business. The owner of the water shop is a lone male in a female fastness. He is not attracting much trade, and has come to the conclusion that the problem stems from customers' reluctance to climb over the market mammies to reach him (he has perhaps seen the scowls and heard the grumbling that greet those who try). A small man whose eyebrows are raised permanently in a look of disappointed surprise, he bravely ventures forth and asks the palm oil seller to move a couple of feet to her right, to create a clear path between the main thoroughfare and his store. At first the woman is silent, her frown hardening slightly, like drying cement. Her defence begins quietly, as she explains gruffly to the man why it is impossible for her to budge, but rapidly gathers momentum as the effrontery of his request sinks in. She lifts herself slowly off her haunches and looms within inches of his face, loudly asking what gives him the right to ask her to move. Before long she is joined by her colleagues, the fishwife and the vendor of plantains. The women stand around him shouting, like footballers haranguing a referee, outraged that he has disrupted their business and challenged their occupancy of the street. The poor man cowers timidly before them, evidently regretting his imposition. He soon retreats to the safety of his shop. 'Women are problematic,' he sighs as he shuffles past us, defeated, his eyebrows raised higher than ever. The three mammies, far from being pleased at seeing him off, continue chuntering crossly among themselves for some minutes after his surrender.

33

While their women are working or shopping in the market, the men of Bo are out at the diamond fields. Diamonds account for half of Sierra Leone's exports. Most are found by small artisanal miners who dredge river beds or dig deep pits in the hope of finding the one large stone that will lift them and their families out of poverty. It is dangerous, backbreaking work - a few days before we arrived in Bo, a river bank had given way, drowning a dozen men who were digging in its lee - but in one of the poorest countries in the world the risks are deemed worth running. 'It would take five years to earn in farming what you can make in one second from diamonds,' says a young miner we meet in a bar. 'It's the only way you can raise yourself up.'

Over a breakfast of tea and omelettes one day in our hotel, we are joined by Johnny and Lucy, who are mining to the east of Bo. Johnny, a strong, bulky former security guard in his forties, was born in Sierra Leone but has spent most of his life in southern England. He is cheery and enthusiastic, full of energy, and talks about his work with a childlike innocence. Lucy, his pretty, brunette Australian wife, is calmer and more businesslike, her focus on the nuts and bolts of the mining operation a foil to her husband's grand plans. They have been in Sierra Leone for a year now, learning the ropes - neither has worked in mining before. 'We'd been thinking about it for a while,' Johnny says in his thick London accent, his large eyes and round cheeks making him appear younger than his age. 'Neither of us had jobs in England that we were desperate to keep so we just thought, why not? You've got to take the risk.'

On arriving in Sierra Leone they took advantage of Johnny's family networks and found a one-acre plot of land beside an ancient watercourse in the forest near Bo. They paid the local chief a few hundred dollars for a five-year lease, and then went to Freetown to acquire a mining license. The licensing process is part of the government's post-war effort to clean up the diamond trade, but the message has not yet permeated officialdom. 'The bribes we had to pay doubled the cost of the license,' says Lucy with a resigned laugh, already attuned to the country's ways. 'The officials just asked us for bribes outright. "Do you have something for me?" they'd say, and if we wanted to get anything done we'd have to hand them some cash.'

Although the new measures have made it harder for warmongers to smuggle and sell diamonds, they are not yet universally applied - two of the plots neighbouring Johnny and Lucy's mine are being dug by unlicensed foreign miners, who are hoping that bribes they have paid to local chiefs will protect them from government inspections. There is little incentive to play by the rules. Possessing a license gives you responsibilities but not rights – it obliges you to declare the diamonds you find and have their provenance certified, but does not give you exclusive ownership. Local people have advised Johnny to evacuate Bo in haste if he finds a large stone. 'If the authorities hear about it they come in a helicopter and confiscate it,' he says. 'You have to hurry to Freetown to have it certified and wrapped up. If you're too slow you'll lose it. Even if you have a license, there's nothing you can do.' On the plot next door last year, a Lebanese miner found a thirty-carat stone, worth several million dollars. Aware of the danger he was in he immediately fled, without paying the chief or his employees the commission they were owed. The chief, scarred by the experience, no longer gives leases to Lebanese.

Stories like the latter give Johnny, Lucy and all the other speculators hope, and the motivation to plough on despite the obstacles (other stories, like that of the American who mined nearby for two years and found not a single small stone, are quickly forgotten). Johnny is also staking out a gold mine in the north, but it is diamonds that keep him awake at night. 'Gold is easy,' he says, his words echoing Ali's. 'It's there in the ground, there's plenty of it. It's a steady income. Diamonds are risky, but you might hit it big.'

They invite us to accompany them to their mine for a day (Johnny, revealing his gambler's mentality, says he hopes we will bring them luck). They have to be there to oversee the sifting of diamonds from the gravel dug up from the pit. This process only happens in Johnny and Lucy's presence, for they do not trust their workers sufficiently to allow them to sift without supervision – 'they would steal from me in a second if I turned my back,' Johnny says. Before we leave he asks us not to tell anyone in the hotel where we are going, for it can be dangerous to let people know you are mining. We jump into his jeep and head east along the Chinese road.

Before we visit the mine, we must first stop to pay our respects to the chief. We turn off the highway onto a jagged red-dirt track which winds through the jungle to a small village. Little mud houses with conical straw roofs crouch in the shade of palms, cassia and ironwood trees. The trees' foliage is so thick that only a few slender shafts of sunlight filter through, dispersing into an ochre haze as they bounce off the dry earth. As our car pulls up, a crowd of children and women quickly gathers around it. They stare silently at us as we climb out. There are no men to be seen – they are all out at the diamond fields - until somebody calls the chief, who emerges from a doorway and greets us with a handshake. He is of middle-age, wizened and unsmiling, and wears only a pair of ragged trousers. He invites us to sit with him on a large tree stump. Johnny would rather be at the mine and seems restless, but he goes through the motions and asks the chief how things are going, and they talk without warmth for a few minutes. Lucy, her long hair tied back from her broad, olive-skinned face, fetches a bottle of rum from the car, and Johnny hands it to his landlord. Although they have paid him for the lease, they explain later, the chief is very demanding and always asks for gifts or money. Knowing that he could tear up the contract at any time, Johnny and Lucy reluctantly pay up.

The chief accompanies us to the mine. It is a few hundred yards from the village in a clearing in the forest. Around it is an area of low scrub, perhaps once used as farmland before being abandoned in the diamond rush. We park the jeep and approach the mine, the rhythmic clink of metal on rock punctuating the silence of the forest. The pit, a forty-foot deep inverted pyramid the size of a small football pitch, is a large brown scar, a blemish in the bright green of the bush. It has been dug by hand, with pickaxes and spades. Its steep walls reveal the different layers of rock, darkening from a tan colour at ground level to slate-grey lower down. At the bottom lies a pool of greenish water. It is down here that the richest "gravel" is found.

The pit walls are terraced but have no supports – mine-owners here are under no obligation to ensure the safety of their employees. Dotted around the narrow ledges, barefoot and without helmets, are Johnny's diggers, fifty lean, well muscled men from nearby villages who work six days a week for a daily wage of ten thousand leones (this equates to less than three dollars, but Johnny tells us it is fifty percent more than most mine-owners pay).

The men rotate tasks. The diggers in the pit fill metal, wok-shaped pans with gravel, which to the untrained eye looks like mud. These pans are transferred on porters' heads to the washing area, a large pool of brown water down the hill from the main pit. It is in this stagnant pond that Johnny and Lucy's fate will be decided, for to finance their venture they have borrowed money from family members back in England, and if the washers do not turn up any diamonds they will be unable to repay the debt, much less live a life of opulence.

Johnny shows me yesterday's haul. The first stone resembles an undistinguished lump of glass, the second a tiny brown rock (this one will be sold not as jewellery but for industrial use in cutters or drills). I try to hide my sense of anticlimax, but then Johnny pulls another stone from his pocket. Although uncut, it is beautiful, flawless, and already looks like a diamond. As I hold it in front of my eyes and turn it in the sun, its different facets glitter beguilingly. Lucy tells Ebru that it is worth several thousand dollars. Her face glows with pride, as if she is lauding the achievements of a beloved child.

I begin to see the allure. You come to Africa, hire cheap and easily replaceable labour, and with minimal equipment and no need to worry about safety regulations or trade union pressure, buy yourself a shot at a life-changing fortune. The costs are low, the potential profits stratospheric. The excitement, moreover, is constant: from one minute to the next you could get rich. Johnny and Lucy have been coming here day after long day for several weeks now, but each time one of the washers finds something in the mud and holds it up for inspection they jump from their seats and rush over, hearts pounding, to take a closer look.

Of all the workers at the mine, the six or seven entrusted with washing the gravel are the stars of the show, the fourth leg in the relay. All the diggers' heavy toil, all Johnny and Lucy's years of planning boil down to this. Unlike the other miners, the washers have names, identities. One is called Whiteboy, because his skin is paler than the rest. Tall, languid and expressionless, he wears a torn Brazil football shirt and, despite the intense heat, a green woollen cap. Another is Commander, who fought with the rebels in the war and wears a khaki hat and combat trousers to prove it. They work under the watchful eye of Mohammed the foreman, who has been employed by Johnny's family in various roles for years. In contrast to those he supervises, Mohammed is conspicuously lacking in brawn, but his eyes are shrewd and piercing under his broad-brimmed straw hat and he has little trouble keeping control of the fifty recruits.

We take seats in front of the washers, like film directors on a movie set. The atmosphere is serious, businesslike, urgent. Johnny, as superstitious as any gambler, asks for yesterday's lucky washer to be brought from the pit. Dressed only in black shorts, the young man trots over to us and takes his place alongside Whiteboy, Commander and another strapping youth. They wait while the gravel is hosed down to separate out any large and valueless rocks before being dumped onto their sifting trays. The trays are wide and round, with a gauze base and bamboo frame. The washers stand in the brown pool, bend at the waist and submerge them in the murky water. Gripping the frames tightly they begin tipping them, from side to side and front to back. The loads are heavy, but the washers make it look as easy as winnowing corn. As they sift, the excess mud floating off into the pool, they slowly lift the trays above the water's surface, occasionally, and heart-stoppingly, tossing the entire contents a few inches into the air so that any diamonds, which are the heaviest of stones, will sink to the middle of the gauze base. Once most of the mud has been removed, leaving just a scattering of pebbles of different sizes, the washers rest the trays on the bank of the pool and examine what remains. Johnny, nervous, stands up to watch more closely. The washers sweep their fingers from side to side over the bigger stones, their hands moving lightly and swiftly like metal detectors. If there is no large diamond among these stones, they are discarded and the washers turn their attention to the thin layer of remaining gravel. It is here that a diamond is most likely to appear. The washers know that if they find anything valuable they will receive bonuses – cash, a mobile phone, a CD player, perhaps even a car – and their concentration is intense. Amid what to us appears an amorphous crust of pebbly wet sand, they can discern even the tiniest gem. 'They have been doing this all their lives,' Lucy explains, less impressed than we are. 'They have an expert eye.'

When a diamond is found it is held up for Mohammed to inspect. He brings it over to us, and Johnny, his face glistening with sweat in the heat, grabs it excitedly and passes judgement. When a good stone is unearthed, he yelps with joy and wonder and enthusiastically chivvies the washers to produce more, as if they have some influence over what is in their trays. More often, however, he is disappointed. 'It's so small, so small,' he groans, unable to comprehend why the life-changing stone he knows is in there somewhere has once again refused to reveal itself.

During our day at the mine, the washers find six diamonds. Two are tiny grey pebbles that will be used for industrial purposes; the other four, which at present look more like sugar crystals than shimmering jewels, will be sent to India to be polished. Larger stones are sent to a polisher in England, who is more expensive than the Indians but cuts with greater care, and if a very large diamond is found it will be sent to Antwerp to be laser cut. So far, Johnny admits, the harvest has been steady but unspectacular. In nine months of washing they have yet to find anything bigger than a five-carat stone. This is not negligible, but nor is it enough. They have not sold a single diamond, and have had no income for two years. They are considering switching their attentions to the gold mine in the north in search of more reliable returns. 'It's not easy,' says Johnny with a grimace. 'We need to make money soon or we'll run out of funds and won't be able to keep either the gold mine or the diamond mine going.'

Closure of the mine would be bad news for the workers, and towards the end of the day, perhaps sensing Johnny's anxiety, Commander and Whiteboy, the star washers, begin loudly to discuss their future. Commander remarks that it would take him a year to earn what the tiny stone Whiteboy has just turned up will fetch in the diamond dealerships of Freetown. He talks about leaving Sierra Leone for Guinea in search of a better life (like his peers, he is always for hire, always on call: a rebel fighter one minute, a diamond miner the next, an exile as soon as a better offer comes along). Their talk makes Mohammed and Johnny nervous. Fearing that Commander may be plotting theft to fund his escape, perhaps by hiding a diamond between his toes, in his mouth or in his upturned trouser leg, Mohammed moves the troublemaker to a new position directly in front of him, under his nose. As we leave the mine Johnny tells his foreman that hereafter Commander must dig the pit, and should not be allowed in the washing area. Mohammed agrees, and the indiscreet rebel's plans are for now snuffed out.

A few weeks later in Freetown we would meet Johnny and Lucy again. This time they seemed fraught. The largest diamond they had found since our visit was of only two carats. Because they had had to dig so deep to find any worthwhile stones, both the cost and the time taken had exceeded expectations, and to keep the diamond operation afloat they had had to dip into funds they had set aside for the planned goldmine. They had now decided to cut their losses and close the pit near Bo for a few months, and were preparing to travel north in search of gold.

The experience had scarred them. They talk of gold fondly, as if discussing a loyal friend. Towards diamonds their feelings are more complex. Diamonds are capricious, elusive, an unrequited love. When they talk about them they appear perplexed, unable to understand how such a deep mine at such a fertile site can refuse to throw up the gems they seek. They cannot banish from their minds the thought of their Lebanese neighbour - visions of him holding aloft his huge, multi-million dollar rock haunt their dreams, forcing them to persevere. After the rainy season, they tell themselves, it will be their turn to celebrate (for a moment they even consider reopening the pit before then, despite the high risk of pit walls collapsing during a downpour). All it takes, as they repeatedly remind each other, is one stroke of luck, one little glint of light in the mud.

We spend our last afternoon in Bo drinking warm beer in an outdoor bar. As we are about to leave, two middle-aged Russians swagger in and sit at the table next to us. They resemble villains from a James Bond film. One is pot-bellied and balding with bad teeth, the other wiry and lean and hard, with leathery skin and violent, icy blue eyes that look like they have seen and shrugged off many things. The men are in jocular mood, and talk loudly to the waiter in Krio. They order beers and tequilas, and raise their tequila glasses in a toast before downing the contents and shouting to the waiter to bring more. Between bouts of raucous laughter they sit quietly, looking smug, reflecting on the deals they have done or the treasures they have found. They order a third tequila, and then a fourth. It has been a good day out at the diamond fields.

34

Kenema, a small town in the far east of Sierra Leone near the Liberian border, is a relatively short *sept places* ride from Bo. Our journey to it is unusually comfortable. Ebru and I have the front passenger seat to ourselves, while the driver shares his seat with another customer. A few hundred yards before every checkpoint we stop to set this passenger down, so that the driver will not be fined for overloading. The passenger walks through the checkpoint and then jumps back in once we are out of sight of its guardians.

Although an attractive place, bordered as it is by the forested Kambui hills and with mango, palm and cotton trees lining the road into town, Kenema, even by Sierra Leonean standards, is hot. The hills trap the heat and block out any breeze. Most buildings are of one storey, so there is little shade. And there is no electricity, and therefore no fans. Stepping out into the street, the dense, broiling air hits you like a sandstorm, leaving you drenched in a permanent coating of dust-speckled sweat.

We spend most of our time immobile, attempting to conserve energy and keep from overheating. Fortunately, opposite the hotel in whose echoing corridors we are the only guests, a friendly tea shack allows for just such stasis. Squashed between a bicycle repair shop and a hut selling mobile phone top-up cards, the tea shop, sheltered by a tin roof held up by poles, is a haven of shade. In front of its small, enclosed kitchen area on a tiny covered veranda sits a single table flanked by two wooden benches and covered by a pink plastic cloth. A low surrounding wall protects this area from the dust of the street. Above the open entranceway, on a wooden board, the legend, 'Welcome to Patteh's Attaya, Tea and Coffee Base,' welcomes sun-weary visitors.

We order attayas (the local name for green tea). The owner of the establishment introduces himself with a handshake as Mr

Patteh. Diminutive and wiry, his small, almond-shaped face lit up by squinting but bright eyes, he is dressed casually in tracksuit trousers and a white vest. He is young and serious, obviously eager for his business to succeed, and stays to chat after serving our drinks. He stands before us on the opposite side of the table as we talk. Before long the conversation turns to the secret societies in the villages around Kenema, which as we speak are rounding up young men for this year's initiations.

Patteh has never undergone the initiation rites and is critical of the societies' power. 'It is very expensive to send your children to secret societies,' he explains, his voice high and slightly strained. 'My parents do not have enough money.' His mother and father are farmers, and therefore poor, but the societies insist that initiates' families send enough rice to feed them for the full three or four weeks of their seclusion, and enough fuel and clothes to keep them warm. 'They make life very hard for farmers,' Patteh says. 'You grow rice but you have to send most of it to the societies. You might have two sacks and you have to send one of them, so you run out of rice yourself. If you want to eat you have to ask someone else for a bag on credit, and tell him you will pay back two bags from the next harvest. So next harvest you go hungry again and have to take more credit.'

The societies' demands sink farmers into a cycle of hunger and debt, but few can elude their clutches. 'My brother still lives in our village,' Patteh says, 'but every year when the time comes for people to be taken into the forest he comes here to Kenema. He is here now. In the big town we are safe, but if you are in the village they can physically force you to go. You can be sleeping in your house at night and they come and surround the house. They bark like dogs. It's frightening. You have to jump over the wall to escape.'

Patteh, who is a Muslim, says the societies are so powerful that Islamic leaders are reluctant to criticise them. 'Imams say that those things you are doing are bad and that you shouldn't do them. They mean the secret societies, but they do not say it openly because it would be dangerous for them.' As a non-member, Patteh is ostracised when the time comes for making community decisions. 'They do not even think you are a man,' he says, vexed by the unfairness of the system. 'You cannot become a chief or a village elder unless you are a member, and when they are having their discussions they do not even want you around.'

He tells us about the war. When it started he was in his village in the south-east, close to the border. 'The rebels came from Liberia. We had heard rumours about them. We thought they had horns, that they were not human, that they were beasts from the forest. When they came through our village wearing red bandannas and carrying guns we realised they were human beings, but they were so violent. They burned down our village and started killing people. Many of my friends were killed.' Patteh was just six at the time – too young even for the RUF to conscript. Later in the war he fled to Gambia. 'It was a senseless war,' he says softly, peering into the distance, remembering who knows what atrocities. 'It started off as a fight for diamonds but became a fight over nothing. Everyone was fighting each other. You didn't know if the person standing next to you was a rebel, a Kamajor or an SLA soldier.' Another of his customers, who has taken a seat opposite us at the table and joined in the conversation, nods in agreement. 'Everyone behaved badly,' he says. 'The Kamajors helped us, but they did terrible things too. One day I saw them killing a Sierra Leone Army soldier in the street outside my house. They tore out his heart and took it away to eat it.'

Kenema and the surrounding villages were the scene of heavy fighting, for along with Kono to the north the district is the hub of the diamond industry. The town is replete with diamond dealers, its environs pockmarked with mines. Rebels, mercenaries, military juntas and Kamajors all took their turns at pillaging its treasures. By some estimates, the RUF earned over a hundred million dollars a year from diamonds, while exports from Charles Taylor's Liberia mushroomed, even though Sierra Leone's eastern neighbour has few diamonds of its own. So many of the rocks were plundered from the earth that today's miners are left to feast on scraps. In Patteh's tea shop, most of whose customers are linked in some way to the trade, the talk seldom strays from the scarcity of worthwhile stones. 'You need heavy machinery these days, to dig deep or dredge the rivers,' says a miner down from Kono. A Fula diamond dealer named Ahmadou tells us that you used to find gems by the side of the road, but that those days are long gone. 'You need a lot of luck now,' he says. 'Some people are even going back to farming.' Like Ali in Bo, Ahmadou has had to diversify into gold trading to tide him over until – 'inshallah' - the diamond price recovers.

Nothing in Kenema is untouched by the diamond industry. Everyone you meet is a diamond miner, or has tried his hand at digging for the stones in the recent past. Hangha Road, the long street which stretches north from the centre, is lined with the squat white bungalows of Lebanese dealers, with four-wheel-drive vehicles parked in their forecourts and generator-powered air conditioning units cooling the men negotiating inside.

Even the town's medicine men cannot ignore the precious rocks. Near the busy main market we meet Dr Abdulai Alai, who exults in the unusual alias of Mortalman Garage. He sits on a low stool in the dust by the roadside with his wares laid out before him. Behind him, tied to a wire fence, two large white sheets advertise the many services he provides. Mortalman, bald and round-faced and wearing baggy white pyjamas which give him the air of an Indian guru, describes himself as 'the only international herbalist in Sierra Leone.' 'The only one?' I ask, shouting above the noise of the traffic. 'Well, there are others,' he concedes, 'but I am the best.' The international dimension of his work involves travelling to Guinea, Mali, Liberia and Gambia to find herbs. He has just returned from a trip to Gambia, he tells me, turning down the radio next to him so he can hear me better.

His potions are arrayed on a sheet on the ground. Most consist of grey powder wrapped in little polythene bags. They look alike, but appearances are deceptive. Mortalman Garage has medicines for all ills. One of his powders will bring you luck in finding diamonds, another in digging for gold. He has herbal remedies that will fend off madness, relieve frustration, make you a good lover, cure bedwetting and dysentery, stop vomiting, heal snakebites, ease pregnancy and labour, and rid of you of nasty irritants like rashes, itching and ulcers. Each of these treatments is depicted in a colour drawing on the white sheets behind him. A diarrhoea potion, for instance, is illustrated by a squatting, half-naked man with a pained expression on his face, a tonic for bushmeat hunters by a smiling man holding up a dead rat. There are potions, too, for those subjected to juju curses. To be cured of 'damage from witch,' you must fork out thirty thousand leones, the equivalent of the average Sierra Leonean's weekly income. Relief from 'nightmares of bush devil coming into your dreams' will set you back a similar amount.

Mortalman finds the ingredients of his medicines himself. 'Cures come to me in dreams sent by God, and then I go into the bush to forage for the herbs and roots I need.' As we talk, a young Muslim man in a white skullcap comes up and purchases a small bag of grey powder. After he leaves I ask Mortalman what the powder was for. 'The boy is weak,' he replies gravely. He holds up a bent index finger and then straightens it to make sure I understand what he means.

In the street around us an audience has gathered - herbalists always draw crowds, and a herbalist talking to a white couple is doubly interesting. I express an interest in his tonic for gamblers, a ground-up purplish root. His rheumy grey eyes light up at the prospect of a sale, for this is one of his most expensive products. He tells me you must rub it into your cheeks late at night and then pray to God or Allah (his medicines do not discriminate). It costs a hundred thousand leones. 'It's very expensive,' I complain. 'Yes,' he nods enthusiastically, 'but it can make you billions!' I refrain from asking why he has not used the elixir himself.

Back in the tea shop, Patteh is dismissive of Mortalman's powers. 'There are many fraudulent juju men,' he sniffs. 'If he was good he would be at home with customers visiting him, not sitting in the street in the dust and fumes.' Although wary of charlatans, however, Patteh has no objection to genuine witch doctors. If he had the means, he says, he would go to Guinea to visit the medicine men there. They are the best in the region, and he believes a blessing from them would be of great help to his business.

While he was in Gambia during the war, Patteh had earned a good salary working in a clothes shop owned by his "brother" (brothers and sisters here may or may not be siblings – the terms can encompass more or less anyone you have ever had anything to do with). Then, towards the end of the conflict, he heard that Sierra Leoneans were being flown out to Australia. Such an opportunity was too good to pass up: Australia meant modernity, Westernisation, comfort – West Africa cannot compete with its lure. He returned via Monrovia to Kenema, but arrived too late for the evacuation. He tried diamonds instead, digging in the nearby Tongo fields with two friends. 'It didn't work out,' he says. 'We only found small stones. It wasn't enough to live on. I lost all the money I had saved in Gambia, so I came back to the town and started buying and selling kola nuts. I sold them to Fulas who would take them north and sell them in Guinea.' Patteh had briefly become part of the ancient kola trade, which as far back as the twelfth century stretched from the forests of Sierra Leone and Liberia where the bitter-tasting nuts are grown to the parched wastes of the Sahara, where they would be exchanged for salt, cloth, iron and slaves.

He gradually traded up, from kola to cocoa, which he sold to

Lebanese merchants in Kenema. Then, after the war ended, he had what appeared to be a lucky break. He left one war zone and landed in another, this time in Iraq, where along with a number of his compatriots he had been offered a job in a laundrette. 'I thought this would bring me good money. It was dangerous going there but we are poor - we have no choice. I earned a hundred dollars a month, but Jordanians doing the same work were earning a thousand dollars. We had been told that we too would be earning high wages, but they tricked us. They treated Arabs much better than Africans. So after five months we came back. I had saved two hundred dollars, and I used that to set up this tea shop.'

We sit on his veranda drinking attaya from large glasses. Children are draped over the low walls around us. Out front by the road, standing in the full glare of the afternoon sun, girls sell egg mayonnaise rolls and peeled oranges. The bicycle repair shop next door does a steady trade, its customers leaning against Patteh's shack while they wait. Patteh, who is now twenty-eight, learned the attaya business as a young boy. 'I went to school until I was thirteen,' he says. 'It was my ambition to learn and get educated. I loved school and I wanted to finish my studies.' It was not to be. His parents ran out of money. 'They told me I had to go out and earn a living. I wanted to stay in school but there was no support. It was a shame. Do you think I'd be sitting here in this tea shop if I had finished my education? No, I'd be out doing a proper job.' His story recalls that of Ibrahima back in Kolda – they toil hard, striving to push their boulder up the hill, only for some sadistic spirit to knock it from their grasp and send it tumbling back down to the bottom.

Like Sisyphus, they have no choice but to start again. Patteh left school and had his first spell digging for diamonds, then became an apprentice to a coffee and attaya seller. After the war interrupted that stage of his career, the hot drinks business was a logical next step when he returned from Iraq. It is not going badly, he says, although the last few months have been quiet. He works from eight in the morning until midnight, seven days a week. A few months ago he married a Fula girl from the north: 'Let me marry and get some help, I thought.' His wife sits in the darkened kitchen behind the seating area. She smiles gently at us, pretty and fine-featured like all Fulani women. On a good day, the newlyweds will earn twelve thousand leones between them (less than three dollars). 'We spend whatever we earn on food,' Patteh says. 'We are fighting for our stomachs.' I ask him if they plan to have children. 'Yes, but only two. I want to be able to look after them well and educate them. If we have more than two we won't be able to send them to school.' As we get up to leave, he refuses to take payment for the drinks.

35

Paul Collier, an economist at Oxford University, has calculated that half of countries that endure a civil war slip back into conflict within a decade of peace breaking out. Within twenty years, the majority have relapsed.

Sierra Leone has made it peacefully through the first post-war decade, but its prospects of remaining stable for a further ten years are in the balance. The Truth and Reconciliation Commission which was set up to investigate the causes and consequences of the war has observed that living conditions today are no better than they were before the conflict. Poverty, inequality and corruption continue to bedevil the country and cause intense frustration to the worst off. The divisions between rich and poor, city and village, east and west and young and old remain, and are reflected in the bitter rivalry between the two main political parties. On our return to Freetown we hear rumours that the governing APC is arming and giving military training to supporters in advance of the next election, and will fight to stay in power if it loses. Rudderless ex-combatants, many of whom have been only superficially reintegrated into society and are not yet accepted by their still-damaged communities, provide a fertile recruitment pool. Alfred, our downtown bar-owner friend, warns of the dangers posed by these multiple potential flashpoints: 'It is like an oil spill on the road,' he says. 'You never know where the spark that sets it alight will come from.'

Many Sierra Leoneans believe their compatriots are too scarred by the war to entertain the idea of taking up arms again, but even if that proves true of those who fought last time, it is easy to see how the next generation might grow restive. I remember Alex's villagers, unable to resolve disputes without resorting to violence. I see and hear the fierce and jarringly frequent arguments in the streets of Freetown. And in thinking about the rush to modernise, which has filled the capital to bursting point and stripped its new inhabitants of their identity and sense of belonging, I recall the ominous words of Kapuscinski, who observed that 'the person living in a mass society is typified by anonymity, lack of social ties, indifference towards the Other and, as a result of losing his cultural identity, defencelessness and susceptibility to evil, with all its tragic results.'

A meeting with the head of the Sierra Leone Women's Movement a couple of days after we arrive back in the capital deepens my unease. We visit the Movement's headquarters above a downtown café in the hope of finding out how women are recovering from the war, and are surprised to be met at the door by a bald man with a paunch. He shows us into his flat, which doubles as an office, and introduces himself in a clipped, precise English accent as Nestor Cummings-John. He is dressed casually in a loose white vest, tracksuit trousers and flip-flops; with his clear green eyes and small, delicate mouth, he gives off a slightly feminine air. His office is a clutter of books, papers, radio equipment, and wires. He takes a seat on a black armchair and gestures to us to sit on a sofa facing him.

I ask him why the Women's Movement is run by a man. 'Faute de mieux,' he replies with a shrug. Having trained in Britain as a lawyer, he returned here to take over the Movement when his mother died. 'She was a founding member,' he says. 'She set it up with some colleagues in 1951. It used to have thousands of members, but today there are fewer than a dozen. Younger women didn't take up the mantle from my mother's generation and we can't find a woman to lead it.' Nestor is highly critical of the young. He believes they have been contaminated by a warped version of Western individualism which demands that you push others down at the same time as you yourself rise up. 'Running or joining a movement like this would require people to have ideals,' he says, 'but today people think only about their personal gain. They can't see beyond themselves, they can't think about bigger issues unless there is something in it for them.' When Ebru wonders aloud whether perhaps today's women do not have time to engage in activities that will not put food on the table, he is dismissive. 'That might be a part of it, but the people are not civilised. They have no consideration for others. It's all about what you can get for yourself. People want power and wealth, and they want it so that they will be in a position to harm others.' This is not the first time I have heard such a disturbing analysis. Nestor's words echo those of several other Sierra Leoneans I have spoken to, and also those of a Dutch woman I had met in Bo who had spent many years in the country working for an international human rights agency. 'People here are cruel,' she had said. 'They like to hurt each other. They prey on the weak.'

One can only speculate as to why this should be so. It may be that in such an insecure environment those who do well, who can never be sure that their success will last, feel they need to put distance between themselves and everyone else, to push others down so that they will have further to climb to dislodge them. Or it may be that the war has done away with innocence and community, and replaced them with a dog-eat-dog mentality. 'It is not enough that I succeed,' as Genghis Khan is reputed to have said. 'All others must fail.'

Nestor is bleakly pessimistic about the future. 'There is no society, no social cohesion,' he says. 'Men steal, women sell their bodies. Relationships have nothing to do with love - if you talk about love to a girl she will think you are a dreamer or a madman. The only thing that matters is what you can get financially from a man, whether he can buy you clothes or give you money to get your hair done.' As he talks I think of Musa, whose wife only smiles at him when he gives her money, and of Lamin, who cannot find a wife because of his poverty. 'Even three-year-old girls know their body is an economic asset,' Nestor continues, shaking his head in disbelief. 'In the nursery school we run, little girls flirt with me or with their male teacher and then ask us for money. Everybody thinks this is normal – even their mothers!'

The country's leaders set the example. 'There is corruption at all levels. It started under Siaka Stevens. He deliberately corrupted all levels of government, and the corruption worked its way down and infected the whole society. Then the war made it worse and got rid of any public spirit that remained. It has become every man for himself.' Even once-respectable professions have been tainted. 'Look at the judges. They are totally corrupt, but they know that if they are investigated they will be reprieved because the judges examining their case are corrupt themselves, and they won't want to open up a can of worms. Or look at university lecturers. They write or copy pamphlets instead of teaching, and sell the pamphlets to students. If you don't buy the pamphlet, they fail you.' He holds his bald head in his hands, laughing at the absurdity of it all. 'You have to become part of it or you will not survive,' he sighs. 'If you don't cheat, you will be cheated.'

Even the vaunted African family has come under strain. While in many cases it remains a vital source of sustenance – I think of Musa's warm relationship with his teenage daughter, Basheru supporting his parents back home in Guinea, Lalas looking after his mother and sisters, and Mame in the Bijagós sending money to her daughters in Senegal - cracks are appearing elsewhere. Parents send young children onto the streets to beg or hawk or rob. Mohammed the diamond miner's uncles and aunts steal from him in his sleep. Husbands desert their wives and refuse to support their children's upbringing. In-laws haggle over dowries. The RUF's targeting of the family institution by forcing recruits to murder, maim or rape their relatives quickened the pace of breakdown, but the process was already underway. As the competition for jobs, food, water and space heats up, the temptation to shed the familial burden, to strike out on your own, is growing. 'There is complete disorder,' says Nestor, rolling his eyes. 'The whole society is falling apart.'

Politicians make a show of melding the country back together by drumming up national pride. While we are in Freetown the government unveils a memorial to the war, a small park next to the Cotton Tree littered with kitsch, brightly-painted sculptures of village scenes, slave ships returning over the ocean, soldiers advancing bravely, and a judge holding up scales of justice. Beneath the soldiers is a plaque. 'For those who gave up their yesterdays for us to enjoy our todays,' it reads. Above the entrance to the park is another plaque, welcoming visitors to this 'Monument in Remembrance of our Fallen Heroes and Heroines.' It is not clear to whom these inscriptions refer. Who are these heroes? Where were these great sacrifices? Did anyone emerge from the war with his reputation enhanced? Are the soldiers not better remembered for allying with the rebels, plundering the diamond mines, and massacring and maiming civilians? The politicians trumpet this effort to hoodwink their people as an example of how they are improving the country. Surprisingly, it seems to work: in the days before the opening ceremony large crowds gather to gawp at the garish sculptures. For a tiny outlay, the government – a government whose ministers travel abroad for medical treatment because their own country does not have functioning hospitals, whose leaders fly around in helicopters because the roads are too hazardous for driving, and whose subjects cannot understand the sculpture park's slogans because they have not been taught to read - has convinced the masses that it is doing something.

But it will take a lot more than sculpture parks to create a nation. Although a faint glimmer of national pride occasionally breaks through the gloom when the country's football team is in action or when people discuss the problems in neighbouring Guinea and Liberia, Sierra Leone as a nation has little reason to be pleased with itself. The pictures on the five thousand leone note – presumably intended to show off the country's achievements - tell a sad story. The first shows Sengbe Pieh, who led the revolt on the *Amistad* slave ship. This was undoubtedly a great achievement, but it took place back in 1839. The other pictures depict more recent happenings. One shows a diamond – the stone that fuelled the civil war. Another shows the Bumbuna Dam in the hills near Freetown, whose construction, beset by corruption and delay, became a symbol of government failure, and which still fails to provide the capital with a reliable supply of electricity or water. The final drawing shows the crumbling ruin of Fourah Bay College in the East End, one of modern West Africa's earliest universities - today only a third of Sierra Leonean adults can read and write. It occurs to me that the only things Sierra Leone has ever had to celebrate have been endings – the end of slavery, the end of colonialism, the end of dictatorship, the end of war – but that any rejoicing was quickly cut short as a new blight replaced the old. Throughout the country's existence, new beginnings have proved false dawns. There is no reason for its citizens to feel national pride, no reason to feel united, and as history barks its stark lessons from every corner, it is difficult for the modern-day visitor to be optimistic.

36

In the absence of any serious efforts by politicians to knit the country together, some sections of society have taken it upon themselves to rebuild. Musa is chairman of the market traders' association on his street. He resolves disputes, punishes miscreants (bad language and fighting incur fines), helps organise a savings club, and manages a disaster fund for traders in urgent need. Another group, which calls itself "Operation Wash Lunatics", collects madmen from the streets of Freetown and gives them a bath and a haircut to make them more presentable – the young street traders involved pay for shaving materials and soap from their own savings.

But perhaps the most palpable evidence that reconstruction is possible is provided by the Dollar Boys. Illegal, belittled by the formal banking sector and derided by their better-educated peers, these young entrepreneurs have come together, with no outside assistance, to create a thriving, well organised industry which not only lifts them and their families out of poverty but oils the wheels of the entire economy. The hope their example inspires, indeed, gives me pause, and makes me question whether my pessimism after speaking to Nestor may have been not so much a cool and impartial judgement as a nettled, irrational response to my own experiences here, to the repeated frustrations of daily life and the corroding effects of the heat, the hustlers and the assailing poverty.

It is impossible to move more than a few yards in central Freetown without hearing the words, 'Hello sir, change?' as a Dollar Boy accosts you, brandishing a large wad of greenbacks or leones. Day after day they are there with a smile and a propo-sition, just in case this happens to be the day when you need to avail yourself of their services. In their determination to do a deal they are tirelessly persistent, never giving up and never looking downcast as you reject their offer for the umpteenth time.

'Tomorrow then,' they shout after you confidently, before swiftly turning their attentions to a more promising target.

The Dollar Boys (they are all men, all young) owe their existence to the weakness of Sierra Leone's economy. One of the poorest countries in the world, its currency, the leone, is not highly prized abroad. Since it broke from its sterling peg in 1978 its value has plummeted: at that time, one pound sterling would have cost you two leones; today it would set you back six thousand. Sierra Leoneans with money are understandably eager to lay their hands on more stable currencies, as are importers and the few who are lucky enough to travel overseas. Foreign diamond dealers, on the other hand, as well as aid workers, tourists, and local people who receive remittances from relatives abroad need leones in cash (only the top hotels accept credit cards and there is just one international ATM in the whole country).

Those who wish to use legal channels for changing their money have the choice of banks or foreign exchange bureaus, but the spread is much narrower and the transaction therefore much cheaper if you use a Dollar Boy instead. Everybody knows this, and although their activities are illegal and they perform them openly and in broad daylight, Dollar Boys provide such a valuable service and have so many high-level clients that they have little fear of arrest.

Our Dollar Boy of choice is named Ahmed. He is in his mid-twenties. Like most of his colleagues, who often have to run alongside passing cars while conducting transactions with their passengers, he is slim and compact. On his temples, close to his lively, alert eyes, there are whisker-like scars, dark brown notches on the lighter brown of his face, from his days in the secret society bush. He walks the streets of the capital with a swagger, but in person is polite and shy. One day we take him to lunch at a shady outdoor café near the law courts, and he tells us about his career.

He started out five years ago, when a "brother" lent him some leones and encouraged him to find himself a patch. 'I started in the East End, but before long I moved to the business district downtown,' he says in his soft, respectful voice. 'I moved to a spot outside a foreign exchange office on Siaka Stevens Street. Our presence disturbed the forex people, and in the end they moved away to Howe Street. I've moved too since then, and I'm now at Russia Base.' Each Dollar Boy has a "base", a fixed point in the city from which he carries out his business. The bases are named after countries. Russia Base is on Siaka Stevens Street, near one of the country's largest banks (the Dollar Boys have no qualms about setting up in close proximity to the competition). 'It's a good spot,' Ahmed says. 'There are a lot of businesses around there and plenty of visitors from the western area of Freetown.'

He numbers among his clients importers and exporters, government ministers, and even banks ('sometimes banks do not have enough cash,' he explains, 'or their staff want a better rate to change money for themselves'). When I tell him I have visited the Ministry of Foreign Affairs for a visa extension, he says he knows the building well, since he provides a delivery service to officials there. He has customers, too, at the country's Central Bank, and tells us that every day the latter's governor sends an emissary to check the street rate of the leone. 'Sometimes the governor comes himself,' Ahmed smiles. 'He tells us to find jobs instead of undermining his currency.' These conversations usually end in laughter, with the Dollar Boys politely reminding the governor that there is no other work available to them.

Ahmed makes around twenty thousand leones (almost five dollars) each day, a decent sum by Sierra Leonean standards. On his best day ever, someone (probably a diamond dealer but he never asks questions) wanted to change fifteen thousand dollars into leones. Ahmed had to bring in other Dollar Boys to amass the requisite cash. 'I had to walk through downtown Freetown to deliver the money,' he says. 'I carried it in a big box on my head. I was pretty nervous, but it was OK.' He likes his work, but is worried about the future. 'The job is not forever. Today I have the ability to move around but tomorrow it might not be so easy for me to chase all these cars and run to all these customers.'

He sits at the table with his black sports satchel, full of money, on his knees. I ask him about the Dollar Boys' management committees. 'They started a few years ago,' he says. 'Some Nigerian soldiers who had stayed behind after the war asked a Dollar Boy to come to a hotel room. They killed him and stole his money. We carried the dead boy's body around the streets of Freetown so the government had to do something.'

Among the users of the Dollar Boys' services are senior policemen. After the incident with the Nigerians the chief of police advised them to set up a committee to protect themselves against physical threats and fraudulent customers. Each base now has a boss, who oversees the activity of all the Dollar Boys stationed there. The bosses sit on district committees, and at the top of the pyramid sits a central committee, headed by a tough Fula. The committees provide security to their members, ensuring customers treat them with respect - there have been no attacks since they were formed. They have also put in place a surveillance system, which warns those at other bases about suspected con artists. If a cheat slips through the net, an insurance pool into which all members make regular payments provides a financial cushion for any Dollar Boy defrauded of a large sum of money.

The committees have two other important roles. The first is to protect the industry's reputation, by investigating customer complaints, punishing bad behaviour and weeding out bad apples. The second is to vet new entrants to the market. In Sierra Leone, even to become an illegal moneychanger you need the right connections. The committees decide who to allow in and who to exclude. Too many Dollar Boys would reduce the profits of those already working in the industry, so the incumbents collude to keep out potential competitors. 'You can only become a Dollar Boy if somebody recommends you,' says Ahmed. 'If anybody tries to start up without a recommendation you ask him to leave. If he refuses, the committee asks him to leave.' If even that does not work, the central committee reports the interloper to the police and tells them he is 'acting illegally.' The police, who respect the committees, are usually sympathetic.

The contrast between the organisation and mutual support of the Dollar Boys and Nestor's forlorn women's movement is stark. Sierra Leone teeters between these two extremes, remaining at peace but remaining unstable. Out at Lumley Beach, the long strip of white sand which adorns the wealthiest part of Freetown, a handful of young men make their living by providing small change to taxi drivers. They are known as Coin Boys. The standard taxi fare from Lumley to central Freetown is eight hundred leones. Most passengers give the driver a one thousand leone note, meaning the driver must give them back two hundred in coins. Drivers buy their change from the Coin Boys, who charge three hundred leones for every two thousand they sell to a driver. Not long ago, the standard taxi fare went up, to a thousand leones. The Coin Boys immediately went out of business - from one day to the next their living was snatched away. Fortunately, after a few weeks, the fare was lowered again, but not before the Coin Boys had had another taste of life's uncertainty, of the fragility of control in this chronically unpredictable part of the world.

We spend our last two days in Sierra Leone at Lungi, near the airport. To get there we must take the rusting ferry. The boat's metal gangplank, over which cars and foot passengers must pass to board, does not quite reach dry land on the sloping ramp of the dock. This is not a problem for cars, but those on foot must negotiate a narrow strip of seawater, perhaps two yards wide and three or four inches deep, before they can reach the deck. Naturally in a country full of entrepreneurs, this creates an employment opportunity. Two teenagers stand by the edge of the water and give piggybacks to passengers who wish to board without drenching their feet. Hefty women straddle the thin boys' backs like sacks of grain as they are carted through the waves. Once deposited, they hand over a small tip and the boys come back for more. It crosses my mind that if the ferry's owners buy a longer gangplank the boys will be out of work, but for now they earn a steady, if painful, living.

From our hotel in Lungi we walk to the airport, carrying our luggage on our backs. As we approach the airport gates we are suddenly accosted by a tall, middle-aged woman. She is dressed in trousers and a loose shirt and carries a heavy-looking suitcase. She is screaming hysterically at us in Temne, her saliva splattering our cheeks. Her face is desperate, pleading, her eyes brimming with tears. She has lost her mind. Who knows what horrors she has endured? Within seconds she is chased away by shouting airport guards. One of them, a woman, ushers us inside the gate and slams it behind us. Two of her male colleagues grab the madwoman by the arms and fling her hard at the gate's iron bars. She crumples to the ground like a punctured lung. The female guard is holding a long stick. She asks us if we would like her to beat the woman with it. We beg her to desist, and she smiles and tells us the woman wants us to take her with us on the plane. 'She is crazy,' she says. 'She always does this. She has her bag packed, ready.' Outside the gate, meanwhile, back in the real, unprotected world, the woman, her dreams of escape once again thwarted, rises to her feet, picks up her suitcase, and walks silently away.

Burkina Faso

37

We fly back to Dakar, over the jungles of still-troubled Guinea and the winding rivers of Guinea-Bissau. In the plane we order two orange juices. After the Nigerian steward hands us one of them, Ebru and I, in unison, ask him for the other. 'I know,' he replies, surprised and slightly offended, 'you ordered two so I will give you two.' In Sierra Leone, alas, where such efficiency cannot be taken for granted, receipt of a second glass would be far from guaranteed; we have grown used to having to spell everything out in detail.

In the Senegalese capital, where we make a brief stopover, the young bargirl in David's hotel tells us her boss has returned to England for treatment on his legs. He has been gone for over a month, and she does not expect him back. Although we realise that it is better for him to be at home and within reach of functioning hospitals, we are sad to have missed him and his expatriate tales, which had given us a taste of what it would be like to carve out a new world for ourselves here. David's drinking, of course, he had brought with him from elsewhere, but his stories of touring Dakar's food markets picking out fresh produce and haggling in French over prices, of watching and learning from local cooks, and of the travails of setting up a business, with all the concomitant hassles, bribes and jocular arguments with officials, had provided an attractive glimpse of the life we could expect.

From Dakar we fly to Bamako, the noisy, traffic-choked capital of Mali, and from there catch a bus to Burkina Faso. Ten minutes outside Bamako the bus breaks down, and we settle down for a long wait in the dry heat of the Sahel. Accustomed by now to these things, we are less perturbed by the interruption to our journey than we might have been a few months earlier. We have water, there is shade in the lee of the bus, we will eventually reach our destination; there is no hurry. What else is there to do but wait? After only an hour or so another bus pulls up. It is headed not for our planned destination but a different Burkinabe city, Bobo-Dioulasso. The driver offers us a ride. Adaptability, we have learned, is a key survival mechanism in West Africa, and we gratefully jump in and bed down for a twelve-hour journey.

A good paved road takes us through the wilds of southern Mali. Big, hump-backed cows roam across flat fields between mangoes, bushy shea trees, eucalyptus and the occasional muscular baobab. The trees are spaced like oaks in an English deer park, but here there is no grass, just the hard red earth of Africa. The flat landscape is vast and open under a hazy, grey-brown sky, the pale ball of the sun obscured by a gauzy blanket of Saharan dust. After the dense hills and dark, snarled forests of Sierra Leone, the feeling of space and airiness is like freedom.

The Malian border guard, with whom we sit under a tree while he checks our passports, invites us to his wedding in Bamako the following month. He tells us it is high time we had children, and then allows us to resume our journey. Our bus continues southwards, down through the villages of north-western Burkina Faso, towards the country's second city.

There is no compelling reason for Burkina Faso to exist as a country. It has no overwhelmingly dominant ethnic group, no unifying religion, there are no obvious geographical barriers dividing it from surrounding nations and, unlike the Portuguese and British enclaves of Guinea-Bissau and Sierra Leone, five of the six countries it borders share the same colonial heritage. Landlocked and lacking significant natural resources, the French only occupied the territory because it provided a convenient bridge between their coastal colonies to the south and their desert holdings in present-day Mali and Niger (then known as the Soudan). For a time, indeed, in the 1930s, the land the French named Upper Volta ceased to be, carved up between more important neighbours and only re-emerging as a country when her colonial masters grew worried about the increasing influence in the region of radical nationalists from the Ivory Coast.

But despite these flaky beginnings, and despite six coups d'état in the first thirty years after independence, Burkina Faso's sixty ethnic groups have held together peacefully. Although they live in one of the poorest countries in the world, and although a massive increase in population and the steady encroachment of the Sahara have intensified the struggle for food, water and jobs, Burkinabes, unlike the citizens of many other West African countries, have neither risen up in armed rebellion nor plummeted into civil war. And whereas their peers in Sierra Leone and Guinea-Bissau are rushing to the cities in search of modernity and the bounties of the West, the vast majority of Burkinabes, few of whom have ever switched on a light or turned on a tap, still reside in their ancestral villages, growing or rearing their own food, battling the hard soil, the merciless sun and the Saharan dust storms, getting by. Burkinabes, like the working-classes described by George Orwell in 1930s England, have 'neither turned revolutionary nor lost their self-respect, but merely have kept their tempers and settled down to make the best of things on a fish-and-chip standard.'

In the villages we pass through, set back from the road and reached by narrow trails between the trees, women stand outside their compounds and pound millet with long pestles. The square or rectangular compounds vary in size. Some contain just one house, others two or three; the tan, single-storey mud houses grow out of the earth like giant termite mounds. Each compound is enclosed by a chest-high mud wall, with a thatched, round granary where food is stored between harvests sitting like a turret in one corner. Chatting to the Malian man sitting next to me, I praise the beauty of these dwellings, huddled like little fortresses against the desert winds. 'They are not beautiful,' he replies brusquely, surprised at my naiveté. 'They are hard work. They have to be retouched every year, before and after the rainy season. It takes a lot of time. If you have a brick house it lasts for years and you don't have to do anything to it.'

It is a land of dry riverbeds, nibbling goats, pecking guinea fowl and wandering cows. In the late afternoon light the infinite plain is cloaked in a warm, comforting glow. Twists of smoke rise from the compounds as the evening meal is prepared. Small groups of people sit under trees, talking. The villages have mosques in the Soudanic style, built of mud and with little wooden poles jutting like the thorns of a cactus out of the crumbling, spear-shaped minarets. Only the larger villages have roadside stalls - the inhabitants of smaller settlements eat what they grow or what they can barter for.

Nearing Bobo-Dioulasso the sepia landscape is suddenly interrupted by the brilliant green of a strip of rice fields, swaying in the breeze under a thin white mist. Flanking the fields is a line of darker green: spring onions. Effusive banana trees are dotted around. Trucks carry marrows and mountains of yellow tomatoes towards the city. As we move into the south-west of the country, closer to the jungles of the Ivory Coast, the land is growing more fertile. Some of the riverbeds contain water. The rice fields are inundated. The aridity of the north gives way to greener, lusher pastures.

We arrive in the city as night falls. After elbowing our way through the usual bus station scrum, we stand in the unlit road working out our bearings. In the darkness this is difficult, and we are relieved when a young Frenchman whom we will never see again offers us a lift to our hotel in his jeep.

38

Bobo-Dioulasso is Burkina Faso's second city. Although more sizeable than Bafatá, its counterpart in Guinea-Bissau, it too is little more than a large town, inhabited only during the part of the year when there is no planting or harvesting to be done in the countryside. At these times, villagers abandon their compounds and flood into Bobo's shady streets, eking out a living by trading and bartering or doing odd jobs in hotels and restaurants. 'People see the villages as home, not the city,' says Abdoulaye, a young man who runs a café near our hotel. 'As soon as it is time to plant the millet and the yams they will go back there.'

Although Bobo is an attractive, leafy town, replete with good, French-style cafés and eating houses and with a steady trickle of European tourists bolstering the local economy, there is tragedy everywhere you look. Gangs of barefoot boys roam the streets carrying tin can begging bowls. Impossibly young prostitutes wait for business outside bars. A young child sick with malaria stares listlessly from a doorway. A madman jumps up and down in the night-time traffic.

The town is full of madmen. One, whom we see often, is permanently naked, his gaunt body covered in a layer of yellow dust. One day we see him throw a nut or small stone onto the ground in front of him. He bends over, his naked buttocks exposed to the traffic, and peers intently at the object for several minutes, smiling mysteriously, before eventually walking away without it (his condition is not uncommon in this part of Africa; it is known by the Yoruba in Nigeria as *were*). Another man lies in the street in a red woollen hat, masturbating into his dungarees. One or two sing songs and dance, to the amusement of onlookers, but most sit on the pavement or walk around in silence, an absorbed look clouding their eyes.

Abdoulaye tells us that although the men appear placid, a few occasionally become aggressive. 'It is safer not to approach,' he warns. He says their families cannot afford to keep them or have them treated, and that while passersby give food and sometimes money, the government offers no help at all because mental health problems are not taken seriously here. I ask him if he thinks it is the stress of poverty that has made the men like this. He narrows his dark eyes and nods. 'Poverty, the heat, hunger. You have to be strong to live here,' he says.

Within a couple of days of arriving in Bobo I find my own resilience weakening. After the trials of Sierra Leone and our enervating experiences with the missionaries and phantom drug dealers, I had hoped that Burkina Faso, the last stop on our trip, would be reinvigorating. But the surrounding misery, the constant, guilt-inducing demands for our business or money, and the relentless high temperatures, which on most days climb above forty degrees in the shade, have wearied me. Instead of exploring a new land I want to have absorbed everything already; the prospect of going through that long process again holds little appeal, and I am too tired now to start up fresh conversations to find out how the country works. I sit with Ebru at a pavement bar, and things and people pass before my eyes without registering. Sights that a few weeks before would have enthralled me – the flowing robes of a Tuareg, Muslims at prayer in the dust, the grand old mosque near the river, and the buzz of the markets and the dimly lit night-time streets – these things that I had longed for years to see are now just a blur. Instead I think of home and family, of cool air and comfort, of anonymity and freedom from hustlers. The latter are the source of particular disquiet. After so many months of incessant attention it is difficult to maintain poise, to treat the latest hawker or beggar with the courtesy you showed the first. Pity the hustler who finds himself the last straw, the receptacle into which you pour your accumulated ire. He is not to know that it is not him you are raging at but the travails, the collected slights, of his continent. As he backs away, stunned, you curse yourself again: West Africa has won another little victory against you.

For respite we hire a motorbike one lunchtime and ride out on dirt tracks through dry forests to a river. We swim in the shade of bamboo stands, the cool, clean water speeding past us over its sandy bed. Red and blue damsel flies crouch on rocks in the shade. Tiny bats swoop to drink. In the still of the early afternoon there is complete silence, interrupted only by the croak of a frog or the buzz of a fly.

While we are sitting drying on the riverbank, a young man approaches and takes a seat on a tree trunk a couple of yards away. We greet him, and he sits watching us. He looks sheepish, bearing none of the confidence of youth, but after a few minutes he plucks up courage and asks if we have anything to give him. We tell him we have brought nothing with us, and he accepts our refusal as if that is what he was expecting. As he gets up quietly and walks away, another slow-worm of guilt burrows through us, for he has asked politely and with reluctance. Despondent and slightly ashamed, we get on the bike and ride back to the city.

The next morning I wake up feeling tense, and over coffee my mind takes a sudden dive. It is as if – and there are no doubt less hackneyed ways of putting it but this is the image that comes into my head - a small dark cloud has come over the sun. Despite the forty-degree heat a shiver courses through me as a feeling of cold dread ensconces itself in my mind. I have been through this once before, and the youthful suicide of a close friend has left me with an inordinate fear of its consequences. I start to shake, terrified of that spiralling descent into depths from which you cannot be sure you will resurface. Madmen drift by in the street, their hair matted and clothes hardened by dried dirt. They are the ones whose resilience has given out, who have been unable to withstand the strain. Am I to end up like them? Will the pressure in my head, too, reach bursting point, and my mind come loose from its moorings? My stomach tightens with fear, and I run to the bathroom at the back of the café. The large, bare room stinks of excrement. The latrine is in the far corner, impossibly far away across a glacier of filthy white tiles (I think afterwards of a scene from *Trainspotting*). I lunge across to the sanctuary of the toilet bowl and vomit around it.

For a few minutes this relaxes me, but on the way back to the hotel it happens again - the tension, the heat, the knotted stomach, the fear racing far ahead of its cause. This time I make it to the shade of a mango tree before vomiting in the dust (I look around to see if anybody has witnessed my capitulation, but fortunately the streets are quiet). The journey from slight tension to panicked desolation has taken just minutes, but the road back to stability seems dauntingly long. I can think of nothing else: escape from the mesh of bleak thoughts is the only thing that matters. I try to focus on making it through the next hour without deteriorating, then the hour after that. I try to come up with reasons – sunstroke, heatstroke, fatigue – to persuade myself that it is just a wobble, a physical rather than a mental problem, and that control, momentarily lost, can be regained. After many hours and several more vomiting fits, and buttressed by Ebru's constant reassurance, this ploy eventually slows my fall (I am in no state to argue with myself). We make plans to move on from Bobo and to head for the capital, Ouagadougou, where there is an international airport within a few hours' flight of home.

I am not the first traveller in West Africa to be brought low by the trials it puts in your path. The French colonists had a word for the condition, "soudanité", a feverish state brought on by the isolation, the ennui, the debilitating heat of the Soudan, and the accumulated effects of alcohol and disease. Large numbers of colonial administrators and military men succumbed - usually, of course, after much longer and more taxing stays in the region than my own. Writing during the colonial era, Auden described the tropics as a 'test for men from Europe.' Of those who undertake this trial, he added, 'no one guesses who will be most ashamed, who richer, and who dead.' Sometimes the fever spilled over into insanity, and Conrad's fictional Kurtz became terrifyingly real.

The explorer Mungo Park may have been an early victim. On his first expedition to the region in 1795, the Scot, travelling alone, had displayed almost superhuman patience and tolerance. Despite being robbed by bandits and village chiefs, beaten by fanatical Muslims, and held hostage for four months by Moors, he maintained an extraordinary equability and understanding of his assailants' motives. 'It must not be forgotten,' he wrote, 'that the laws of the country afforded me no protection; that everyone was at liberty to rob me with impunity; and finally that some of my effects were of as great value, in the estimation of the Negroes, as pearls and diamonds would have been in the eyes of a European.'

Park had a limitless store of courage. After escaping from the tyrannical Moors he had to hide out for weeks in the bush, avoiding all human contact for fear of being turned in to his former captors. He wandered with his horse through the parched Sahelian scrub, with nothing to eat or drink for days. With the scorching sun showing them no mercy, man and beast soon came to the brink of death, but even at his lowest point the explorer was able to muster compassion for his equine companion. 'As I was now too faint to attempt walking and my horse too fatigued to carry me,' he wrote, 'I thought it but an act of humanity, and perhaps the last I should ever have it in my power to perform, to take off his bridle and let him shift for himself.' The effort of removing the bridle made Park dizzy and nauseous. He fell to the ground, feeling as if 'the hour of death was fast approaching.' As he lay there on the burning sand, his mouth as dry as acacia bark, he contemplated his fate: 'Here, then, thought I, after a short but ineffectual struggle, terminate all my hopes of being useful in my day and generation; here must the short span of my life come to an end. I cast, as I believed, a last look on the surrounding scene; and whilst I reflected on the awful change that was about to take place, this world and its enjoyments seemed to vanish from my recollection.'

He was saved, miraculously, by a freak thunder storm – he quenched his thirst by sucking on the clothes he had laid out to soak up the rain – and was rewarded for his forbearance when a few weeks later he located the Niger and established that, contrary to European belief, it ran from west to east. 'Looking forwards I saw, with infinite pleasure, the great object of my mission: the long sought for majestic Niger, glittering to the morning sun, as broad as the Thames at Westminster, and flowing slowly to the *eastward*. I hastened to the brink, and having drunk of the water, lifted up my fervent thanks in prayer to the Great Ruler of all things for having thus far crowned my endeavours with success.'

Park's second trip to the region, nearly eight years later, was not so blessed. On this mission he had two objectives: to chart the entire course of the Niger and to find the fabled city of Timbuktu on the edge of the Sahara. From his first visit he had learned the importance of coming prepared, and this time he arrived at the Gambia not alone but accompanied by forty-five European soldiers, servants and carpenters (the latter would build the boats in which they would descend the great river), and with plentiful supplies of food and gifts. Crucially, however, the voyage was delayed until the rainy season, when dangerous diseases flourish, and by the time Park reached the Niger for the second time three-quarters of his men had died of malaria or dysentery. The handful of bedraggled survivors boarded canoes at Bamako. One had been driven mad by the soudanité, the remainder were weakening by the day.

On his first trip, Park's apparent love of Africans was undimmed by their repeated attacks on his person and posses-sions ('whatever difference there is between the Negro and

242

European in the conformation of the nose and the colour of the skin,' he had written after observing a tearful reunion between an aged mother and her son, 'there is none in the genuine sympathies and characteristic feelings of our common nature'). But by now his attitude had changed, and he made a decision which betrayed his deteriorating mental state. Instead of continuing to haggle his way out of trouble with gifts and money, he switched to a murderous scorched earth strategy whereby he and his men would avoid all contact with 'natives' and shoot on sight any who hinted at malicious intent. Dozens of those with whom he would once have patiently reasoned and negotiated were felled by his muskets; the great explorer had finally lost his equilibrium, his spirits at last worn down.

When he reached Timbuktu, the city of which he had dreamed for so long, Park did not disembark from his canoe, but instead rowed past without so much as a glance. In his last letter to the British Colonial Office there are none of the fascinated descriptions of local customs and geographical features that had lent such colour to his earlier missives. Reaching the end of the river had now become the sole object of his thoughts; his bravery had degenerated into a suicidal recklessness. 'I shall set sail for the east,' he wrote, 'with the fixed resolution to discover the termination of the Niger or perish in the attempt. Though all the Europeans who are with me should die, and though I myself were half dead, I would still persevere, and if I could not succeed in the object of my journey, I would at least die on the Niger.'

Die he did, either drowned when failing to negotiate a treacherous stretch of rapids or, more likely, murdered by a hostile tribe. He had covered over a thousand miles by canoe, but was still hundreds of miles from the mouth of the river (within a few decades of his death the discovery of quinine as a treatment for malaria would enable later travellers safely to chart the river's course, down to its swampy delta on the steaming coast of modern-day Nigeria). Park's exact fate remains unknown. When, several years after his last letter, reports of his demise reached Scotland, his son, Thomas, did not believe them, and in 1827 he made for West Africa himself, intending to rescue the missing explorer from captivity. Days after arriving on the Guinea coast, however, Thomas was dead, having fallen victim to malaria. No further attempts were made to locate his father.

39

Perhaps the most notorious of the soudanité's victims was Paul Voulet, who in 1898 led an expedition to acquire the western Sahel - the vast strip of semi-desert that linked the coast of Senegal to distant Lake Chad - for France. A young, ambitious officer who saw in the enterprise an opportunity to cement his growing reputation and accelerate his rise through the ranks, Voulet had fought in what is now Burkina Faso two years previously, defeating the king of the Mossi and razing his capital, Ouagadougou, to the ground. These exploits had drawn widespread acclaim in Europe, and Voulet was a logical choice to lead the new campaign.

France's motives for colonisation were complex. As well as the usual economic considerations – her West African colonies exported palm oil, rubber, timber, cotton and cocoa – there was also a "mission civilisatrice", a civilising mission, the effort to remake Africa in France's own image. Under slavery, the Europeans had wanted Africans' bodies, which were set to hard physical labour until they dropped dead of exhaustion. Now they wanted their minds. The Victorian-era urge to tame nature found its natural expression in the attempt to curb the native's wildness, to put an end to his barbaric traditions. 'For colonialism,' wrote Frantz Fanon, 'this vast continent was the haunt of savages, a country riddled with superstitions and fanaticism, destined for contempt, weighed down by the curse of God, a country of cannibals.'

Such a vision was buttressed by science. As late as the 1950s, in a report published by the World Health Organisation, the psychiatrist J.C. Carothers described the African as a 'lobotomised European,' who 'makes very little use of his frontal lobes.' Half a century earlier, A.R. Wallace, who had collaborated with Darwin to unveil the secrets of evolution, predicted that the 'lower races' would soon be wiped from the earth, for they would be unable to modernise in time to withstand the onslaught of civilised peoples (in a similar vein the British Prime Minister of the time, Lord Salisbury, proclaimed that 'one can roughly divide the nations of the world into the living and the dying'). Colonialism would hasten this evolutionary inevitability: either the inferior races would be assimilated or they would disappear, their extinction leaving the way clear for the enlightened human society that had annihilated them to roam the earth in peace.

Those Africans who refused to be civilised were brought into line by force. In 1849 the French massacred the entire population of the Algerian town of Zaatcha. Three years later they repeated the feat in Laghouat. Paul Voulet learned from these tactics; after capturing Ouagadougou during his first visit to the region, he used summary executions to instil fear and respect into his new subjects. These techniques were lauded back home, and on his second expedition he ratcheted up the violence. This time, however, his methods would prove unpalatable even to his superiors.

Voulet began in Senegal with just a small band of men. His government was reluctant to provide a large army, and it was left to the young officer to gather whatever troops he could on arrival in Africa. Using a combination of force and promises of pillage and power, Voulet, a short, moustachioed, slightly rotund man who carried in his luggage books about the military triumphs of Julius Caesar and Alexander the Great, gradually amassed a significant fighting cohort. The army expanded as it advanced, adding to its numbers at every village it passed. On reaching a settlement Voulet would send out a patrol to surround it. Anyone who tried to escape was shot dead, his head impaled on a stake to strike terror into the survivors. The Europeans carried machine guns and rifles, the villagers either slow-loading muskets or mere arrows and spears; surrender was inevitable, and the patrol would return to camp with a fresh supply of fighters, porters, concubines (the thousand-strong force had a harem of six hundred women), and slaves.

As the army grew, it became more violent. At one village, after six of his soldiers had been killed while attacking its inhabitants, Voulet took revenge by having twenty women and babies speared to death. At another, in retaliation for the wounding of two of his men, he took thirty women and children captive and ordered the extermination of the entire male population (as proof that they had carried out his orders, Voulet demanded that his men bring back their victims' hands, a custom that would be mimicked a century later by Sierra Leone's rebels).

Early in 1899 the campaign reached its nadir (at around the same time, Joseph Conrad was finishing *Heart of Darkness* in far-off southern England). At the village of Birni-N'Konni in modern-day Niger, Voulet's men went on a murderous rampage. They made their way along its little lanes, raping, burning and looting. By the time they had finished, not a single inhabitant was left alive: hundreds of men, women and children had been killed. It was one of the worst massacres in French colonial history.

Voulet himself was becoming increasingly unhinged. When he heard that his superiors, worried that their *mission civilisatrice* had gone astray, were sending a more senior officer to replace him, he announced that he was breaking his ties with France. 'I am an outlaw now,' this real-life Kurtz told his men. 'I disavow my family, my country. I am no longer French. I am a black chief. Africa is large; I have a gun, plenty of ammunition, six hundred men who are devoted to me heart and soul. We will create an empire in Africa, a strong impregnable empire...They will never dare to attack me.'

Voulet's replacement, a Lieutenant-Colonel Klobb, made his way down through the Sahel with a force of fifty men. He pursued his quarry for fifteen hundred miles, accompanied at every turn by the acrid stench of death. He came across burned out villages, charred corpses, cooking fires strewn with children's limbs, and hanged women dangling from trees 'like black husks.' The remains of guides and porters who had displeased Voulet were dotted along the route like milestones; they had been strung up alive at a height where their feet could be reached by hyenas' hungry jaws. At Birni-N'Konni, the site of the massacre, Klobb and his men were horrified to find more than a thousand corpses rotting in the afternoon sun.

When he finally caught up with Voulet, Klobb addressed the renegade's men, reminding them of their duty to uphold the honour of France. Voulet responded by ordering them to shoot the intruder, and Klobb fell dead on the sand. This was not the end of the matter, however, for within two days rumours of mutiny reached the young officer's ears. Furious, he gathered his troops together and harangued them, berating them for their disloyalty. As he raved at his men he began shooting at them with his pistol. Eventually they shot back, and Voulet's reign of terror was over. When news of the atrocities committed in the name of France reached Paris, there was a public outcry. The embarrassed government ordered the Minister of Colonies to conduct an inquiry. Its conclusions were published three years after Voulet's death. They blamed his actions squarely on the soudanité.

40

We take the bus to Ouagadougou. Unlike Guinea-Bissau and Sierra Leone, Burkina Faso has coach companies plying the main routes between towns - there is no need here to cram into the back of a *sept places* or stew for hours waiting for a minibus to fill up. Miraculously, our bus leaves Bobo on time, and we settle into our comfortable, pre-assigned seats for the six-hour journey.

It was Bruce Chatwin, I think, who wrote that the psychological benefits of movement are a legacy of our nomadic past, and an hour or so into the journey I am less fraught, my mind less cluttered as the slight rocking of the bus lulls me into calm. After several days of grey apathy (Ebru would later tell me that my state of mind had so worried her that she had hidden our penknife for my protection), I even feel a little of my enthusiasm for the trip returning, and begin again to take in something of the country.

A few miles outside Bobo-Dioulasso there is a military checkpoint. This is burdensome for travellers: our bus is stopped for a few minutes while the driver's papers are checked, and passengers of smaller vehicles must get out and show their identity cards. The checkpoint lengthens journey times, increases costs for business traffic, and hurts the pockets of those whose documents are not in order. As it takes away, however, it also gives, for sitting on the ground around it are a dozen market women, selling peanuts, onions, fizzy drinks, mangoes, bananas and other provisions. There is also a small café. If the checkpoint closed, all these women and the owner of the café would go out of business, but while it is in existence it helps share out some of Burkina Faso's meagre wealth. Bus and car passengers could, of course, buy mangoes and bananas in the markets of Bobo instead, and if they did, the economic effect of closing the checkpoint would be neutral. But they surely buy more than they otherwise would merely because the women are there and the buyers have time to kill while waiting for their papers and vehicles to be examined (I, for one, buy a bottle of fresh yoghurt that I do not need). Since those who can afford to drive or travel by bus are in general better off than those who hawk in the dust, therefore, it seems likely that the checkpoints play a part, however small, in smoothing the country's economic imbalances. Thinking thus, moreover, makes the delays easier to tolerate.

The long journey to Ouagadougou gives one more than enough time to examine the village architecture of western Burkina. The houses and compounds are smaller and scruffier than those in Mali. Many of the mud walls are crumbling or have collapsed, and each village has a scattering of dwellings that have been abandoned, perhaps when they became too dilapidated to repair, perhaps because the inhabitants moved away or died. But in contrast to Sierra Leone and Guinea-Bissau, where we saw entire villages lying empty, here there are new houses being built, and new urn-shaped granaries topped with fresh yellow thatch. For Burkina Faso is one of Africa's least urbanised societies. Whereas almost half of Sierra Leoneans and Guineans live in towns or cities, four in five Burkinabes live in the countryside. The rural areas are crowded - the country's fertility rate, at an average of six children per woman, is among the highest in the world, and in the past half-century the population has increased five-fold. Everywhere you look, even in the remotest regions, you see people, tilling the parched fields, pumping at wells, driving herds of cows through the scrub, or simply walking or sitting.

As we leave western Burkina behind, the land begins to dry out. The trees shrink and become more scrub-like, the fulsome mango, its still-green fruits hanging like yo-yos, replaced by squat acacia whose bright yellow flowers provide a rare injection of colour. Under the trees the ground is bone dry. Lakes are reduced to large puddles, rivers to chutes of sand. When we stop for a refreshment break and step out of the bus, we are knocked back by what we think is a gust of hot air but soon realise is the normal weather of central Burkina Faso. It is as if you are stepping into the blast of a giant hairdryer. The air is so thick with heat that if you reach out you feel you will be able to grab big handfuls of it, like mounds of burning ashes. People we had met elsewhere in West Africa had warned us about Burkina's cripplingly high temperatures. Are you sure you want to go there at that time, they had asked. You know it's going to be hot? It's even hotter than Mali! You like the heat then? Having planned the trip for years, we had had no choice but to come, and we hoped that if we respected the heat it would treat us kindly in return. We had been worried about its physical effects, from which we thought wearing hats and keeping covered up would protect us, but had not bargained for its effects on our minds.

41

Only the most sadistic psychiatrist would recommend Ouagadougou as a retreat for a patient recovering from the soudanité. The city is one of the oldest on the planet. It feels like the end of the world.

Look at Ouagadougou on a map and you will see an orderly design, a grid of long, straight avenues punctuated by parks and the occasional monumental square or large government building. The map, however, is deceptive. In reality, the wide, flat avenues trail off into nowhere, attractive only to the winds of the surrounding plains. The parks are nothing more than empty brown wasteland, neither a blade of grass nor a tree to be seen. But the biggest deception of all is that for long periods each year the visitor to the city can see none of this, for the cartographers have neglected to make reference to the harmattan, the great Saharan sandstorm which for several months each dry season, as it carries its grainy load from the dunes of the desert out into the Atlantic, smothers the whole of West Africa in a choking, ochre haze.

Ouagadougou is on the harmattan's frontline. Day and night the city is caked with grime. As you haul yourself through its asphyxiating heat, thick clouds of dust rush down the avenues to embrace you. Women pull up scarves to cover their mouths, men don plastic facemasks. The sounds of cars and motorbikes are muffled, as if they are gliding along with their engines switched off. You can see no more than a hundred yards. We watch a street sweeper shuffling along in a black headscarf, black mask, black overalls and with a black broom cradled in her arms like a rifle. Only her eyes are visible. It resembles the set of *Blade Runner*. The entire city is shrouded in a permanent grey-brown fog. Even the sun, normally so fierce, is blotted out, a pale disc behind a dirty muslin veil. The defiant can eyeball it with comfort, although the sun will not quickly forget this slight and will re-emerge with still greater fury once the storm has passed.

Ouagadougou's hawkers are unbowed by the dust. At every turn you are greeted with a loud 'Mon ami!' or 'Mes amis,' a 'Bonjour!' or, less judiciously, a 'Les blancs!' There are hundreds - no, thousands! - of them, on every street corner, at every junction, outside every eating house or hotel, or just ambling along the pavements. In my fragile state I find it harder than ever to treat them all equally, politely, without rage. We try crossing the road when we see them approaching, but they cross too! We decline their offering but they keep walking with us, cajoling and pleading, pulling other objects from their satchels - other rabbits out of the hat - to tempt us into a purchase. 'Looking is free!' they say. 'Just have a look!' I wonder how they do it, how they can keep going through so many rejections, how they feel at the end of a bad day, and how they muster the energy to go out and do it all again the following morning.

None of these questions makes me feel any better. Retreating from the streets to our hotel room one afternoon, the guilt, the fear, and the shame at my weakness in the midst of so many far more difficult lives suddenly return. It is as if a switch in my brain has flicked the wrong way, plunging me back into gloom. As I sit on the bed, sweating onto sodden sheets, here again is that feeling of bleakness, of being drained, enthused by nothing, of being weighed down under a granite cloak. Here too the all-consuming selfishness, the harmattan of self-absorption, as recovery once again becomes the only thing that matters. I grow irrationally impatient with Ebru when she tries to help by talking and diverting my thoughts, and respond curtly to the hotel receptionist when he asks how my morning has gone. As the minutes pass and my loss of control reaches its extreme, disturbing violent impulses enter my head and clamour for my attention; I have to shut myself in the bathroom to calm down.

I begin to half-wonder if I might have been cursed, if one of the many hawkers or beggars I have spurned over the past few months has cast a juju spell on me. Perhaps they felt that they had given me something – a greeting, a smile, the wish for a good day, company – and that by rejecting their requests for help I had broken the ancient code of reciprocity. Kapuscinski wrote that 'the unreciprocated gift lies heavily on the head of the one who has received it, torments his conscience, and can even bring down misfortune, illness, death.' But it is too late now for me to heed the wise Pole's warning.

I seek distraction in a dry political science book, discarding a more risky novel in which any allusion to breakdown or depression might pitch me deeper into turmoil. I cling to small improvements. The book occupies my mind for a while and this brings temporary relief. When it stops working, however, and my thoughts again wander, it is as if another rung on the ladder back to safety has snapped, and I fall a little further. I realise, of course, that as a writer all this angst puts me in distinguished company, that it will make me appear a more sensitive and tortured soul, but this provides no consolation; all I can think of is getting back on an even keel, back to the shallow contentment of old.

In the late afternoon we decide to make for the airline office, to enquire about bringing forward our flight home. It feels like defeat, and I am at first reluctant, but when Ebru reminds me that it might be prudent for us to be in a country with a functioning health service I grudgingly agree. As we emerge from the hotel into the furnace of the Ouagadougou streets, we pause for a fatal second to adjust to the change in temperature. I look to the right, and a seated hustler shouts, 'OUI!' at me, confidently and firmly, as if it is him that I have been looking for, as if he has the solution to all my problems. For the first time in days I laugh, and resign myself to my fate as he rises to sell me a model motorbike he has made from a recycled mosquito spray can.

42

The man in the Air France office tells us that changing our flight will be straightforward, and that once we have decided on a date we need only give him a few days' notice. This reassures us, and we resolve to take a few days to think it over.

The next morning dawns under the same grey fog. Mopeds and taxis ply the streets quietly, tentatively, as if after a snowfall or an air raid. Pedestrians inch along, covering their faces against the swirling dustclouds. It is easy to imagine a sudden powerful gust burying the entire city, perhaps the entire country, beneath a mountain of sand, to be discovered centuries later by excited archaeologists.

We take a bus to the outskirts of town. We are in search of a cemetery, of a man's grave. On the bus we meet Maurice, a civil servant who works in the finance ministry. Short and sturdily built, with a broad, weary-looking face, he is dressed in a smart shirt, pressed trousers and flip-flops, as if he grew tired of putting on clothes by the time he reached his feet. We fall into conversation. He seems surprised and pleased that we have chosen to spend our morning at the grave, and tells us that he himself visits it every year on the fifteenth of October, the anniversary of its occupant's death. When the bus breaks down a mile short of our destination, he says he will accompany us the rest of the way on foot.

The graveyard is one of the most desolate places on earth. We turn off the main road down a dusty alley between shabby brick buildings. The alley opens out onto a wasteland. Ahead of us lies a colossal heap of smouldering refuse. It is the size of a football pitch. Next to it a black tent under a tree houses a family, whose members peck among the rubbish, scavenging for scraps to sell. To the left of this festering pile the cemetery stretches off into the far distance. There is no gate, no grass, no flowers, a few dust-covered weeds the only colour amid the unremitting brown dirt.

Smoke from the burning tip billows over the mean, poor graves, most of them marked only by a brick or perhaps a little iron crescent moon. Some are unmarked, just small crumbling mounds of dry earth. The sky is veiled in the grey-brown dust of the harmattan. It is the same colour as the parched ground and the distant surrounding houses. As we walk through, the gritty wind batters our faces, mingling with the smoke from the tip. Black plastic bags flap around our legs like the giant crows of hell.

Maurice leads us over a small rise, and in the distance, through the fog, we make out a low cluster of whitewashed graves. Rectangular stone boxes under simple white headstones, they look spectrally pale in the brown haze. The twelve tombs, a few of them already crumbling, stand in a line, huddled together against the wild wind and swirling sands. In front of them, but very close, is another grave, this one painted in bright colours. A scattering of red pebbles on a background of military-fatigue green and brown decorates its surface. On one side of the grave is daubed the flag of Burkina Faso, a yellow star dividing horizontal strips of red and green; on the other the words, 'Père Fondateur de la Révolution,' Founding Father of the Revolution, are emblazoned in capital letters. And on the headstone is the name of a president.

The history of Africa in the second half of the twentieth century is strewn with dead revolutionaries. Lumumba in the Congo, Cabral in Guinea-Bissau, Biko in South Africa, Mondlane in Mozambique: all were feted as the saviours of their people; all were felled by colder, worldlier foes. These idealists, these visionaries with plans for the improvement of their countries were snuffed out before they could see their projects through. Their fervour, their energy, and the love they inspired in their people would prove insufficient defence against the Machiavellian manoeuvrings of the old guard, those grim-faced, calculating rivals who were still in cahoots with the hated colonial masters.

In Burkina Faso the revolutionary torch was taken up by Thomas Sankara. A charismatic, handsome army officer with an intense gaze and a burning zeal for change, it is he who lies here before us, beneath the headstone whose inscription reminds us of his humble rank of "Capitaine". Dynamic, impulsive and passionate for his country to be free, this ill-fated young firebrand is seen by many as Africa's Che Guevara, and still inspires adulation a quarter of a century after his death.

Sankara becomes president of Burkina Faso in 1983, after ousting the repressive military government in a bloodless coup d'état. He takes over a people whose hopes have been muzzled. Independence, that great eruption of optimism and joy, has been and gone, and Burkinabes are no better off, no freer. Two decades of corrupt and incompetent leadership have left their country penniless and indebted; to stay afloat it has been forced to beg for loans, first from the World Bank and the International Monetary Fund, and then, most humiliatingly, from France, the former colonial power.

Sankara, who sees these moneylenders as neo-colonialists engaged in a "reconquest" of Africa, dreams of throwing off the chains. Although he is just thirty-three years old and has no experience of high office, he tackles the task with relish. As soon as he comes to power he launches his revolution. He promises to bring development to all Burkinabes, and not just to the elites who are in league with the French. His people will no longer need foreign handouts or be fleeced by their own leaders. 'We do not want this aid that turns us into beggars and dependents,' he thunders, pumping his fist in the air. Peasants, women, the working classes and the young will break free and lead their continent to a self-sufficient, dignified future. 'Down with imperialism!' he cries as he rallies his spellbound followers. 'Down with the embezzlers of public funds! Down with toadies and thieving rats! Down with the ravenous jackals!'

The young leader has revolution in his bones. As a child he had celebrated independence by lowering his village's French tricolour and raising the new flag of Upper Volta; as president he replaces his ministers' Mercedes with the humble Renault 5, the cheapest car on the market. While other African leaders stash millions in foreign bank accounts, Sankara, whose cheques often bounce, draws a monthly salary of less than five hundred dollars and needs a mortgage to buy a home. While other African leaders buy private jets and lounge on luxury yachts, Sankara's most valuable possessions are a refrigerator, three guitars and the battered old bicycle he rides around Ouagadougou. And while other African leaders wear the finest suits flown in from Paris and Milan, Sankara, echoing Gandhi, dresses his ministerial team in homespun Burkinabe cotton. The youth of Africa lap it up.

It is Sankara who gives the country its name. The French had called their colony Upper Volta, a dry, geographical description taken from the three rivers that rise to the west of the capital. Sankara renames it Burkina Faso, the Land of the Honourable People. He wipes the colonial stain from the map and puts his countrymen proudly in its place. Burkinabes revel in their new-found importance, thrilled that one of their own sons is daring to stand up to Africa's historic oppressors, amazed that they, humble peasants, are in the vanguard of a movement that will transform the entire continent.

But the Revolution is not only about symbols. The corrupt institutions of power must be brought to heel, and Sankara is fearless in his choice of targets. He takes on tribal leaders by abolishing the tribute payments and forced labour they exact from their subjects. He takes on the political classes by cutting civil servants' salaries and launching an anti-corruption drive. He tells haughty army officials that they must 'live among the people,' and drags ambassadors out into the countryside to explain their raison d'être to mystified villagers. And he rattles foreign donors, and in particular the French, by telling them his country does not want their help and cannot afford to pay back its debts. 'Those who lent to us were playing a game of chance,' he explains unapologetically. 'As long as they were winning there was no problem, but now they've lost they squeal "unfair". They played, they lost. Those are the rules of the game. Life goes on.'

Having torn down, he sets about building up. Burkinabes lack the skills and physical strength to carry the Revolution forward, so Sankara builds schools and invests in healthcare, vaccinating millions of children against killer diseases. To boost agricultural productivity he breaks up feudal landlords' estates and parcels them out among the peasants. He plants trees to hold back the encroaching Sahara. Lithe and fit and rarely seen out of military fatigues, he darts around, full of energy, driving his people on and exhorting them to work harder, to produce more, to haul their country out of poverty. 'Consommons Burkinabe!' he cries, and backs his words by slapping a ban on fruit imports.

There is room on the revolutionary juggernaut for women, too. Africa will never develop, Sankara says, if half its people are treated like chattels. He promotes women to key government positions, reforms inheritance laws to give equal rights to male and female children, bans polygamy, and rails against female circumcision, a painful rite of passage for girls that can lead to fatal complications during childbirth. He instigates a national day for husbands to do the family shopping, and takes an all-female presidential motorcade with him when he tours upcountry. Already bewitched by his youthful good looks, the women of Burkina swoon.

We sit with Maurice on a rock by the grave, buffeted by dust, the only sounds the wind and the rustling of the flying plastic bags. A brown goat walks across one of the whitewashed tombs. People cycle past from time to time, wearing masks to keep out the dust and toxic fumes from the tip. There is a strong smell of burning plastic. A young mother walks by with a baby on her back, seemingly unaware of her proximity to history. 'She knows about him,' says Maurice when I wonder aloud whether today's younger generation are still interested. 'Everyone loves him except those who killed him.' I have heard many similar senti- ments. 'He was unique,' Maurice continues, staring wistfully at the gaudily-painted grave. 'He was the only African leader who worked for his people and not for himself. He was a martyr.' Back in Bobo-Dioulasso, Abdoulaye had given a similar endorsement. 'All African leaders are the same, except one,' he told me. 'Thomas Sankara wanted people to work, to prosper, to make Burkina Faso and Africa better. He was loved not just here but all over Africa, and even in Europe. But he was the last one.'

Sankara's dauntless optimism and attacks on the estab- lishment galvanise his people and give them renewed hope, but progress on the development front is slow. The Marxist economic policies adopted by many African governments had failed their people – as the rest of the world had grown richer, Africa had grown poorer. Sadly for Sankara, who embraces Marxism with gusto, the policies prove no more effective in Burkina Faso.

Marx called for industrial armies to improve the soil. Sankara, who idolises the peasantry, draws up a five-year plan for agriculture. Cotton and grain production duly increase, but where are the storehouses to preserve the extra stock? Where are the roads to take it to market? Where, indeed, are the markets? The president has not had time to build up the nation's infra- structure, and a third of the annual harvest is destroyed.

Marx called for the elimination of the wealth gap between town and countryside. Sankara obediently raises consumption taxes, paid mainly by urban dwellers, to fund the rural investment his country desperately needs. But urban Burkinabes are poor, too. How can they afford the higher prices of goods, and how can industry cope with the inevitable decline in demand? The president, putting ideals before pragmatism, has overlooked these concerns, and manufacturing and commerce plunge into recession.

Sankara is impatient to drive his country forward, but the eternal African barriers stand in his way. Decrepit infrastructure, an unskilled populace, a hostile climate and the quirks of colonial cartography which left Burkina Faso detached from international trade routes thwart his ambitions. To his bewilderment, and despite his tireless efforts, living standards barely improve under his watch.

As the economy stalls, rumblings of discontent are heard in the towns and in the countryside. With the decline of manufacturing, jobs in the cities dry up, and the urban middle classes emigrate to Ghana and the Ivory Coast. Muslim merchants, already irked by the Catholic Sankara's ban on polygamy, are given further cause for resentment when the state takes control of commerce. And in the villages, as the fruits of revolution fail to ripen and poverty continues to bedevil the population, the complaints of tribal chiefs grow louder and more defiant.

West Africa can warp even the purest intentions, and Sankara, frustrated by the country's slow progress, responds harshly. He sets up People's Revolutionary Tribunals, which inflict brutal punishments on critics of his reforms. He shuts down national newspapers, fires striking teachers, and executes trade unionists suspected of plotting a coup. His Committees for the Defence of the Revolution, which are sent into the rural areas to keep his people to the right path, administer justice randomly and violently, and use force to bully the peasants into working harder. Unrest in the villages grows.

Sankara, who although as nervous of criticism as any dictator has no desire to rule by force, admits that mistakes have been made. He attempts to rein in the Committees' excesses, but their degeneracy has added fuel to the fire of his growing list of enemies. At home, tribal chiefs and the urban elites; abroad, France and his fellow African leaders, whom he berates for their corruption ('there is a crisis in Africa,' he says, 'because some individuals deposit sums of money in foreign banks that would be large enough to develop the whole continent'); powerful forces are ranging against him, none of whom would regret his demise.

In the end, as in all great tragedies, he was betrayed by those closest to him. Blaise Compaoré had risen through the ranks with Sankara, and the two men were close friends. When Sankara had been arrested by the previous government, his friend was among those who freed him. When he had seized power shortly after-wards, his friend led the military wing that ensured the coup's success. And while Sankara governed as president, his friend served as his second-in-command and Minister of Justice.

But Compaoré was a pragmatist, Sankara an idealist, and in Africa it is the pragmatists who survive. An old black and white photograph shows the two men saluting a military parade. Sankara seems out of his depth, looking uncomfortable, even slightly schoolboyish, in a high-collared army jacket. His youthful, fresh face is rapt with concentration as he puffs out his chest and gamely tries to act out a part for which he is unpre-pared. Next to him, tall and wiry, stands a stern Compaoré, his feminine lips pursed as he haughtily surveys the troops. Although he is two years younger than his comrade, it is Compaoré who appears the worldlier, the more suited to his role.

While his boss was busy with revolution, Compaoré plotted to replace him. He curried favour with the dictators his colleague had spurned, strengthened his ties to the army's disaffected officer class, and secured the crucial support of the French. These power blocs were neither popular with nor concerned for the Burkinabe people, but their backing was all Compaoré needed. With the imperial powers and their African stooges ranged against them, Sankara and his impoverished masses stood little chance of holding their ground.

The young president was aware of the danger his friend posed. In his later photographs he is sombre, his large eyes narrowed in thought. In an interview in the autumn of 1987, while talking of Che Guevara, he said: 'While revolutionaries as individuals can be murdered, you cannot kill ideas.' A few weeks later his mood was darker still. 'The day you hear Blaise Compaoré is preparing a coup against me,' he advised a group of journalists, 'do not try to warn me – it will be too late.'

Within seven days he was dead, gunned down on a sunny October afternoon by a military hit squad. Twelve of his colleagues perished with him. They lie here in the cemetery with him now, as close in death as they were in life. The plotters took over the airport and the state radio station, and that evening, as the dead men were being dumped in an unmarked grave, Blaise Compaoré declared himself president.

The assassination is shrouded in silence. According to his death certificate Sankara died of natural causes, and despite years of campaigning by his family and supporters there has never been an official inquiry. Compaoré always denied being involved in the murder that brought him to power. Seemingly oblivious to the coroner's verdict, he expressed his shock at the 'brutal attacks' on his comrade. He claimed that although Sankara had betrayed the Revolution, rendering his removal from office unavoidable, the transition was intended to be peaceful, and his soldiers had disobeyed orders. To this day many observers, including the French and supportive leaders elsewhere in West Africa, accept this version of events, describing the assassination as a coup attempt that 'went wrong,' an accident. Few openly hold Compaoré responsible for his colleague's death.

Maurice has no doubt who was to blame. 'How could thirteen deaths be an accident?' he scoffs. 'Everyone knows he was killed deliberately. He was too popular just to be left in prison. They had to kill him.' The exact truth may never be known. Several of the soldiers thought to have carried out the shootings have since died in mysterious circumstances, their testimony accompanying them to the grave. The only survivor of the attack, who escaped because the plotters thought him dead, still lives in Ouagadougou but does not talk. What is not in doubt, however, is that Compaoré was both the driving force behind the coup and its main beneficiary. He would have known better than anyone that his comrade remained popular, and that if he had been allowed to live the clamour for his reinstatement would have been impossible to quell. Compaoré needed Sankara off the scene, and his soldiers obliged. As so often in Africa, his supporters looked the other way.

As we are about to leave the cemetery, an old man in a mask and a red woollen hat pulls up on a moped. He dismounts, nods at us in greeting, and walks over to one of the whitewashed graves. It bears the name of Somda Der, Sankara's young driver. The man stands over the grave with his eyes closed and his head bowed in prayer, the dust swirling around his fragile frame. Twenty-three years after his relative – perhaps his son, perhaps his brother - was shot dead, he has not forgotten him. After he leaves, Maurice tells us that if a dead person comes into your thoughts or dreams, you should go to visit his grave. 'He must have had a dream last night,' he says, as the old man and his moped fade away into the haze.

Once the fallout from the assassination had subsided, the new regime began to co-opt the dead men's memory in an attempt to give itself legitimacy. Sankara is now a "Hero of the Revolution", and he and those murdered with him were reburied in the individual graves we see before us. But the graves are untended; they do not look like those of a president and his men. The anniversary of the deaths, moreover, is marked by no official ceremony (on the twentieth anniversary in 2007, when Sankara's wife returned to the country for the first time since his death, the internet was closed down for several days, dissenting voices gagged). It is as if Sankara, all his energy and fervour extinguished, has been left behind by his erstwhile friend, consigned to the silence of history.

Burkinabes have not forgotten, however. Sankara's legend has grown in the years since his demise. His economic failings and the brutality of his revolutionary committees are largely overlooked; what has remained is the memory of the hope he instilled in his people. In Ouagadougou's main market the day after our visit to the cemetery, I ask a young stallholder if he knows where I can find a Thomas Sankara T-shirt, as a souvenir of my trip. The boy is delighted, and excitedly relays my request to his neighbours. A crowd quickly gathers to tell me about the great man, as one of them is sent off to hunt for the prized trophy. Most members of the crowd were not yet born when Sankara died, but each has something to say about him, about his honesty, his stand against the French imperialists, his rejection of foreign aid, his criticism of his corrupt peers, and his untimely death. Eventually, after half an hour of enthusiastic discussion, the T-shirt hunter returns, breathless but happy. He has found me a perfect fit, with a grainy photograph of a fist-waving Sankara on the front and his immortal words, 'When the people stand up, imperialism trembles!' emblazoned on the back. He presents it to me proudly. I ask him what he thinks of Sankara. 'He was a great man,' he replies, 'but he didn't last. To last in African politics you have to lie, but he told the truth.' The boy, made cynical beyond his years, is no more than sixteen.

43

Our hotel room in Ouagadougou, unlike all the other rooms we have stayed in on our trip, has a television. This allows us to watch the celebrations marking fifty years of Burkina Faso's independence, which are being held on a football field in Bobo-Dioulasso. Blaise Compaoré is the guest of honour.

Compaoré has ruled his country for much longer than the man he replaced, but he remains a sullen, unloved figure. Sankara has streets named after him in African capitals, with pilgrims trekking to his grave from all corners of the continent. Compaoré, on the other hand, inspires only suspicion and fear; like a stepfather replacing an adored father, he has never gained his people's affection.

In the first months of his presidency he attempted to mend fences. He disarmed Sankara's revolutionary committees, legalised political parties, and declared an amnesty for political prisoners. Still he was not trusted, however: he had too much blood on his hands. Realising that he would not win any popularity contests and that holding fair democratic elections would therefore leave him vulnerable, he tightened his grip on power by other means. The media was silenced, rivals locked up or executed, ballots rigged, and opposition parties ground into insignificance. When he stood unopposed for election in 1991, three-quarters of his countrymen abstained from voting.

On the television, a soldier presents his president with the Burkinabe flag - the flag Sankara designed – while the master of ceremonies tells the audience of seated dignitaries that the red half of the flag symbolises the blood spilt for the freedom of the country. Compaoré, balding but still physically robust, looks humble, almost shy as he joins in the singing of the national anthem (which Sankara composed on his guitar). Dressed in a dark suit, crimson tie and polished black shoes, he steps up to a podium to deliver his speech.

It is not easy being an African dictator. Attaining and then holding onto power require resourcefulness, cunning, patience and endurance. You can never drop your guard, must never lose sight of your single overriding imperative of clinging to office. All your energies - your entire existence - must be permanently focused on this. It is an exhausting choice of career.

To acquire power, you first need to gather around you a loyal band of supporters. You can start with family members, but as you rise through the ranks in the army or the political party you will need to branch out. Colleagues who admire your charisma and respect your obvious leadership qualities will be your first port of call. You will need to grease their palms from time to time, either with financial rewards or promises of high office when you reach your goal (be especially generous with military officials, whom you will rely on to stage your coup d'état). To obtain the financial rewards and to bolster the long-term solvency of your project, take the time to garner the favour of a handful of wealthy businessmen; you can repay these benefactors with public works contracts once you have your hands on the national purse.

You will need support in the wider population, too. It is possible to lead a country without universal popular backing, but with no support at all from your citizenry you will be defenceless when rivals move to unseat you. You turn, therefore, to the people from your village, your town, your tribe. You promise them that you will give them jobs when you assume power, and in the meantime you must give them sweeteners - food, cash, land or assistance in resolving disputes.

To really make certain that your push for glory will prevail, you must obtain the sponsorship of a Western power, for only they can provide the financial muscle that will guarantee your success. During the Cold War this was easy. However incompetent, corrupt and bloodthirsty you were, however many of your innocent fellow citizens you tortured and murdered, as long as you claimed to be fighting off the communist tide or resisting the capitalist oppressor you could count on financial and military aid from the United States or the Soviet Union. This option is now closed off, although perhaps with the growing presence of the Chinese in Africa it might one day open up again.

Today your best hope is the former colonial power. France in particular is happy to support dictators in return for influence, business contracts, and access to your country's natural resources. The Ministère des Affaires Etrangères has been a steadfast ally to a panoply of West African dictators, from the mad cannibal Jean-Bédel Bokassa to the kleptocratic Omar Bongo and Félix Houphouet-Boigny. France has even supported dictators whose countries it never colonised, propping up ruthless tyrants like Teodoro Obiang of Equatorial Guinea and the doyen of all despots, Mobutu Sese Seko, who while appropriating two-thirds of Zaire's national budget for his "discretionary spending" openly advised members of his party not to steal too much at once but to 'steal cleverly, little by little.' Most of these men (including Blaise Compaoré, who quickly turned his back on the austerity of the Sankara years) have villas in the south of France, palaces in the Parisian suburbs, and penthouse apartments in the City of Light itself. They have fleets of Mercedes and Bugattis to ferry them around when they visit the metropolis. As a budding dictator you have all this to look forward to, and you can count on the French to assist your rise with money and arms, confer legitimacy by recognising your government, and help you quash opposition once you have attained the presidency.

Now that you have the French, your tribe, a few wealthy businessmen and a cadre of military and party colleagues onside, you are ready to make your push for power. In West Africa coups d'état are often bloody. Your opponent will not go down without a fight, so you must be ready to use extreme violence. If you do not eliminate him outright, you must at least force him into exile, preferably after seizing his assets (while Charles Taylor's rebel soldiers were relieving Samuel Doe of his ears, they yelled at him to give them his bank account numbers). When he is gone, to nullify the risk of a counter-coup you must immediately purge his followers. Siaka Stevens executed dozens of potential rivals during his first few years in power, and Nino Vieira and Compaoré himself were quick to do likewise whenever they smelt a conspiracy brewing.

Once you are ensconced in office, your travails intensify, for you must always be alert to the threat of sedition. This danger is real, your paranoia fully justified. From the 1960s to the turn of the millennium, three in five African leaders ended their rule in a coffin or in exile. 'I expected a coup any day,' said the former Nigerian dictator Ibrahim Babangida. 'From day one I was there, I knew that somehow, some day there would be a coup. Because we took it by force, somebody is going to try and take by force.' You will need eyes everywhere – in the villages, in the cities, among your friends and close colleagues, even within your own family - to protect you against usurpers.

While you are watching your back, you must not take your eye off your supporters. Now that you are president, their expectations skyrocket, and you must continue to slake their thirst. The French demand mining contracts and free rein for their businesses. Your military colleagues expect promotion and power (you will have to create new positions, new battalions, to give each of them the status and access to national funds he requires). Nor must you forget your tribe and your village. They are your rock, the critical mass which will give you the numbers you need to fend off rebellions or popular revolt. You need them to love you, everybody else to fear you.

To satisfy these grassroots followers you must first provide them with a source of income. This is likely to mean expanding the government bureaucracy to create jobs. This makes your administration less efficient, but by increasing the number of hoops citizens and businesses must go through to accomplish anything, it also multiplies the opportunities for your supporters to extract bribes. Further demonstrations of your largesse will come in the shape of grand projects in your home community. The Ivory Coast dictator Houphouet-Boigny built the world's largest cathedral in his provincial hometown of Yamoussoukro. Compaoré has opened a wildlife park in the grounds of his palace in the dusty backwater of Ziniaré, and has drawn up plans to relocate the country's main airport there from Ouagadougou. The town, unlike those around it, has schools, a hospital, and numerous development projects, all in the service of cementing its inhabitants' loyalty to their leader.

Although your task as a dictator is never straightforward, however, neither, as many of your predecessors have shown, is it impossible. There are a number of advantages to pursuing your choice of career in Africa as opposed to a less benighted part of the world. Chief among them is the weakness of your subjects. The masses are too poor, too hungry and too busy finding food to eat each day to plot rebellion; they are uneducated, and therefore easy to manipulate once you gain control of the media (Compaoré's first act after dispatching Sankara was to take over state radio); and they are accustomed to repression - to them, one despotic leader resembles another (Western governments take a similar view, and exert only half-hearted pressure for you to step down).

The weakness of your country's economic and political institutions is another blessing. The business sector, for example, is undeveloped, and laws to protect its assets nonexistent – this makes it easy for you to appropriate your nation's natural resources to enrich yourself and your cronies. The authority of chiefs was hollowed out by colonialism, making it easier for you to centralise power in the capital. And political parties, if they exist at all, are often mere husks, vehicles for their leaders to amass wealth and furnish the demands of their supporters; they are in no position to stop you plundering state finances and siphoning off foreign aid. You can use the fruits of your pillage, indeed, to guarantee their silence. They will happily comply, for their people must eat too: Compaoré's own coalition contains more than thirty other parties.

That you are not alone is a further advantage bestowed on you by your continent. Once you have established a reputation as an effective custodian of power, your fellow dictators will rally to your cause. Charles Taylor gave Compaoré conflict diamonds from Sierra Leone, and received weapons and men for the RUF invasion in return. Compaoré also befriended Libya's Gaddafi and Gambia's Jammeh, who claims to be able to cure AIDS (but only on Thursdays). The late Houphouet-Boigny gave the Burkinabe leader his daughter's hand in marriage. If a rebel group somehow manages to elude your all-seeing eye and make a grab for power, you can usually count on your neighbouring despots to help you extinguish the threat.

Solidarity with your peers is essential, for like them you are in this for the long haul. This job, once embarked upon, is for life. Even if you weary of spending all your time smoking out opponents and attending to supporters' needs, even if all the extrajudicial executions and betrayals of close friends finally breach your psychological defences and envelop you in guilt, it will be impossible for you to step down. Your power is a prison. If you allow someone else to take the reins, your life will be at his mercy - in the unlikely event that he does not send you to the gallows or the firing squad, at the very least he will target the assets you have so patiently accumulated.

But let us imagine that you can be sure of your survival, perhaps after reaching an agreement with your successor to stand down in return for being left alone. Maybe then you can fade peacefully from the political scene and slip into a quiet retirement. But wait! You cannot! You have forgotten the most important thing! If you step aside, what will become of your villagers, your tribespeople, your long-standing political and military allies? They will all be cast out onto the street, penniless. You cannot do this to us, they will say, an appalled look on their faces, their palms upturned in a pleading gesture. After all we have done for you! This is Africa – you have obligations. You cannot just turn your back on your people! Did your venerable ancestors bring you into the world for this? To spit on us, to betray those who gave you everything? No, you must stay the course, they agree, nodding sagely, the wisdom of generations on their side. We are in this together. You have no choice. You wanted power, we put you in power, and in power you must remain.

The French anthropologist Emmanuel Terray, drawing on his experience in the Ivory Coast, identified two distinct but parallel systems of government in Africa. The first is the world of the air-conditioner. This system, which is inspired by the Western style of government, gives off an impression of bureaucratic and technocratic efficiency. It is a world of presidents, constitutions, parliaments and laws, and speaks the language of democracy, development and modernisation. It pertains to certain places and certain hours of the day, to 'office hours (as long as one defines these relatively flexibly),' to government buildings made of cement and steel and glass, to presidential palaces and airports with VIP lounges, to 'glorious official soirées in illuminated gardens.' While the air-conditioner hums in the background, the leader, in his three-piece suit and tie and speaking in fluent metropolitan French or the smooth American burr favoured by Charles Taylor, announces grand development plans to his spellbound foreign backers: hydroelectric dams, a new motorway, airports, universities – the appurtenances of a modern state. He promises elections free and fair, and looks businesslike, not awestruck, when he takes his seat at the United Nations.

But much of this is display. As Terray observed, the principal function of the world of the air-conditioner is not to govern, but 'to show, particularly to the outside, that the country works, that it holds rank in the concert of nations' (recall the Sierra Leone government's gift to Haiti's earthquake victims, and its explanation that the country needed to play its part as a member of the international community). The serious business takes place not here, but amid a second world, the world of the veranda. This is a world of palavers under baobab trees, of sharing what you have, of the impenetrable African night, of obligations – personal, not bureaucratic, obligations - to your ancestors and your community; a world, at its most extreme, of human sacrifices in sacred forests. For our leader's real concern is not democracy, nor the provision of services to his nation, nor that nation's prosperous future. His real concern is in meeting his obligations to his narrow band of supporters, in feeding them in the here and now so that they will sustain him in power. This second system acts as a brake on the pride and greed of the Big Men, who are allowed to enrich themselves only if part of the material and political booty they accrue is generously redistributed. Like Gulliver tied down by the Lilliputians, Terray noted, the Big Man is 'far from being entirely the master of his choices.' As long as he produces the goods, the little people will sing his praises, vote for him, pass on rumours and render him other services. But if he fails to deliver, and to keep delivering throughout his time in power, they will jump ship. It is a tit for tat relationship, which requires the leader to be permanently on his toes.

As the anniversary celebrations in Bobo reach their climax, Blaise Compaoré concludes his speech. It is possible that my imagination is deceiving me after spending the past few days thinking about Sankara, but I detect in his successor a great, crushing sadness. His eyes, sloping down at the outer edges, look careworn, lacklustre. His shoulders are slumped, his brow furrowed. His speech, fluent but turgid, has merely gone through the motions, its repeated references to 'solidarity' and the Revolution containing none of the vigour and excitement that filled his predecessor's proclamations. Compaoré is in the process of amending the constitution to allow himself to stand for yet another five-year term in office. If he finishes that term, he will have ruled Burkina Faso for thirty-three years. Thirty-three years of looking over his shoulder, fielding demands, nurturing loyalty - thirty-three years in a jail of his own making. As I sit there watching the speech in my new Thomas Sankara T-shirt, I cannot suppress a pang of sympathy for the late revolutionary's nemesis.

44

And so to the north, to the Sahel, the shore, the last sliver of solid ground before the perilous sea of the Sahara. Our journey has become something of a race against time, a quest to see as much as possible while my frazzled mind still clings to its own terra firma. It is all about reaching the end, and we are propelled on by the illusion that movement will hasten that moment, accelerate time itself. We have a sense that our fate is no longer in our hands. When we discuss the remainder of the journey, we append an "inshallah" or a "God willing" whenever we settle on a plan. Nothing is certain any more. Not Ebru and I, but Africa and her capricious gods will determine whether, and in what condition, we make it through the final weeks.

The Sahel, a vast, flat steppe dividing desert from equatorial forest, stretches almost the width of the continent. It is a land where the mighty kingdoms of western and central Africa rose and fell, the starting point from which Mansa Musa, the fourteenth-century ruler of the Mali Empire, set off for Egypt, carrying with him so much treasure that the gold price in Cairo's markets took decades to recover. Traders and their camels have traversed the region for thousands of years, ferrying slaves, ivory and kola nuts northward, salt, iron and Islam south. They moved in camel-led caravans thirty miles long, and sold their wares in the magnificent desert cities of Timbuktu and Agadez. The Burkinabe stretch of the Sahel saw the rise of Askia Mohammed's great Songhai Empire, and then its swift decline and surrender to Moroccan Berbers. After the latter departed at the end of the seventeenth century, it became something of a no man's land, the traders and their thirty thousand-strong camel caravans sharing the territory with bandits, smugglers and, in recent years, desperate migrants headed for fortress Europe.

As kingdoms have waxed and waned, however, one group of people, the Fula, has been a constant presence on the Sahel's broad expanses. Although in recent years they have scattered across West Africa, into the forests and down to the Gulf of Guinea where they make a living as traders in coastal cities like Bissau and Freetown, it is to this strip of dry, beige semi-desert that the Fula belong. For centuries, perhaps millennia, they have roamed its lonely plains with their herds, always on the move, never laying claim to any particular place. In the dry season they migrate to the southern reaches. When the rains come they begin the slow return northward, to the edge of the desert. It is a life, as the 1930s French traveller Odette du Puigaudeau described it, 'divided into days of pasture and days of wandering, into days at watering holes and days without water, a humble, quiet life full of long dreams, moving slowly across infinite, empty plains, outside the walls of towns.'

The English explorer Richard Jobson encountered Fula herdsmen on the Gambia in 1620. 'Their profession is keeping of Cattle,' he reported. 'Some Goats they have, but the Heards they tend are Beefes, whereof they are aboundantly stored.' Every day their women - 'streight, upright, and excellently well bodied' - would bring to Jobson's camp, 'in great and small gourds like dishes, made up very handsomely, new milke, sowre milke and curdes, and two sorts of butter, one new and white, the other hard and of an excellent colour, which we call refined butter, and it is without question, but for a little freshness, as good as any we have at home.'

Then as now, the Fula were semi-nomadic, never staying anywhere for long. 'In some places they have settled Townes,' Jobson observed, 'but for the most part they are still wandering...Where they find the ground and soyle most fitte for their Cattle, there, with the Kings allowance of the country, they sit downe, building themselves houses, as the season of the yeare serves.'

Today, the old Fula ways are under pressure. On the bus heading north, the Fula man sitting next to me says that many of his brethren are quitting the nomadic life and settling in the towns and cities (we had seen some of them in Ouagadougou, listlessly hawking leather bags and sandals). 'There is not enough pasture and the boreholes are drying up,' he explains. 'I used to be a herder myself, but it's difficult spending all day under the sun looking for water or grazing land only to find it has all gone.' He now works for a development agency as a livestock expert, teaching herders how to treat sick animals and how to stock grass to tide them over during lean periods. 'They don't have education, so they don't know about modern techniques,' he says. 'When their cattle fall sick, they just die. The herders can do nothing about it. We are trying to improve their knowledge so that they can continue their way of life.'

As our bus trundles northwards, the country grows ever drier. Stunted acacia are dotted sparsely around, intersected by long lines of denuded baobab spaced like electricity pylons. Scrubby, grey-green thornbush offers a faint trace of colour. The rest is dust. 'There used to be many more trees,' says my neighbour, 'but people have cut them down. Wood is their only source of energy, and when the population exploded there was deforestation and the desert advanced.' From time to time in the distance we see herds of scrawny cows, driven on foot by a lone Fula in a dark robe and conical straw hat, man and beast united in the eternal search for water and pasture.

You know you are approaching a Sahelian town when the country about you becomes pockmarked with black plastic bags, strewn around like toxic chocolate chips on a cookie. An ugly ring of these bags surrounds every settlement, thickening as the first buildings come into view. We reach the small town of Dori, which is no exception, late in the afternoon. The harmattan has eased off for now, and the high, gaping African sky, white tinged with blue, has reappeared. The people have come out of their dust-strafed shells and cheered up. 'The harmattan makes you sick. It gives you colds,' says the man in our hotel, relieved that the siege has lifted. 'You don't have dust in your country, do you?'

Dori was once a punishment posting for civil servants. The hottest town in one of the world's hottest countries, it has the feel of a remote frontier outpost teetering on the brink of the desert, cut off from the rest of humanity. The few cars and trucks that ply its streets rarely look like they are going anywhere else. The telephone lines are down. The occasional bus penetrates the moat of plastic bags, but otherwise the town is contained in its own little dustcloud. Here, as we are reminded every time we venture out into its sandy lanes, we really are 'Les' Blancs. There are no other white people. The only other outsiders are a couple of shopkeepers from the south. It is a world apart.

Dori's remoteness breeds solidarity among its inhabitants. Everybody seems to know one another, and salutations and smiles are freely given. On our second afternoon we find a yoghurt shop, on whose veranda we can sit, drink thick, sweet yoghurt, and watch the life of the town. Passersby – stately Fula women in heavy silver earrings, teenagers in jeans, old Muslims in white kaftans, and Tuareg, the people of the desert, in flowing indigo robes and turbans – stop to exchange greetings and news. As they continue slowly on their way, many of them greet us too. Nothing else happens. Cows mooch around, goats snooze in the shade of mud walls, boys career past on donkey carts, women pound millet in pairs outside their compounds. Later, towards dusk, the call to prayer wafts gently down the lane from a nearby mosque.

The young man who runs the yoghurt shop pulls up a plastic chair beside us and introduces himself. His name is Abdoul-Karim. In his late twenties, tall and light-skinned, with deep brown eyes and a slightly aquiline nose, he wears jeans, flip-flops, a Muslim skullcap and, despite the forty-degree heat, a thick red lumberjack shirt. Originally from Bobo-Dioulasso, he came here a few years ago after dropping out of school, rescued from unemployment when a friend of his brother's offered him a job in the yoghurt shop. He works all day and sleeps on a mat outside the shop at night. He earns a pittance, barely enough to live on. Like so many others, his life has been blown off course. 'I had big plans,' he says, 'but I ran out of money and had to give up school. That set me back, and for a while my head was all over the place.'

It must be easy, if you are a Burkinabe, a Sierra Leonean or a Guinean, to become downhearted. Of the planet's seven billion people, you and your compatriots are the unluckiest. Through pure accident of birth, ninety-nine of every hundred people in the world have a head start on you; your entire time on earth will be spent trying to claw back ground. 'For three years I have been trying to save enough money to resume my studies,' Karim continues, 'but it's difficult. I have to make new plans now in case I can't go back to school. I need to regroup and think about what to do next. But I am an optimist. I will get out of this.'

The security guard outside the bank next door has been listening to our conversation. Sprawled drowsily over a metal chair, he leans towards us and joins in. The bank is closed (it does not open at all during the fortnight we spend in the town), but he tells us he will nevertheless be there all night guarding it. 'Nobody comes. It's very quiet,' he says. I ask him if he sleeps during his watch. 'Of course!' he replies with a toothy grin.

The guard, a Mossi, changes the subject to tell us about the laziness of the Fula. 'They don't know how to work,' he says. 'The Mossi work hard. They go out to the fields at five in the morning and come home at ten at night. The Fula go out at seven with their cows, come back three hours later and call that a day's work!' He then tells a joke about perceived Fula greed. The old Sahelian rivalry still simmers. As crop farmers, the Mossi and other settled tribes depend on the Fula's herds for vital protein. The Fula, meanwhile, cannot survive for long without the grain they acquire from farmers. But the relationship is strictly transactional, rarely straying into warmth or friendship. While the farmer mocks herding as the work of the indolent, for the herdsman, free as a bird, the shackled, cattle-less farmer is an object of contempt.

There are deeper reasons, too, for the antipathy. The Fula were enthusiastic slavers, sweeping down from the mountains of Guinea to harvest captives for the Atlantic and North African markets; the Mossi successfully defended themselves, but other settled tribes of the Sahel were less fortunate. The Fula were also keen jihadists, using the profits from slaving to fund holy wars. Themselves converted to Islam by Arab and Berber traders, they launched numerous raids to cow the sedentary peoples of the region into submitting to their God. The victim of slave raid and jihad was the settled farmer, the perpetrator the itinerant herder. This historical divide has yet to be fully bridged.

Another ancient fault line is also still in evidence. When they bring their livestock south in the dry season, herdsmen inevitably run up against land occupied by peasants. Most of the time this does not create problems - the cattle fertilise the farmers' soil, and the nomads exchange milk products, meat and hides for grain. In periods of scarcity, however, competition for water and pasture intensifies, sometimes boiling over into conflict. Farming in such a barren region is difficult at the best of times (Robert Delavignette, a colonial administrator serving in Upper Volta, noted that while the French peasant had 'made of France a garden in which rare islands of wilderness still persist,' the African, on the contrary, had laboured and suffered 'to occupy a few islands of cultivated land in an encircling ocean of bush'). When drought forces the farmer to use every last square inch of soil and eke out every last drop of available water, he becomes less accommodating towards his old adversary. The collision can be explosive. 'There is often violence when the herders trespass on farmers' land,' the livestock expert on the bus to Dori had said. 'In recent years there have been many droughts, and the conflicts have grown more frequent and more violent. The rainy season starts late and finishes early. There is not enough water for everybody.' We will hear this complaint frequently in the coming weeks.

45

We quickly settle into an agreeable routine in Dori. In the mornings we sit with a friendly Songhai outside his shop and drink green tea. After a lunch of fish with spiced rice or peas with tomatoes at one of the town's two eating houses, we spend the hottest part of the day in our room, reading and sleeping (as usual, we are the hotel's only guests). In the evenings we sit with the languid Karim outside the yoghurt shop, watching the activity in the street and chatting with him and various passersby about the country. After the assault that was Ouagadougou, the slow pace of life is a welcome relief.

This being West Africa, however, ugliness lurks amid Dori's charms. The Sahel is Burkina Faso's poorest region, and the poverty here is Dickensian. Starving, pot-bellied toddlers sit quietly in the dust. Beggars roam the streets - everywhere we go, children and sometimes adults ask us for a "cadeau". The shops have no stock, the market scarcely any food. In the late dry season desiccation, even the cows and goats look emaciated.

One morning we have breakfast at the town's lone coffee shack. Sitting outside on a long bench with our backs to the road, we dip dry bread in coffee whitened by condensed milk. While we eat, five boys not yet in their teens hover behind us, silently staring. From time to time one of them moves closer to our shoulders, seemingly checking to see if we are leaving anything. When we look round he retreats to the group. The boys, their faces ghostly pale, wear torn T-shirts and shorts. Their entire bodies are caked in dust, their bones jutting out through their chapped skin like a fight in a tent. They stand there for twenty minutes, like seagulls waiting for scraps (failing once again Auden's test for men from Europe, I grow impatient with them for intruding on our meal). As soon as we get up to leave, they run to the table and hoover up a few crumbs of bread. When we look back, we see one of them gulping down the dregs of Ebru's coffee.

The boys are talibé children. They are ubiquitous in West Africa. In the towns of Guinea-Bissau, Senegal, Mali and now Burkina Faso, posses of these boys – uniformly skinny, dirty and with a look of fraught desperation in their eyes – have been our constant companions. They work the streets in packs, empty tomato tins or little plastic buckets dangling from their shoulders, and ask everyone they see for money or food.

The Muslim African tradition of parents sending their sons to be educated by Islamic scholars dates back centuries. The children were given instruction in Arabic and Koranic studies and a place to sleep, and were expected to feed themselves by farming or begging for alms. After a few years, armed with knowledge and wisdom, they would return to their villages and disseminate the Prophet's message.

Today, many of the holy men are frauds. 'They go to the market, buy a cap and gown and a Koran and say they are Koranic masters,' says Karim as we sit with him one evening. The men focus their recruitment efforts on the rural areas, using promises of food and shelter to persuade destitute families to send them their male children. Parents, uneducated, gullible and relieved at having one less mouth to feed, are tricked into allowing their sons to be taken. Often it will be the last they see of them. Some of the boys are as young as five or six.

The children are a cash cow for their masters. 'It is pure child exploitation,' says Karim, a devout Muslim. Every morning they are sent out into the streets to beg. They are expected to come back with at least a hundred and fifty francs (fifty cents). If they do not hit their target, the holy man will beat or torture them, so towards the end of the day those who have not raised enough through begging are forced to steal. 'They know what is waiting for them otherwise,' says Karim darkly.

Few of the talibé children receive any form of education. Their masters, these modern-day Fagins, want them on the streets instead. Some have twenty or thirty boys in their care, a potential revenue stream of more than ten dollars a day. This is big money in these parts, and the masters, who anyway know little of the Koran, cannot afford to waste time teaching. At night the boys sleep on crowded floors in their captors' homes. They do not get enough rest – we often see them in Dori in the afternoons, sleeping on the ground under trees (they look young and vulnerable, with an innocence that disappears from their faces as soon as they awake). Nor do they have enough to eat. The boys who surrounded our breakfast table were underfed, their bodies too small for their heads. In Ouagadougou the previous week another talibé child had asked us for money. 'Give me something so I can eat,' he demanded through swollen lips. We refused, and he began to stare intently at Ebru's bag, his eyes desperate, feverish as he homed in on it. When he made to snatch it I pushed him away. I could feel his ribs like a radiator through his T-shirt.

When they are old enough to stand up to their overlords, or too old to garner almsgivers' sympathy, the boys escape or are released, or set up as masters themselves. Their future is bleak. 'They get used to this life of begging and stealing,' says Karim, 'so when they grow up and run away their only option is delinquency.' It occurs to me that the boys would make easy prey for extremists and warlords. Across Africa, it is to young male outcasts that those plotting rebellion or brutality turn first. The talibé boys, hopeless, hungry and made amoral by years of abuse and alienation, fit the bill. West African governments are worried by this prospect, but their half-hearted efforts to put a stop to the practice have had little effect. 'It is a river that cannot be dammed,' opines Karim. 'Families are too poor, they have no choice.' When I suggest that free education might help, by providing children with a daily meal and thereby reducing the economic burden they place on their families, he laughs. Burkina Faso's performance in this area is abysmal: fewer than half of rural children ever go to school.

46

The people of Dori are worried about famine. Over coffee one day we meet a man whose job is to teach adults to read and write. Three-quarters of Burkinabe adults are illiterate, and the teacher believes that by learning these skills of the modern world the herders of the Sahel will be better able to diversify away from what is an increasingly precarious occupation. He tells us that drought and famine have become cyclical in the north of the country: 'The last rainy season was poor, so there is not enough water or pasture. People are already hungry, and in the next two or three months, until this year's rainy season begins, the situation will get worse.' The Fula will be the worst sufferers, he predicts. 'Herders will not be able to feed and water their cattle. Many animals will die. Maybe people will die too.'

The Burkinabe Sahel has suffered regular and crippling droughts throughout the past half-century. In the 1970s a decade-long famine claimed the lives of a hundred thousand people and tens of millions of cows and sheep. In 2005 the failure of the rains left the entire population of northern Burkina on the brink of starvation. '2005 was very bad,' says Ousmane, our Songhai shopkeeper friend. 'There was no millet and the prices of maize and sorghum doubled. We had to import food, which was much more expensive. Everywhere was affected, even the towns. You were lucky to have one meal a day. Whole herds of cattle were wiped out.'

Three years later the spectre of hunger loomed again. A worldwide spike in food prices put even basic staples beyond the reach of most Burkinabes. In the cities, riots broke out in protest against "la vie chère". Karim, who at the time was visiting family in Bobo-Dioulasso, saw crowds of looters fighting with police, ransacking shops and petrol stations, and destroying vehicles and public buildings. He was shocked at what he saw, and does not believe the rioters had good cause. 'There were a few problems with food vendors taking advantage of the situation and hiking up prices,' he says, 'but the people didn't understand that it wasn't the government's fault that prices were so high - it was a global problem.'

Droughts hit the Fula especially hard. In good times, they make a living selling milk and sometimes leather products in the markets of the Sahel, and buy grain from sedentary farmers with the proceeds. But in times of scarcity, when boreholes dry up or grain prices rise, they are vulnerable. Other tribes, like the Songhai, might combine herding with a little crop-farming, which spreads the risk for the hard days. But the Fula cannot do this. They have been on the move for centuries, since time immemorial. They cannot suddenly call a halt to their wanderings and settle down, chaining themselves to one place. 'It is not in their culture,' says the Songhai Ousmane. They know no other way of living.'

When drought bites and food prices soar, therefore, the Fula cannot fall back on home-grown crops. Nor, with their starving cows now unable to produce milk, do they have anything with which to barter. The only option left to them is to sell off their animals. But this too is unthinkable, for their animals are their future, their prize asset. And besides, they love their animals – selling them would be no less painful than selling a child. 'A Fula will do anything for his cows,' Karim had told us. 'He would treat a sick cow before a sick wife.' The adult literacy teacher concurs. 'They won't sell their animals even to buy corn to save their families,' he says. 'Even when their cows are sickening and dying they hold onto them. They prefer to keep the animal and die rather than part with it. Many Fula die in droughts.'

In centuries past, when food and water were easier to come by and conflict over resources was uncommon, the Fula's single-mindedness was a rational response to a perilous environment. Experimentation with new techniques was considered too risky – it would divert time and energy from tried and trusted pursuits and the eventual rewards were uncertain. Mungo Park observed that although the "Foulah" drank plentiful milk and ate copious amounts of butter, they knew nothing of how to make cheese, and showed little interest in learning. 'A firm attachment to the customs of their ancestors,' Park surmised, 'makes them view with an eye of prejudice everything that looks like innovation. The heat of the climate and the great scarcity of salt are held forth as unanswerable objections; and the whole process appears to them too long and troublesome to be attended with any solid advantage.'

The customs of the ancestors, however, are no longer fit for purpose. The Fula are being forced to quit their roaming, to leave behind the tall skies, the endless plains and the rumbling herds and relocate to the cacophonous, crowded cities. The modern world is dragging them into its vortex, severing their mystical ties to the open spaces of the Sahel. The people of Sierra Leone and Guinea-Bissau cannot escape their villages quickly enough, but the Fula are different. They are happy where they are. They have no yearning for change. The Fula, like a recalcitrant herd, are being driven into the twenty-first century by phenomena beyond their control.

There are two great forces lining up to push the herders off their land. The first is the changing climate. 'You in Europe have made all this pollution and we in Africa are feeling its effects,' says Ousmane accusingly one morning. 'The weather is less predictable now. The harmattan goes on longer and the rainy season is shorter. Life has become very difficult for everybody here - farmers and herders.' Burkina Faso is on the climate change frontline. The Sahel will be one of the world regions hardest hit by global warming. Average temperatures, already the highest on the planet, could rise by over three degrees in the next century. Rainfall has decreased by a quarter since 1950, and even if it does not decline further the rise in temperatures will mean that rainwater evaporates more quickly, before the Fula and the settled cultivators of crops can make use of it. The changing weather is likely to bring more droughts, more floods and more pests. It threatens to make food, water and pasture scarcer. Already the Sahara desert is advancing several miles into the Sahel each year, smothering valuable grazing land. As it continues its relentless march and the rains retreat before it, those trying to eke out an existence on the drying plains will have to travel ever farther to find sustenance.

As they forage, they will run up against a second great force. Climate change is a new problem, but one of its side-effects is the re-emergence as a challenge of a much older problem - the population explosion – which has reared its head as the supply of food and water has dwindled. Population growth need not be a disaster for Africa. Burkina Faso has one of the highest fertility rates in the world, with the average woman mothering six children. Its population has almost quadrupled in the past half-century. But with fifteen million inhabitants the country remains empty in comparison with the United Kingdom or Italy, for example, which are of similar size but have four times the number of people, and in neither of these European powerhouses have dense populations impeded spectacular economic expansion.

There are many advantages to being crowded. More people mean more customers for businesses and farmers and the potential for a more efficient division of labour. As Adam Smith noted of the 'lone houses and very small villages scattered about in so desert a country' as eighteenth-century Scotland, farmers' very isolation required them to carry out a multitude of tasks in addition to herding or growing crops. They had to be baker, brewer, carpenter, mason and smith, 'to perform themselves a great number of little pieces of work, for which, in more populous countries, they would call in the assistance of those workmen.'

The population of Burkina Faso today is similarly dispersed.

An observer of Burkinabe village life will see farmers building their houses, repairing compound walls, thatching roofs, and undertaking numerous other domestic or community tasks that limit the time they can spend in the fields. The village women are yet more versatile. From dawn to dusk they flit from one chore to another – collecting firewood, gathering water, feeding babies, pounding millet, cooking, washing clothes, selling produce in the market, working in the fields or tending their herds. They must do all these jobs themselves because their communities are too small for it to be worthwhile anyone setting up as a provider of such services. Burkina Faso has many villages, but each one is tiny, and a builder, thatcher or baker would seldom have enough custom to justify abandoning his own domestic duties. Since they must carry out all tasks without specialising in any, the villagers' outputs, to put it in industrial terms (and including the children they rear), are inevitably of a lower quality than they would be if they could focus on a single enterprise. Being of lower quality they are also of lower economic value, making it difficult for a family to accumulate wealth and climb out of poverty. More multitudinous societies, on the other hand (and more urbanised societies, if they can overcome the many problems that beset West African cities), are likely to contain specialists in different trades who will produce higher quality goods, and more likely as a consequence to advance.

Although population growth by itself does not deepen poverty, however, when it occurs suddenly, and in locations with limited and shrinking resources, it may heighten the risk. The population of the Burkinabe Sahel has tripled in the past forty years. Despite food shortages and the looming threat of climate change it is likely to triple again in the next forty. How will all these people eat? How will they share out their meagre rations? How will herders and farmers avoid resorting to violence as the scramble for food and water intensifies? Already the amount of food produced by the average African has declined by a tenth since 1960. Already drought and reduced rainfall are leading to increased conflict. How will communities cope when there is still less food, and when there are still more mouths to feed? Not well, according to the American economists Raymond Fisman and Edward Miguel, whose calculations predict a sharp rise in the number of violent clashes in the Sahel in the next half-century. Not well, either, according to the United Nations, which expects the number of hungry people in the region to double in three decades.

It is not just the size of the population that poses problems for West Africa, but the structure. The region is full of children. Everywhere you look there are hordes of them, straddling their mothers' backs, playing in the streets, begging for alms, or herding cows and sheep. In any one year, one in three Burkinabe women will give birth (the proportion in a low-fertility country such as Spain is one in forty). Half the population is aged fourteen or younger.

Children produce nothing but consume everything. Most of what adults grow or earn disappears into their offspring's stomachs, leaving parents with little to eat and less of the time and energy needed to tend cattle or dig fields. The younger generation suffers too. With food shared out among many siblings, each child has less on his plate. Hunger makes learning more difficult – adults who have been malnourished early in life have been found to have lower IQs than their better-fed peers – and means West African teenagers enter the labour force ill-prepared compared with their counterparts in countries with a more balanced age structure. Unproductive, they will earn less and find it more difficult to afford the rising cost of food, and more difficult, too, to feed and educate their own children. And so it goes on, in a vicious spiral that continues down the generations.

But while population growth may be bad news for Burkinabes in the short term, in the longer-term it could offer a glimmer of hope. Many countries have passed through the demographic difficulties with which Burkina Faso is now grappling and come out the other side, and it is not inconceivable that Burkina and her neighbours will follow in their footsteps. Sweden, for instance, now one of the world's wealthiest nations, endured extreme poverty in the middle of the nineteenth century as its small adult population failed to cope with a sudden surge in the number of children. As in West Africa today, child labour was widespread, and the country, forced to borrow from abroad to keep afloat, became one of the most indebted in the world.

As these swarming masses of children grew up, fertility rates plummeted, and when they reached working age Sweden's population became heavy with young adults. This too was a troubled era, marked by mass emigration, rapid urbanisation, and political unrest as poverty continued to bedevil large swathes of society. But the young adults now had fewer children to support than did their forefathers, and more freedom, as a consequence, to work, save and spend. Out of this turbulent period came the beginnings of Sweden's industrialisation, the rise of an entrepreneurial spirit, and an increase in prosperity as the country took its first steps on the road to modernity.

Eventually Sweden's baby boom generation reached maturity. Middle-aged adults are society's great providers. They earn more, save more and invest more in businesses than any other age group. They can support themselves without relying on handouts from older or younger generations. And they fund the education of children and the care of the elderly. When the populations of East Asia reached maturity, their economies took off. Between 1965 and 1990 the number of working-age adults in the region grew nearly four times faster than the rest of the population. The Harvard economist David Bloom estimates that this "demographic dividend" accounted for a third of East Asia's giddying economic growth during the period. Sweden, too, prospered once the balance of its population became adult-heavy. The Swedish demographer Bo Malmberg has calculated that between 1920 and 1970, when the proportion of mature adults was at its highest, the income of the average Swede grew by four hundred percent – more than twice the rate in the decades before and after this boom.

Malmberg's analysis may offer hope for Burkina Faso. 'Countries that for a number of decades have benefited from increases in the middle-aged group,' he writes, 'seem without exception to have entered the club of industrialised nations. Such an increase is clearly associated with a more developed stage of economic growth.' Fertility rates in West Africa have remained stubbornly high, meaning that adults still have many hungry children to support. The pressure this exerts on those of working age has hitherto tended to explode into conflict rather than spark economic advance. But if the countries of the region can first create a baby boom generation by bringing down fertility, and then harness the boomers' potential when they reach maturity, their long-term prospects may be less bleak.

47

For six days of every week, Dori is a sleepy backwater, its wide streets of deep sand mostly empty. The harmattan, which has returned after a brief hiatus, blows lazily through. The only sounds are the regular tom-tom beats of giant pestles on mortars, as women performing their millet-pounding duets rock back and forth with the smooth synchronicity of pairs of nodding donkeys.

Every Friday, however, the tan-coloured town, like a desert blooming after sudden rain, explodes in a riot of colour as hundreds of herders and their families descend on its weekly market. They come from far afield, from the northern deserts, from the barren wastes of Niger to the east, and from all over the Burkinabe Sahel. They come to buy and sell, and also to socialise, to meet up with their fellows who have spent the weeks or months since they last came here roaming in different directions with their herds. The ritual is centuries old. The German explorer Heinrich Barth visited in 1853 and marvelled at the quality of the woven blankets on show, but even by that time the market was an ancient and venerable institution, part of the patchwork of weekly cattle fairs that stretches across the Sahelian plains.

We awake at dawn and head out. The road in front of our hotel, usually quiet with just a few goats or cows, is teeming with life. Along it passes a procession: donkey carts laden with goods, mopeds ridden by turbaned Tuareg, trucks bringing livestock and hitch-hikers from outlying villages, and a dazzling throng of colourfully-dressed pedestrians. We see tall, light-skinned Fula women with shawls billowing behind them and scarification marks on their cheeks; smaller Bella women – the former slaves of the Tuareg – with babies straddling their backs and clay cooking pots balanced on their heads; groups of Fula and Songhai men in long robes, holding hands; and teenage boys at the beginning of an insecure career dragging unruly goats by the ears.

We follow them down past Karim's yoghurt shop, the street now suddenly transformed into a busy, noisy thoroughfare, to the far side of the town, where an avenue of tall, bushy trees borders a vast open maïdan that stretches off into the distance. The near end of the avenue, beside a cluster of straw huts where Fula nomads have struck camp, is given over to cattle. Herds large and small are being led in across the dusty plain. The smaller herds stand in the shade of the trees, penned in loosely by wooden stakes. Herders with larger stocks remain out in the open, struggling to keep their restless charges in order. Many of the animals are scrawny and undernourished, but there are a few magnificent specimens with huge curved horns and noble bearing. One particularly majestic beast with a large hump flopping at the shoulder breaks loose from his comrades and is chased along the avenue, scattering onlookers in all directions. His owner, a young Fula, eventually catches up with him and ties him to a tree, where he remains unhappily for the rest of the day, pacing vengefully at the end of his rope and goring the dry ground and the innocent tree trunk with his horns.

We sit for a while on a tree stump by one of the sandy, bush-lined lanes that lead in from the outlying villages. A biblical parade passes before us. A bearded, rheumy-eyed old man in a black and white keffiyeh floats by on a donkey and salutes us with a wave; goatherds stroll in with their flocks; girls march past with enormous, cloth-wrapped bundles on their heads; a man in a straw hat leads a donkey cart carrying a woman and a pair of tethered goats. All the while, a stream of women and men pass by on foot wearing long robes of dazzling colours - purple, turquoise, lime and dark green, peach and cream, reds and blues and yellows, some of a single colour, many others patterned with flowers, geometrical shapes, or animals. Fula women sport silver earrings and heavy gold bracelets, the Tuareg more subdued indigo and blue. Most striking of all are the girlish Bella women, with silver discs hanging from their thickly plaited hair, glittering sequinned shawls draped across their shoulders, and long multi-coloured dresses flowing in their wake. Anything goes in the quest to add brightness to the monochrome Sahelian landscape. A Bella girl wears a red Manchester United football shirt over a yellow and black patterned skirt. Others prefer the crimson and blue stripes of Barcelona, adopted not just by young boys but by their mothers, on whom the famous Catalan colours merge seamlessly with the riot of reds and greens and silver and gold that adorns every other part of their body.

While the men and boys lead in their animals, the women bring other wares to sell. The influx of livestock and their owners attracts traders in a variety of goods. Some sell millet beer, poured from clay pots or calabashes into little mugs and dispensed to thirsty herders. Tuareg women in straw shacks sell finely worked silver bracelets and stouter bangles and earrings. Bella women sit on donkeys, resting their legs on large bundles of firewood tied to the beasts' flanks. Also on offer in the shade of the trees are rice, smoked fish, grain, cold drinks, straw for fodder or building huts, rope for tethering livestock, fried dough balls, peanuts, succulent mangoes, and the thick woven blankets seen by Barth.

Further along the avenue, away from the cattle, dozens, perhaps hundreds of goats are tied to wooden posts. Young boys have two or three to sell, their elders many more. An old man offers us a healthy-looking black and white specimen, which we reluctantly decline. A group of moustachioed young Tuareg, foot-long daggers in leather sheaths attached to their waists, sit on their haunches by their own herd, waiting for customers and commenting wryly on passersby. From time to time a prospective buyer ambles up and inspects one of the goats, squeezing its haunches to check its strength. A long, patient haggling process ensues, involving much smiling and gesticulating, until at last the satisfied buyer hands over some cash, wrestles his chosen animal away from its companions, and leads it off by the horn.

At the far end of the avenue we come upon the donkey section. Well-groomed and looking well-fed, the meek, virtuous beasts stand in the shade with their secrets. A donkey seller from Gorom-Gorom to the north tells us his day is going well. Another young man comes up and asks if we are buying or just observing. He is a trader, here to buy and sell sheep and goats, 'to make a little profit.' It's going OK, he says, before plunging back into the fray when he realises we are unlikely customers. In our ears are the sounds of chatter, of the lowing of cattle, the rap of stick on animal hide, and the rumble of hooves as a new herd trundles in from the plain and joins the mêlée. Everyone seems cheerful, pleased to see each other, engaging in long conversations even with those they have no plans to trade with, laughing, flirting, lecturing, exclaiming, and filling up on gossip and news to tide them over when the time comes to resume their lonely wanderings.

We move back to where the herds of cattle are stationed and sit on the ground under a tree among a gaggle of high-spirited men. Many of them greet us with a smile or a wave; others stare or pass amused comment to their companions. The chairman of the market crouches down beside us and welcomes us with a handshake. All around is bustle and activity. Whenever a new truck arrives, crammed with goats or cows and sprouting human passengers on top like stunted dreadlocks, a crowd swarms around to watch it being unloaded. Escapee bulls, chased down with sticks, cause a brief commotion, but it is not just these renegades that attract attention. The herds of cattle are the stars of the show, the Venuses de Milo in Dori's Louvre. Each individual beast is apprised, admired and commented on. The Fula's love of their cows shows no sign of weakening – it is a love that is passed down from one generation to the next, part of their genetic make-up. White-haired old men nod in approval as they stroke a tan-coloured flank or stand back to size up the curve of a horn; their sons discuss prices, grazing sites or the vagaries of the weather; and their grandsons, dreaming of future meanderings, look on with awe and envy as another huge lowing herd is brought in across the plain, kicking up clouds of dust.

But appearances are deceptive. Despite all the excitement, trade in cows is non-existent. While wads of low-denomination banknotes are occasionally exchanged for a goat or donkey, the cattle stay where they are, revered but unwanted. The mighty herds led in from miles around stand undisturbed, intact. Youssouf, a young Fula herder with whom we fall into conversation, explains why. Confident and friendly, with a round face, a moustache and large, deep-brown eyes under his navy blue turban, he stands before a small herd of eight or ten head of cattle. He does not expect to sell any of them today. 'Business has been bad for the last three years,' he says. 'It's very hard to sell cows because nobody trusts herding at the moment. There's not enough rain and not enough pasture, so it's difficult to keep a large herd. Sometimes you have to travel for three or four days with your cows to find water. Some animals don't make it. It's risky to buy cows, and it hurts you emotionally as well as economically – you are close to your animals, you don't want to see them suffer.' He shakes his head sadly. 'The only people who buy cows these days buy them not to herd but to slaughter. Nobody can afford to tend them. Everyone is saving his *sous*, hoping that the climate will get better and the rains will return.'

Fula herders have no other source of income than their cattle. They can sell milk only on market days (as Youssouf explains, if you are two hundred miles from a market and have no means of refrigeration, you must drink the milk yourself), so most of the money they make comes from selling cows. They do not need to sell very often, of course, for their living expenses are minimal - they have no rent or mortgage to pay, no vehicles bar their feet, and the open spaces, the vaulting skies and the company of their herds provide sufficient pleasure that they do not yearn for the opiates of modernity. 'We only sell when we have to, to buy food,' says Youssouf. 'We don't like to sell. We love our cows, it's hard to part with one.' Today, however, even these fire sales cannot be relied on. The prices of stock are collapsing. Later in the year, as famine tightened its deadly grip, we would hear of aid agencies buying up thousands of sickening cows at rock bottom prices and taking them off for immediate slaughter. Seeing their beloved animals on the point of death and diminishing in value by the hour, the starving Fula would have no choice but to sell.

After an afternoon sleep, we return to the market in the early evening. It has quietened somewhat, but there is still a buzz about the town as the jamboree dies down. In the lengthening shadows under the trees, the inspections of goats continue. A few thin specimens are sold, the deal sealed with a handshake. A man in a red turban and white robes walks off with a small goat cradled in his arms like a baby. He pauses by a group of friends who are sitting in the dust, and puts his purchase on the ground to show them. They nod approvingly, and the man picks the animal up and continues on his way. People start to wander back to their villages in groups, chatting and laughing, discussing the day's business. The rebel bull that was tied to the tree is led off by three wary herders. A thin cloud of dust floats on the air, filtering the fading sunlight. We stand for a while, leaning against a tree and watching as the herds of cattle trudge off into the distance across the endless, dusty plain. An old man in a white robe and skullcap is standing beside us with the small flock of sheep he has brought in to sell, most of them by now sitting quietly on the ground. I ask him how his day has gone. He nods in acknowledgement of my question. 'Un peu,' he says: a little. He seems satisfied with that, and turns to start untying his charges in preparation for the journey home.

48

It is difficult to speak to Burkinabes about the effects of hunger; people are understandably reluctant to talk about it. But food shortages are a reality from which northern Burkinabes in particular can never escape. Many live in a constant state of semi-starvation. 'Even now, before the drought season starts, there is hunger,' says Karim, with whom we spend the last few hours of market day chatting in front of his shop. 'Food prices are still very high, and there is a lot of malnutrition.'

Few places in the world have higher proportions of under-nourished children than the Sahel. Malnutrition accounts for half of the region's child deaths, while those who survive episodes of acute hunger are left more vulnerable both to disease and to the stunting of their mental and physical growth (the spindly children we see in Dori may never fully recover from being denied sustenance during the 2005 drought). But while childhood hunger is a disaster for individuals, it is the effect of famine on adults that can destroy societies. If famine takes the life of a child, he or she can be replaced and the family or community can eventually pick itself off the ground, but if adults die there is nobody to do the replacing, and nobody to feed others, care for the sick, or help a community regroup after the crisis recedes.

Adult malnutrition is an under-investigated subject, with childhood hunger attracting the greater part of research funding. But in 1944 an extraordinary experiment on a remarkable group of young men gave the world a new insight into the effects of food shortages on adults, and showed how a sudden drop in caloric intake can wear down even the strongest of minds and bodies.

As the Second World War entered its death throes and the liberation of Europe began, stories began to emerge that hundreds of thousands of civilians in Nazi-occupied territories were starving. These stories came to the attention of Ancel Keys, a young professor of physiology at the University of Minnesota in the United States. Keys had previously worked with the US War Department to develop pocket-sized food rations for the military, and he realised that the Allied forces had little idea of what they would find in the countries they were about to free, and no idea of how to cope with hordes of malnourished people. To help advance governments' and relief agencies' understanding of the problem, he devised a study. He teamed up with the US Civil Protection Service and placed advertisements for research subjects in its offices and circulars. 'Will you starve that they be better fed?' read the strapline. Thirty-six healthy, robust young men, who had conscientiously objected to fighting but wanted to help the war effort in some other way, came forward as volunteers.

For the first three months of the experiment, the men were allowed to eat normally. After that, their food rations were halved and they were subjected to a semi-starvation regime that would reduce each man's body weight by a quarter (in most famines, semi-starvation, to which the body can with difficulty adapt, is more common than total starvation). For six months the men were fed an unbalanced diet containing approximately sixteen hundred calories per day. This is one-third lower than the caloric intake currently recommended for men by the UK Department of Health, but slightly higher than the average daily intake of the world's poorest people.

The physiological effects of starvation, beamed regularly into our living rooms in television news stories from drought-hit areas, are by now familiar. As Ancel Keys reported in *The Biology of Human Starvation*, his account of the experiment, research subjects' bodies buckled under the pressure of hunger. Their ribs protruded, their skin sagged and thinned, they developed eye problems that would take years to heal, and oedema swelled their limbs (when they were rehabilitated and the swelling in their feet subsided, the volunteers' height decreased). Not surprisingly, there was a sharp deterioration in the men's ability to tackle physical tasks. They suffered from sore muscles, headaches, reduced coordination, dizziness and extreme tiredness. While out walking they looked for driveways when crossing streets, to avoid having to step up onto pavements. Keys calculated that for every ten percent of weight lost, the men reduced their energy expenditure by a quarter. (Unlike West African famine victims, of course, the men from Minnesota did not have to withstand the additional energy-drainer of the African heat, or cope with the accumulated effects of a lifetime of under-eating.)

The experiment also had serious psychological impacts. In conditions of total starvation, hunger pangs subside, but with semi-starvation they are a constant companion. The men could think of nothing but food. It haunted their dreams, dominated their conversation, and became the only topic that could rouse their interest. They read cookbooks, studied menus, and hoarded items of crockery. 'It made food the most important thing in your life,' reported one. 'Food became the central and only thing.' As the experiment progressed, apathy set in. The men grew withdrawn and isolated, unable to muster the confidence to engage in social interaction. A number of them experienced depression, with three suffering severe breakdowns. One man was so stressed he cut off three of his own fingers with an axe. Even the most robust of the volunteers reported heightened anxiety and irritability, and in several cases the psychological damage lasted long after the experiment concluded.

These individual impacts of hunger are mirrored in its effects on communities. Another American academic, Robert Dirks of the University of Illinois, has examined how societies respond to famine. As drought and competition for food in the Sahel make such crises more frequent, what he found may become a familiar pattern.

The first signs of famine are hard to spot. People are used to shortages, and the initial increases in food prices do not cause widespread consternation. As the shortage persists, however, and prices continue to rise, the realisation dawns that this time it is something more serious. A tremor of alarm ripples through the community. People become garrulous and excited as they wake up to the danger. They discuss what is happening and debate what can be done. They talk to everyone, expound their theories, and crowd around those who have opinions or news. They are generous, too, their hunger drawing them together. They share their dwindling resources and hand out scraps of food.

As the famine gathers strength, alarm turns into panic. A few pioneers decide to move in search of food. But where will they go? Anywhere, anywhere but here, it doesn't matter: there is no food here, so we must try elsewhere. In their confusion they do not consider that other places might have even less food, that in those places, moreover, they will be outsiders, strangers, and therefore last in line at the feeding queue. They do not consider, either, that movement itself is dangerous. Their bodies are weakening by the hour, and moving uses up valuable energy. Exhausted, starving, and thirsting for water, some of the wanderers collapse and die on the way.

With fatigue and hunger come increased irritability and anger. As the crisis deepens people begin to look for scapegoats, for someone to blame. Their frustration turns outwards, often towards their governments, which have failed to prevent this disaster. Sometimes their discontent can flare up into violent protest or the rioting and looting seen in Burkina Faso in recent years (were these the first scenes in a long Burkinabe famine?). This is a dangerous time for a country's leaders – many governments have been overthrown during the early stages of famines.

But if they can ride the early storm, leaders' prospects of survival greatly improve. For the protests cannot last. As the hunger continues to gnaw away, relentlessly sapping their energy, the protesters become too weak to maintain their revolt.

Like the young men in the Minnesota Experiment, they quieten and withdraw into themselves. Their anger fades, and they concentrate instead on conserving their strength. They stop working and spend their time sleeping or sitting; restlessness gives way to lethargy. They stop talking - the desire for social interaction, so strong in the initial stages, melts away. They hunker down in smaller groups and share food only with a tiny group of close relatives. Visitors are no longer welcome – even the ancient law of hospitality cannot withstand this cataclysm. And since most ceremonies involve sacrificing animals or donating food, the old religious rituals, too, are suspended. It is hoped that the ancestors will understand that such gifts must be temporarily withheld, and that the offerings will be redoubled if the family makes it through.

Outside, in the dusty lanes of the village or the nomad encampment, the world is descending into chaos. Crime mushrooms - the desperate search for food, and for energy-efficient ways of acquiring it, forces people to steal (another sign that Burkina may be in the midst of a long famine: theft from granaries is increasing, and it is no longer safe to leave stocks of food in the fields). As disorder spreads and the populace yearns for someone to restore stability, leaders who have kept a low profile since the earlier unrest re-emerge as people to be respected (the men in the Minnesota Experiment asked to be subjected to stricter authority halfway through). These leaders, moreover, control most of a country's resources; their subjects have no choice but to bow down before them. During the Russian Revolution political fugitives were forced by famine to hand themselves in to the police. In the nineteenth-century Irish potato famine, hitherto law-abiding citizens committed crimes so that they would be arrested and have access to food. At this point governing becomes easy, and those in power can entrench themselves for when the emergency finally passes.

As the end approaches, even the close family unit, Africa's

most enduring institution, comes under stress. Supplies are so meagre that families can no longer hold. Food becomes more important even than blood ties. First, the elderly are ejected from the home and left to fend for themselves. Then, shockingly, children are cut loose (yet another indicator of Burkina Faso's long famine: the talibé children, cast out when their families can no longer feed them). Parents take their sons' and daughters' rations - in the Irish famine, one observer reported that he had 'seen mothers snatch food from the hands of their starving children, known a son to engage in a fatal struggle with a father for a potato.' Children and adults alike are reduced to beasts, their own survival their sole imperative.

Finally, there is silence. Exhaustion overwhelms the survivors. They sit in the dust, alone under the burning sun, and wait to die.

49

Karim himself may be a victim of his country's prolonged famine. The eldest of seven children, his parents could not afford to keep him, and when he was six or seven they entrusted him to his maternal grandparents and moved away, joining the three million other Burkinabes living in the Ivory Coast. Karim did not see them again for eleven years. 'My grandparents are my parents now - I call them mother and father,' he says sadly as we sit watching the last stragglers from the market making their way home along the darkened street. 'When I saw my mother again after all that time I didn't recognise her. She was very upset and cried because I didn't hug her and didn't show her any warmth, but how could I? They had abandoned me for eleven years.'

Although he knows that what happened to him is a common occurrence in his country, Karim is still bitter about his parents' desertion. The pain seems to have weakened his resolve - he is less stoical than most of his compatriots, more prone to self-pity. 'I have no friends or relatives here in Dori,' he says. 'At home in Bobo I have many, but there is only one who really understands me. The rest are not serious. They go out and mess with girls. They have children too young, and then leave the girl alone with the baby.' His friends do not live up to his ideal of the nuclear family, an ideal perhaps held more strongly because of his own family's disintegration. He himself intends to marry some day, 'but not until my life is stable and I can support my wife and children.'

He says he is optimistic that he will soon be back on track, but his words do not convince. He talks often about making plans, perhaps returning to Bobo-Dioulasso, perhaps to Ouagadougou, but although he has plenty of time to think, with the yoghurt shop seeing only a trickle of customers throughout the day, he has alighted on nothing concrete. Like a young Sartrean existentialist, he talks and dreams of action but takes solace instead in thinking and planning. Thrown off course first by his parents' desertion and later by having to give up his studies, he is still reeling, unable to regroup. The wonder, of course, is that Karim is the exception here rather than the rule, that so many of his fellow West Africans can pick themselves up from setbacks, dust themselves down, and plough on. With my own demons continuing to cast a shadow over the last weeks of our journey (we have decided to bring forward by a month our return home), I can only wish that I too possessed such resilience.

We turn in early that evening in the hope of waking at dawn to catch a ride north. It proves to be a strange night. We are awoken in the middle of it by a maniacal banging on the metal door of our room, accompanied by loud shouts in a language we do not understand. I have been dreaming about being robbed, so I leap out of bed as if on springs. Without thinking, I open the door, but there is nobody there so I dress and walk out to the long balcony that fronts our floor. A petite, pretty African woman is standing there in the darkness. Off to the left, inside, I see a Chinese man lurching drunkenly into another room. The woman apologises in French for the man's behaviour. He had got the wrong room and was yelling at us to let him in. The Chinese owns the photography shop downstairs and is here on a short visit (the shop never has any customers, and I wonder whether it might be a front for something shadier). The woman was his prostitute.

Once the adrenalin has subsided we manage to go back to sleep, only to be woken soon after by a power cut. Burkina Faso's towns (although not its villages) have a more reliable electricity supply than those of Sierra Leone and Guinea-Bissau, but power cuts are nevertheless common. When the ceiling fan stops turning you are immediately soaked in sweat, as if somebody has wrung you out like a sponge and all the water inside you has instantly percolated to the surface. We get up off our drenched sheets and open the window in search of cool air, but since the outside temperature too is in the high thirties, our best hope of relief is to wait for the hallowed fan to resume its circular journey.

Outside is darkness, only the stars providing a faint glimmer of light. The sandy lanes between the mud walls that enclose the compounds appear empty, but after some time staring out of the window, off to the right we see a flame. In a lane on the far side of one of the walls, perhaps a hundred yards away from us, a tall, dark figure has lit a fire under a tree. It is difficult to make out what he is doing (we assume it is a man, although we cannot be sure), and even whether he is alone, for once or twice we think we see another, smaller figure on the opposite side of the fire, half-obscured by the mud wall. The flame gradually gathers strength, until it grows almost as tall as the man. What is he doing? It is three in the morning, and baking hot. Why has he lit a fire? Why under a tree, whose lower branches hang perilously close to the flame? Why, indeed, is he awake at this time of night, wandering the deserted streets? He stands looking at his creation, his shadowy companion occasionally drifting into and out of view, so diaphanous that we eventually conclude that he is not some sacrificial lamb but a trick played by the flames. We worry fleetingly that the tree might catch alight and the fire spread through the compounds, but after perhaps thirty minutes, perhaps fewer - time unwinds at this hour - the flame dies down and the mysterious figure, the evidence of his intentions reduced to ash, recedes into the darkness whence he came.

50

The next day, Saturday, Dori returns to its usual sleepy state. The streets and lanes are empty, the Fula nomads' straw huts have been packed up and carted off, and the only movement on the plain at the edge of town is of dust clouds dancing in the gentle harmattan breeze. It is as if yesterday's great spectacle had never happened, as if it were a mirage conjured up by the dry desert heat.

It is time for us to move on, to wade further into the Sahel, to the very edge of the Sahara itself. We hump our bags down to the bus stand and look for a vehicle to take us north. We are shown to a clapped out pick-up truck with two facing wooden benches out back under a metal canopy. Fortunately, we are among the first passengers to arrive and are given a more comfortable seat in the cabin. We settle down to wait for the truck to fill up.

The rutted road from Dori to the far north was until recently infested with bandits, who would hold up the few passing cars and relieve their occupants of money, jewellery, animals and food. The local government put a stop to this practice by placing police checkpoints along the route, but the bandits were not long in finding other ways to make a living. Two months after our passage through northern Burkina, the region would suddenly find itself on the travel blacklists of the British, French and American foreign ministries. Aid workers would be evacuated in haste to the capital, tourists and businesspeople strongly advised to steer clear. American intelligence had got wind of a plot wherein unemployed former bandits would kidnap Westerners and hand them over to an Islamic terror group linked to Al Qaeda. Northern Burkina Faso was pinpointed as the most likely hunting ground.

The West African Sahel is covered in these black spots. At the time of writing, early in 2011, vast swathes of Nigeria, Niger, Mali, Mauritania and now Burkina Faso are considered unsafe for Westerners to visit. A series of abductions has shaken foreign governments' confidence and put a stop to the region's fledgling tourist industry. Attendances at Mali's great musical showpiece, the Festival in the Desert, have slumped. The Paris-Dakar Rally has had to move to South America. The Sahel is rapidly becoming a no-go zone, and such is the fear Al Qaeda instils that it would only take one kidnapping in a major southern city to put the whole of Mali, Niger or Burkina Faso off limits to foreigners (during our brief stay in the Malian capital, Bamako, when a late night taxi drove us home from a nightclub through the dark, deserted streets, I remember thinking how much more lucrative it would be for the driver if he were to hand us over to kidnappers rather than drop us at our hotel).

The exact provenance of this new threat is unclear. The Afghan arm of Al Qaeda was alleged to be involved in diamond smuggling during Sierra Leone's civil war, and it may also have had a hand in the cocaine trade through Guinea-Bissau and in heroin trafficking through Nigeria. The group's Sahelian offshoot, Al Qaeda in the Islamic Maghreb, is thought to have arisen out of an Algerian Islamist movement and established loose links with the Afghan faction at a later date. Some observers believe Algerian security forces are involved, just as Pakistan's Inter-Services Intelligence agency supports the group in Central Asia, although the government in Algiers vehemently denies this.

These, then, are the rumours. The only facts are a succession of attacks on Mauritanian army barracks, a handful of bombings in Algeria, and a few dozen kidnappings of Westerners. The abducted are snatched in towns or on major roads, sold on to the Islamists, and then marched across the desert to remote camps. Most are eventually freed, their governments either stumping up multi-million dollar ransom payments or persuading their West African counterparts to release convicted terrorists back into their societies in exchange for the captives' liberty. A few, however, have been less fortunate. A French aid worker died or was executed (again, it is not clear) after the French army botched a raid on the camp where he was being held; two others died in Niger after another bungled French rescue mission; and an English tourist had his throat cut in Mali after his government refused to negotiate over his release.

Whether the kidnappers' motives are financial or fanatical is uncertain. There are two factions operating in the desert, only one of which so far has blood on its hands (the other, headed by a former cigarette smuggler known as Mr Marlboro, seems more interested in extracting ransoms than punishing infidels). But as they accumulate wealth and grow in power, the demands on the group's leaders will intensify. Like the region's dictators, they will not be able just to rest on their laurels and enjoy the fruits of their labours; wealth and power bring obligations, and now that they have money they must share it. Those who have helped them will require recompense - cash and jobs must be doled out to relatives, old friends and other community members. If the leaders saw the kidnappings merely as a quick route to riches, they made a gross miscalculation. As the ransom payments roll in and the number of supplicants swells, the pressure to keep going will prove impossible to stave off.

The group has duly begun to broaden its horizons. In 2010 it made overtures to radical Islamists in northern Nigeria, announcing: 'We are ready to train your sons on how to handle weapons, and will give them all the help they need – men, arms, ammunition and equipment – to enable them to defend our people and push back the Crusaders.' Al Qaeda in the Islamic Maghreb appears to be planning expansion, a pan-West African terror network seemingly the goal. The reference to Nigerian 'sons' provides a telling clue to their intended methods. The ransom bounties will buy more weapons, better communication systems and faster jeeps, but if they are to extend their holy war across the region, eject the old colonial powers, and bring down insufficiently Islamic governments, it is young men that the terrorists will really need. Al Qaeda's leaders know that the youth of the Sahel, like the drug mules of Guinea-Bissau and the rudderless fighters in the Sierra Leone war, are for sale. Desperate, poor, and with no other means of carving out a path in life, they have no choice but to sell their bodies to the highest bidder; for jihadists looking to invest their newfound wealth in widening the scope of their operations, they are the obvious first port of call.

As our pick-up truck sets off from Dori, we are unaware that this escalation in Al Qaeda's activity might threaten Burkina Faso; of more concern to us is whether our conveyance will survive the sixty-mile journey. Four miles outside Dori it breaks down for the first time. Unperturbed, the driver and his young assistant haul a jerrycan round to the front of the truck and pour water into the engine. There is a hole in the radiator, they explain; they have come prepared. Four miles later we break down a second time, the vehicle, whose brakes do not work, rolling slowly to a stop on the empty road as the engine gives out. Again, they pour in water and we continue on our way for another four miles before breaking down a third time. And so on. Eventually, in the middle of what appears to be empty desert, they run out of water. With a lack of hesitation which suggests they have done this many times before, the driver and his boy traipse off into the distance with their jerrycans and evaporate into the heat haze. The passengers sit and wait, boiling slowly in the sun. Most of those on the benches out back fall asleep. We are not yet halfway through our journey.

As the minutes extend into hours, we fall into conversation with the gaunt man sitting next to us. He is from Niger, and has come to Burkina to visit relatives. In an evident effort to look smart, he is wearing a jacket and trousers over a white shirt, but the jacket is too big for him and it hangs off his shoulders as if on a coat rack, and the white shirt is grubby and creased. He tells us that he used to be a talibé child, but escaped when the beatings grew too severe. Now he is an independent tour guide in Niger, but business is bad because tourists, frightened off by the terrorists, have stopped coming. He gives me a crumpled business card – "Ismael Baré, Guide Touristique", it proclaims – and tells me to call him when I next visit Niger.

After two hours the driver and his assistant return, their jerrycans full of water that they have somehow found in the desert. We continue on our spasmodic journey. Ismael's destination, Gorom-Gorom, is very close to the Nigérien border, but direct transport is expensive and to save money he has come the long way round, catching a much cheaper bus to Ouagadougou and then heading north from there. This entailed a detour of several hundred miles and an additional fourteen hours of travelling. Unfortunately, however, he has taken inadequate account in his plans of the risk posed by checkpoints. We are stopped twice during the first half of our journey. Each time, scenting a hapless foreigner, and one who being West African and therefore powerless is unlikely to cause them any trouble by complaining, the police manning the barriers summon Ismael out of the truck to question him. His papers are in order, but if he wishes to continue his journey he must nevertheless pay a bribe. The other passengers complain to our driver about the unfairness of it all, but there is nothing anybody can do. Ismael coughs up a total of about eight dollars – almost a week's average salary. All the savings he made by spending fourteen extra hours on the road are wiped out. As he climbs back into the truck after the second checkpoint, he appears on the verge of tears.

At the transport park in Gorom-Gorom, by which time all the other passengers have been dropped off, Ebru and I switch to another vehicle for the final stretch of the journey. This one, a jeep in good working order, belongs to a local Tuareg man, a physician who also owns the *campement* in the remote desert village of Oursi where we plan to stay (without your own car or camel, there is no other way to reach the far north). As we hurtle over low sand dunes on a rough track that is barely distinguishable from the surrounding desert, it does not occur to us, the only white people for miles around, how easy it would be for kidnappers to hunt us down.

51

Oursi is a small village surrounded on three sides by high sand dunes. Its inhabitants are mostly Songhai, but it also hosts an itinerant population of Fula, Tuareg and Bella herders, whose temporary straw shelters abut the periphery of the permanent, mud-brick settlement.

The nomads are drawn here by the lake, the great Mare d'Oursi, which flanks the fourth side of the village. The lake is an oasis. For hundreds of miles in all directions there is nothing but merciless desert, but here, perhaps dug out by a pitying God, this glistening body of water sits like a diamond stud in a woman's navel. The Mare is a magnet for herders from northern Burkina Faso and southern Mali and Niger, who lead their cattle and camels in from the sand dunes to graze and drink. They are joined by women from the village and other nearby settlements, who draw water or wash clothes on the lake's grassy fringes. Young girls bend over the mud, burrowing for roots to take home for dinner. Although the water level at this time of year is low, the lake hosts a steady stream of human and animal visitors, all dependent on it for their survival.

Our *campement*, a scattering of simple straw huts on a low sand dune, lies at the edge of the village. We are separated from the lake by a narrow road and a line of tall, dark trees and low, thorny bushes. To our left as we look towards the water a group of Fula have set up camp, taking advantage of a nearby borehole. The women of the community, who visit the borehole throughout the day to refill jerrycans or clay pots, wear long scarves wrapped over the head and around the neck, for the harmattan here is blowing at full force. Only at night does the storm relent; during the daytime it spews an unceasing horizontal shower of sand along the road, around the straw huts and across the lake. The sun is once again blotted out, although it has left a legacy of intense heat from which the wind provides no relief.

Modernity has made an even smaller imprint on Oursi than on Dori. There are no cars here, no Western clothes, no electricity, television aerials or radios, no foreigners but us. Village life continues as it has for centuries, punctuated only by the weekly market, the advent of the rains, and the dry season exodus of the nomads, whose hemispherical straw huts have not changed since Richard Jobson visited West Africa in 1620. 'The forme of their houses is always round,' the explorer wrote, 'and the round roofes made lowe, ever covered with reedes, and tyed fast to rafters, that they may be able to abide, and lie fast, in the outragious windes and gusts.'

In the early evening we wander down to the lake. Shallow and marshy, its furthest reaches fade away into the dusty haze. With the water level so low we are able to walk far out from shore across the mudflats. Brilliant purple starlings cackle behind us, as if speculating on when we will start sinking. Two Bella women in yellow and blue dresses pass on donkeys, aiming for a waterhole. A few yards ahead of where we stop, a heron stands to attention, while nearby a glossy ibis pecks in the mud. Flocks of small birds wheel above, feasting on clouds of insects. In the distance, only faintly visible in the haze, we can make out the gauzy silhouettes of an untended herd of horses. The heavy scent of mud and grass clogs the air.

Not much happens. We stand watching the birds. The Bella women draw water from a hole in the lake bed. A few boys gather firewood while their sisters scavenge for roots. Back on shore a camel groans plaintively. After a time, two young boys and a girl who have been watching us from afar pluck up the courage to approach us. Barefoot and dressed in scruffy T-shirts and shorts, they walk tentatively in our direction, carving a wide arc in order to bear down on us from the rear. They chirrup at us as they draw nearer. 'Ça va? Ça va? Ça va?' they trill, their voices high as songbirds'. We keep our backs turned, pretending not to hear them, playing the game. When we do not return their greeting they slow down and grow more hesitant. 'Ça va?' they call again, more sheepish this time but still creeping closer and giggling. When they are within a few feet I turn round suddenly, waving my arms in the air and roaring. The children, terrified, flee the white man, hollering and wailing. They run and run, not looking back until they are at least half a mile away. Even then, and although we have stayed where we are and are watching after them guiltily, realising that the game has not been taken in the spirit intended, they do not stop running until they have reached the safety of the lakeside trees. As they finally disappear into the bush and out of our lives, I can only hope that I have not scarred their perceptions of white people forever.

Dusk draws in, and people finish their business and drift unhurriedly homewards. Boys carry their bundles of wood back to the village. Girls skip back happily over the mud, shouting greetings at us. Trains of men and women on donkeys make for the far side of the lake, where a thicket of trees hides unseen hamlets. Behind us, far beyond the village, a lone nomad in dark red robes disappears behind a sand dune, heading home to his makeshift shelter.

Our own hut at the *campement* is designed in the Fula way – a shoulder-height, armadillo-shaped dome with a knee-high entranceway and a woven straw panel acting as a door. Inside is hot and airless, so at night we pull the cane bed out into the open and lie down under a clamouring crowd of stars. We are lulled to sleep by the lowing of cows and the waves of chatter and laughter from the Fula camp, rising and then subsiding, the deep rumble of the men's voices interrupting only occasionally the sing-song burble of the women. The wind has at last petered out, and we sleep peacefully and well.

We are woken just after dawn by the steady drumbeat of pestle on mortar as the women in the camp begin pounding the day's millet. By the time the men and children push aside the door panels of their huts and crawl out blinking into the resurgent dust storm, fires have already been lit and those women who have acquired some food are cooking. The sound of human voices drifts lightly across the dunes as morning greetings are exchanged and plans made for the day. While their daughters sweep inside the huts or collect water from the borehole, the men, aware that today is market day, do not tarry long before taking their cattle or goats off to the lake.

The road that passes the *campement* is a popular route into Oursi's market. As we sit outside our hut watching, a cavalcade of donkey carts passes. On them sit women in colourful patterned dresses, their faces decorated with ritual scars – a gash across the cheek, a notch or two by the eyes, arrow shapes on the forehead. Their husbands either walk beside them or ride donkeys themselves. There is the usual cheerful chatter. At the Fula camp, a group of women have come in from the sand dunes, each with a baby straddling her back. They stop outside one of the huts and crouch by the low entranceway to greet its occupants. When a woman in a red dress and headscarf emerges, they continue into town together, talking animatedly and excitedly.

We take the lakeside route to the market. Sprawling herds of goats traipse in across the marshy flats. Before them on large brown camels trot proud Tuareg, only their dark eyes visible behind their turbans. Ahead of us a family of Bella ride side by side astride donkeys, their feet dangling almost to the ground. Ebru notices that one of the men is wearing Converse training shoes under his long tunic. Another has a mobile phone around his neck - the trappings of Westernisation, from which Oursi's remoteness and poverty have for so long shielded it, have made their first tentative inroads.

The market is in the middle of the village. It is smaller and more modest than the Dori spectacular. Here in the arid far north the herding of cattle is dying out, and the market is dominated instead by goats, sheep and the occasional camel. Amid the bleating animals we are pleasantly surprised to see a Tuareg man selling grey slabs of salt brought in from the Sahara. Salt has been mined in the desert for thousands of years, dug up from the pans at Bilma and the quarries of Teghaza and ferried south across the sands by camel trains. In 1352 the legendary Muslim traveller Ibn Battuta described towns and houses with walls built of rock salt and salt slabs for paving stones. Nearly three hundred years later the Moroccan sultan Moulay-Ahmed el-Mansour, observing that 'the Sahara lives on the salt trade,' embarked on the successful military campaign to occupy Teghaza that triggered the downfall of the defeated Songhai Empire.

The Moroccans abandoned the Sahel at the end of the seventeenth century, but little else has changed. The people of Oursi – those who can afford it – still use Saharan salt to season their millet. They still follow the old camel trails across the dunes. They still dismantle their huts when the seasons change and move off with their families in search of fresh pastures. It occurs to me that the rise of Al Qaeda in the Islamic Maghreb might have the unintended consequence of protecting these rituals, of ossifying the Sahel's ancient traditions. Now that the governments of Europe and America have ruled this part of the country off limits to foreigners, it may be that the old ways will gain renewed strength, that they will hold out against modernity's tide, and that those Converse boots, that solitary mobile phone will remain anomalies, curiosities for future generations, slowly fossilising relics from a different, far off world.

Back at the *campement* in the late afternoon, as the donkey carts and herds of goats make their slow way home, we sit talking to Hassan, the Fula man who looks after the huts. Tall, thin and fine-featured, with the long straight nose characteristic of his people, he wears a white turban over a loose blue shirt and trousers. It is hot, and the harmattan has been blowing all day. Lacking turbans of our own, Ebru and I spend much of our time towelling a gritty film of sand and sweat off our necks and faces.

Hassan is a reluctant employee. When I ask him if he has ever been a herder, he looks at me as if I am stupid. 'Yes. I'm a Fula,' he replies once he has recovered his composure, his ethnicity and the pastoral life inseparable in his mind. 'I had over forty head of cattle. In the dry season I would take them to Mali and stay there until the rains. Then I would bring them back here. But the weather has changed. There used to be grass and water, but not now.' Like many other Fula, Hassan has had to give up the herding life. 'The cows can't survive the long journeys,' he says sadly. 'Most of my herd died, the rest we had to kill to eat. I only have eight cows now.'

Forced to find a job in Burkina Faso's threadbare (and now threatened) tourism industry, Hassan spends his days sitting and staring into space, thinking of lowing herds and patient journeys. He breaks off his reveries only to greet those passing on the road. We sit in silence for a few minutes, our host contemplating, Ebru and I struggling to find words of comfort, as if someone has died. Eventually, he awakes from his daydream. 'The people of Oursi are tired,' he says quietly. 'Many have had to move to Ouagadougou to hawk in the streets. They don't know commerce, they only know herding, but there's nothing for them here.' For the moment, Hassan is resisting the pressure to move south. He hangs on in the Sahel, clinging to the hope that the climate will relent, that his old life will once again become feasible, and that one day he will be able to quit the dull, confining job in the *campement* and go back to his ambling herds.

52

A few days later we make our way back to the capital. In the weeks since we were last there it has warmed up. The harmattan has eased off, reduced to the occasional blast of hot dry wind, and the sun is making up for lost time. The midday temperature reaches forty-five degrees. In the streets, drifts of prone bodies are piled up in the shade of walls, sleeping through the hottest hours. Only towards the tail end of the afternoon does the city stir again, but nobody can do much or walk very far or fast. There is nothing for it but to sit still and stare, conserving the energy that the heat is attempting to suck from you. Even at midnight the temperature remains in the high thirties. Life has slowed to a crawl.

My state of mind is less fragile than during our previous spell in the city, but the heat plays dangerous tricks, and if you do not respect it, it will destroy you. One afternoon, after walking no more than two hundred yards, I feel dizzy and have to sit down on a step outside a bank. The security guard brings me water. 'Next month it will be even hotter,' he warns. 'You can't walk from one side of the street to the other. It's so hot you can go mad.' The following day I am again out walking, in the late afternoon. It feels hot, but by breathing life into the otherwise motionless air the gusts of wind give you the impression of relative comfort. The wind is deceptive, however. In reality it makes no difference to the temperature; it is still murderously hot, the sun still pounds you with its hammering rays. I see a young man marching down the street with a jagged rock in his hand and a homicidal look on his face. He appears to have come down with the soudanité, and four or five other men have to restrain him from smashing the rock into his terrified target's face. Continuing on my way down one of the city's broad avenues, I suddenly find that I have veered off a straight line and drifted into the oncoming traffic. Only after two or three seconds do I realise where I am and steer back, shaken, towards the dusty verge.

It is time, it seems, to go home. I talk about carrying on for a few more weeks, but Ebru, the more sensible partner, has had enough, not least of worrying about me. Defeated, we make for the Air France office to bring our flight forward. We are left with just three more days in the country.

Large parts of those days are spent in our hotel, keeping out of the heat and hoping that nothing else will go wrong before we reach the safety of home. Over breakfast of omelettes and coffee one morning we meet Jan, a Christian woman who works in the hotel restaurant. A mother of three, she has had her job for twelve years, a long time in a region where only a tiny minority are formally employed. A job, however, does not mean financial security; Jan earns in a month what our double room costs for a night. She lives far away in the suburbs, in a district without running water or electricity but where rents are cheap, and comes to work every day on a moped. Before she leaves home she does the housework, fetches water from the well, and dresses and feeds her children. Then she oils and straightens her hair and dresses herself, Western-style, in a skirt and blouse. Her husband, a waiter in a café, takes the two eldest children to school, with the youngest entrusted to a grandparent.

Jan's position is under threat. Business is bad, and the hotel's owners have recently cut staff salaries. This prompted one of her colleagues to quit, and since the owners have no intention of finding a replacement, Jan now has to do two jobs, starting at six in the morning and finishing at eight at night, for the same pay as before. Petrol eats up half of what she earns, and as her wages fall and fuel prices continue to climb she will soon be unable to afford to work here. She has asked for a pay rise to reflect the increased workload, but her bosses told her that if she is unhappy she should leave. 'They told me there are plenty of people searching for jobs,' she says, her brow furrowing in anger.

Unfortunately, they are right.

Like most West Africans, who are eternally concocting schemes to improve their lot, Jan has made plans to get back on her feet. If she has to leave the hotel, she tells us, she will set up as an onion trader. Once a week, she will travel by bus to her ancestral village in the north-west and buy sacks of onions from farmers. After spending a night in the village, she will return with her sacks to Ouagadougou the following morning and sell them to market women. 'It is hard to find jobs,' she explains, 'especially for women. Trading is a better career for women.' From the comfort of the hotel restaurant Jan will be plunged into a life on the streets. I wonder what will become of her. Will she become one of those desperate hawkers who besiege buses or fight – sometimes with their fists – for your custom in the markets? Will her kindly disposition give way to the pushiness and cunning demanded on the streets? Will her soft, warm face become hardened and aged in the struggle? She seems optimistic, taking the imminent upheaval in her stride. How else, after all, can she respond? Events are beyond her control; there is nothing for it but to adapt, to keep going.

She takes comfort in religion. Christians are in a minority in Burkina Faso, but Jan has recently added one to their number by converting her husband from Islam. She is delighted, and as the conversation switches from her problems at work to the glories of Christ the gloom lifts from her face. 'We've been married for fifteen years,' she says in her lilting West African French. 'We got married in church. He was Muslim but he wasn't very religious so he didn't mind. I've been trying to persuade him to become a Christian ever since, but he always said he didn't want to convert or didn't have time. Every Sunday I take my three children to church - he is the only one who doesn't go.' The combined artillery of cajolery and ostracism had no effect; her husband's defences held out. Finally Jan resorted to more radical measures. 'I prayed solidly for three months and every Wednesday and

Friday I fasted, going without food and water.' Eventually her asceticism bore fruit. 'One day he woke up and said he wanted to become a Christian,' she beams. 'He will be baptised on Easter Sunday.'

Jan is a member of the Mossi, the largest of Burkina's ethnic groups. Traditionally a tribe of horsemen, they are ruled by the Moro Naba, the King of the World, who oversees the activities of the country's various royal courts from his palace in Ouagadougou. The Mossi kingdom dates back to the fifteenth century. It was famously close-knit and well organised, with power centralised in its leader, and while other tribes were devastated by slavers and marauding Muslims, the feared Mossi cavalry held out against repeated invasions. Visiting at the end of the nineteenth century, the French historian Louis Tauxier noted 'the absolute security that the population enjoys, where everywhere else war and slave-raiding parties desolate villages. One notices with envy the Mossi peasants who go out alone to their fields, where among other groups the head of the family must have, night and day, his weapon ready in his hand.'

The arrival of the French colonisers put an end to this serenity – the horsemen's muskets and spears could not compete with European machine guns - and Paul Voulet's destruction of Ouagadougou marked the end of Mossi hegemony in the region. But Voulet placed a puppet king on the throne and left the existing power structures largely intact; although gravely weakened, therefore, the institution of the Moro Naba survived the colonial period. The Mossi king remains an influential figure today, and, is regularly consulted by the country's president, Blaise Compaoré (even the most modern and powerful of dictators cannot escape the clutches of old Africa).

On our last day, a Friday, Jan advises us to get up early to attend the Nabayius Gou, the weekly ceremony at which lesser Mossi kings and other local dignitaries pay their respects to their ruler. We rise at six and take a taxi to the palace. Closed to the public, the large, plain building sits behind high walls in the middle of an expanse of dry earth. Although we have arrived at the scheduled time, there is nobody around. The taxi driver points us to a large, tree-lined rectangle of bare ground by one of the walls, and we trudge over and sit in the dust to wait.

After some time, a man with a white horse materialises by the palace. Holding the horse's reins in one hand, the man sits down on the ground, cross-legged, and waits. A little later two older men – dignitaries of some sort - walk in from the road and lower themselves carefully to the ground, facing the palace. They too sit and wait. Other men arrive in dribs and drabs, many on foot, some on mopeds, a few in battered old Mercedes. They wear long gowns and fez-shaped caps; many have swords attached to their waists in tasselled scabbards. They are all men, mostly old, preserving an ancient rite in the face of the weakening interest of the young. The only onlookers are tourists or expatriates - few Africans punctuate the thin line of spectators standing under the trees, and fewer still who are below the age of thirty. In decades past, great crowds of people would have gathered here to pay homage to their beloved leader, but today's disengaged youth see no meaning in the ritual. The ceremony continues without them, the old patriarchs, undeterred, clinging on tenaciously, raging against the dying light, re-enacting the age-old scenes for their own benefit while outside, beyond the rectangle of trees, the modern world rushes obliviously past.

The men in fezzes sit in rows facing the palace. They are digni-taries of different ranks - chiefs from outlying districts, ministers of the Mossi kingdom, and assorted other courtiers. There is a strict hierarchy, with the most important at the front and lesser minions at the rear. Before he takes his place, each new arrival must first sit on the ground in front of the most senior dignitaries, bow until his head touches the hard earth, and then, as he rises, rub his hands together in a circling motion and splash imaginary dust over his face. Having paid his respects in this timeworn way – the splashing of dust as a symbol of deference was recorded by Arab merchants in West Africa a millennium ago - he is free to sit with his colleagues and join in their conversation and laughter, which have not abated since the first two old men arrived.

There are, as ever, conflicting histories of the Nabayius Gou. In the most romantic version, the wife of an eighteenth-century Moro Naba was kidnapped by a hostile tribe while on a visit to her family in the north-west of the kingdom. The ruler of the world set out to rescue her, but before he could saddle his horse he was stopped in his tracks by courtiers, who told him he was needed in the capital to defend his territory against the enemies who were massing at its borders. The king, putting duty before his broken heart, reluctantly stayed, and the ceremony to celebrate such selfless dedication to his people was born.

Once everyone – perhaps two dozen notables – has taken his place, a lone figure, standing not far from the white horse, takes out a crooked stick and begins to beat a drum cradled under his elbow. The man is a griot, from the ancient storytelling caste of West Africa, fulfilling his age-old calling of singing the praises of his king. As he drums, three men beside him chant a dirge. Presently, the Moro Naba himself emerges from a low door in the wall of the palace. A large, imposing man, he is resplendent, but fearsome, in the bright red that symbolises war. He sits on the ground as three of the most important dignitaries break ranks and walk over to beg him not to sally forth to rescue his beloved. They bow, rub their hands together, and douse themselves with imaginary dust, before returning to join their still-chattering colleagues.

A cannon is fired. The Moro Naba withdraws into his palace. He re-emerges soon after dressed in white, the colour of peace. A collective sigh of relief is breathed, and the King of the World, closing the door on this glimpse of old Africa amid the din of the modern city, disappears for the last time. The ceremony is over;

our journey too. The dignitaries rise to their feet, say their farewells, and we and the other bystanders disperse with them into the teeming streets.

Acknowledgements

There are many people without whom it would have been impossible to write this book, and to whom I am immensely grateful.

My most obvious debt is to all those in West Africa who provided me with hospitality, contacts, stories and company. Many of them are mentioned in the book (some with names changed to protect their safety), but there are others – Osman Sankoh, Peter Aaby, Ben Lyon, Bertin, Lenny, Suzy, Tim, Missa, Fred, Mohammed – who probably have no inkling of how valuable their help was. It is thanks to them that despite the difficulties, I came away from this wonderful region knowing that I would soon – God willing - be back.

In the writing of the book, I am deeply beholden to Paul Godfrey, Mick Fealty, Jane Turnbull, Charlotte Weston, Colin Freeman, Fatosh Deniz, Jane Frewer, Alex Roberts, Steven Bonnick, Alex Mitchell, Idris Williams, Victoria Collis, James Helsby, Lol Middleton, Jane Morley, and Gemma and Magnus Willis for giving me their time and wisdom; to David Bloom for teaching me most of what I know about development; to Lynne Spencer for her inspirational enthusiasm (as well as her time and wisdom); and to David Steven for priceless advice and encouragement throughout.

Finally, my writing abilities are inadequate to express my gratitude to my father, who set me on the road; to my mother, who as ever could not have been more supportive and helpful; and most of all, of course, to Ebru, who still refuses to accept that this is her book too.

Select bibliography

Chinua Achebe: Things Fall Apart (1958); A Man of the People (1966); Anthills of the Savannah (1987)

Sharman Apt Russell: Hunger: An Unnatural History (2005)

Tim Butcher: Chasing the Devil: The Search for Africa's Fighting Spirit (2010)

David Bloom, David Canning and Jaypee Sevilla: The Demographic Dividend: A New Perspective on the Economic Consequences of Population Change (2002)

Richard Burton: Wanderings in West Africa (1863)

Robert Calderisi: The Trouble with Africa: Why Foreign Aid isn't Working (2006)

Patrick Chabal: Amílcar Cabral: Revolutionary Leadership and People's War (1983)

Patrick Chabal, Jean-Pascal Daloz: Africa Works: Disorder as Political Instrument (1999)

Paul Collier: The Bottom Billion (2007)

Maryse Condé: Segu (1987)

Robert Delavignette: Service Africaine (1946)

Robert Dirks: Social Responses during Severe Food Shortage and Famine (in Journal of Current Anthropology, February 1990)

Richard Dowden: Africa: Altered States, Ordinary Miracles (2008)

Jónina Einarsdóttir: Tired of Weeping: Mother Love, Child Death and Poverty in Guinea-Bissau (2004)

Frantz Fanon: The Wretched of the Earth (1961)

Raymond Fisman and Eduardo Miguel: Economic Gangsters: Corruption, Violence and the Poverty of Nations (2008)

Toby Green: Meeting the Invisible Man (2001)

Graham Greene: Journey without Maps (1936)

Robert Guest: The Shackled Continent (2004)

Danny Hoffman: The City as Barracks: Freetown, Monrovia and the Organization of Violence in Postcolonial African Cities (in Journal of Cultural Anthropology, March 2007); Like Beasts in the Bush: Synonyms of Childhood and Youth in Sierra Leone (Journal of Postcolonial Studies, November 2003)

Samuel Huntington: Political Order in Changing Societies (1968)

Uzodinma Iweala: Beasts of No Nation (2005)

Michael Jackson: In Sierra Leone (2004)

Richard Jobson: The Golden Trade or A Discovery of the River Gambra (1623)

Ryszard Kapuscinski: The Shadow of the Sun (2002); The Other (2008)

Ancel Keys: The Biology of Human Starvation (1950)

Ahmadou Kourouma: Waiting for the Wild Beasts to Vote (1998)

Sven Lindqvist: Exterminate All the Brutes (1992)

Michel Leiris: L'Afrique Fantôme (1934)

Matthew Lockwood: The State They're In: An Agenda for International Action on Poverty in Africa (2005)

Karl Maier: This House Has Fallen: Nigeria in Crisis (2001)

Bo Malmberg: Global Population Ageing, Migration and European External Policies (2009)

Katrina Manson, James Knight: Sierra Leone (Bradt Travel Guide, 2009); Burkina Faso (Bradt Travel Guide, 2006)

Albert Memmi: The Coloniser and the Colonised (1957)

Harry Mitchell: Remote Corners: A Sierra Leone Memoir (2002)

Shiva Naipaul: North of South: An African Journey (1980)

VS Naipaul: The Masque of Africa: Glimpses of African Belief (2010); The Middle Passage (1962)

Nathan Nunn: The Long-term Effects of Africa's Slave Trades (in Quarterly Journal of Economics, February 2008)

Mungo Park: Travels in the Interior of Africa (1822)

FJ Pedler: Economic Geography of West Africa (1955)

Odette du Puigaudeau: Le Sel du Désert (1938)

John Reader: Africa: A Biography of the Continent (1997)

Walter Rodney: A History of the Upper Guinea Coast 1545-1800 (1970)

Abd al-Sadi: The History of the Sudan (1655)

Emmanuel Terray: Le Climatiseur et la Véranda. In Georges Balandier, Alfred Adler (eds.) Afrique Plurielle, Afrique Actuelle (1986)

Richard Trillo and Jim Hudgens: The Rough Guide to West Africa (2008)

Barry Unsworth: Sacred Hunger (1992)

Henrik Urdal: The Devil in the Demographics: The Effect of Youth Bulges on Domestic Armed Conflict, 1950-2000 (World Bank Social Development Paper, 2004)

William Vollmann: Poor People (2007)

Contemporary culture has eliminated both the concept of the public and the figure of the intellectual. Former public spaces – both physical and cultural – are now either derelict or colonized by advertising. A cretinous anti-intellectualism presides, cheerled by expensively educated hacks in the pay of multinational corporations who reassure their bored readers that there is no need to rouse themselves from their interpassive stupor. The informal censorship internalized and propagated by the cultural workers of late capitalism generates a banal conformity that the propaganda chiefs of Stalinism could only ever have dreamt of imposing. Zer0 Books knows that another kind of discourse – intellectual without being academic, popular without being populist – is not only possible: it is already flourishing, in the regions beyond the striplit malls of so-called mass media and the neurotically bureaucratic halls of the academy. Zer0 is committed to the idea of publishing as a making public of the intellectual. It is convinced that in the unthinking, blandly consensual culture in which we live, critical and engaged theoretical reflection is more important than ever before.